W9-AXH-610

The Power Economy

Books by John Oliver Wilson

After Affluence: Economics to Meet Human Needs (1980)

Middle Class Crisis: The American and Japanese Experience
(with Fumiaki Ibuki, in Japanese, 1983)

The Power Economy: Building an Economy That Works
(1985)

The Power Economy

Building an Economy That Works

JOHN OLIVER WILSON

LITTLE, BROWN AND COMPANY — BOSTON   TORONTO

FIRST EDITION

The author gratefully acknowledges the Organization for Economic Cooperation and Development, Paris, for permission to
reprint data and quote from its publications; and the Brookings
Institution, Washington, D.C., for permission to quote from "Japan
and the World Economy," by Lawrence B. Krause and Sueo
Sekiguchi, which appeared in *Asia's New Giant: How the Japanese
Economy Works,* edited by Hugh Patrick and Henry Rosovsky
(copyright © 1976).

Library of Congress Cataloging in Publication Data

Wilson, John Oliver, 1938–
 The power economy.

 Bibliography: p.
 Includes index.
 1. United States — Economic policy — 1981–   .
 2. Great Britain — Economic policy — 1945–
 3. France — Economic policy — 1945–   . 4. Germany
 (West) — Economic policy — 1974–   . 5. Japan —
 Economic policy — 1945–   . I. Title.
 HC106.8.W55   1985   338.9   85-169
 ISBN 0-316-94502-1

MV

Designed by Patricia Girvin Dunbar

*Published simultaneously in Canada
by Little, Brown & Company (Canada) Limited*

PRINTED IN THE UNITED STATES OF AMERICA

To Jacquetta Ruth Wilson,
who long ago instilled in me
an insatiable curiosity
about the world

Contents

Introduction

On May 14, 1984, readers of the *Chicago Tribune* were greeted by headlines suggesting that Continental Illinois National Bank was near collapse. Similar headlines were repeated in nearly every major newspaper in the country, and panic began to grip the average American, whose savings and bank deposits suddenly seemed in jeopardy. Was this the beginning of a repeat of the great banking crash of October 29, 1929? Were the nation's financial institutions really in dire trouble? What was happening to an economy that had seemed immune from catastrophes for so many years?

The possible failure of the nation's eighth largest bank was certainly cause for great concern. But it was not just Continental Illinois National Bank that had been capturing the headlines. Out of the industrial Middle West, news stories had been appearing for months suggesting that the economic heartland of the United States was in deep trouble.

In the nation's midsection (long the pride of Carl Sandburg, beloved poet of the "stormy, husky, brawling" steel mills, wheat farms, and hog butchers), times were not so good. International Harvester — the oldest of our industrial-equipment companies and the proud successor to the McCormick Harvesting Machine Company, which traced its origins back to the invention of the reaper by Cyrus McCormick in 1831 — had teetered on the brink of bankruptcy for many months. The automobile companies in Detroit were struggling against declining markets and foreign competition, and in the process had laid off one-third of their work force. Many of the steel mills of Indiana and Ohio had been shut down. Tire manufacturers, automobile parts producers, retailers, and wholesalers were terminating thousands of workers.

The disaster was so great that Americans were beginning to wonder what had happened to the nation's once powerful manufacturing base. Or as Democratic presidential candidate Walter Mondale put the issue: "What do we want our kids to do? Sweep up around Japanese computers?"[1]

Although the experts point out that we are going through a period of structural adjustment from a manufacturing economy to one more dependent upon services and high technology, those of us affected by the change — and that includes nearly everyone, for no job is secure in this time of industrial turmoil — are not so certain that we like the upheaval.

For the displaced automobile- or steelworker who packed the furniture in a U-Haul, loaded up the family, and drove south, the job prospects have been far fewer than advertised. A few fortunate expatriates from the North have found jobs in the energy industry, earning as much as $450 a week working on the offshore oil rigs. But most are working at minimum wages of $4 an hour or less, clerking in department stores or working at other low-skilled service jobs. Unions are few and far between in the South. Low wages, lack of public services, and high living costs have made life miserable for the vast majority of the new immigrants. Nor are the northerners welcome, as they have encountered "a brand of Southern hospitality that is more Southern than hospitable — something like Yankee Go Home."[2] And many of them have done just that: they have packed up and driven back north to Detroit and Toledo, preferring to be unemployed among family and friends rather than fruitlessly search for nonexistent or low-paying jobs in the hostile Sun Belt.

High-technology jobs on the West Coast and along the resurging corridors of Boston are not the pot of gold that many would like to believe. In the first place, most of the new jobs in the future will not be in such industries as computers, pharmaceuticals, office machines and information-processing equipment, biotechnology, robotics, electrical components, and advanced military hardware. It is estimated that only 17 percent of all of the new jobs created from now through 1995 will be in such high-technology industries. And second, most of these jobs will be low-skilled and low-pay occupations. While the high-tech industries will employ engineers, mathematicians, and computer scientists, the bulk of the labor force will be composed of clericals, secretaries, assemblers, and warehouse personnel. Since few of the high-tech firms are unionized, these workers are paid wages well below the national average.

According to a recent study from Stanford University,[3] just one million of the expected twenty-six million new jobs that will be added to our economy by 1995 will be high-tech occupations requiring a college education and paying good salaries. The fastest-growing occupations will be building custodians, cashiers, secretaries, office clerks, waiters and waitresses, and nurses aides — jobs that will pay no more than two-thirds of what the average worker will earn.

It is not just those who are looking for new opportunities in the Sun Belt or high-tech industries who are feeling threatened. Every job in America is in jeopardy. Bankers, who long thought they were secure in their conservative and stable world of finance, are suddenly faced with the threat of increased competition from the likes of Sears, Roebuck and Merrill Lynch, as well as hordes of foreign banks who are moving into our lucrative domestic markets. Jobs in government are being curtailed. The airlines have been deregulated, and many are struggling to survive. Bankruptcies among small businesses reached postwar highs in 1983. Farmers are losing their land at a rate not seen for many years. Unemployment has struck at the core of the middle class, casting unprecedented numbers of white-collar, middle-management, and middle-aged workers out of work.

The American economy is undergoing massive structural changes that will dramatically affect the future of everyone. Many of these changes are well known. Large numbers of women and youths have entered the labor force in recent years, straining our economy to provide new jobs in sufficient numbers to prevent rising unemployment. The centers of economic growth are shifting from the Middle West to the South and the West. The potential of our economy to grow has diminished from what it was in the past. The costs of maintaining existing social services, including such popular programs as Social Security and Medicare, are increasingly becoming untenable.

Other structural changes are not nearly so well known and understood. These involve what is going on in the international economy. The American economy is no longer the dominant force it once was, accounting for one-half of the output of goods and services of the entire world. Our relative size has shrunk from one-half to one-quarter, and in the process we find that we must compete with many other countries for world markets. And our competition is not just the Japanese and the Europeans, but a group of nations that have been given the name "newly industrialized countries." Manufacturers based in Hong Kong, South Korea, Taiwan, Singapore, Brazil, and Mexico have become intense competitors, challenging our steel and shipbuilding industries, taking the leadership in textile, television, and other electrical-goods manufacturing, and even threatening our computer industry. To a far greater extent than we realize, or maybe want to acknowledge, our future is becoming inextricably tied to economic developments abroad. Like it or not, we are now part of a global economic community.

Nowhere is our dependence upon the economic fortunes of other countries more apparent than in jobs. The loss of automobile and steel jobs to foreign competition has been well publicized. (Signs in parking lots in Detroit announce to would-be customers: PARK YOUR DATSUN IN TOKYO.) Far less publicized is how many American jobs are created because of our exports: far more jobs than are lost to foreign-import competition. Today over five million jobs are directly related to trade, and between 1977 and 1980 an amazing eight out of ten new manufacturing jobs created in the United States were linked in some way to exports.

The extent to which the future of our economy is tied to that of the world economy is even more evident when we examine the importance of exports to some of our major industries, and our reliance upon imports. It is expected that during 1985 we will export about $415-billion worth of goods and services. These exports are critical to the survival of computer-equipment manufacturers, who export 27 percent of their total output; semiconductor companies, who export 33 percent; and the producers of oil-field machinery (46 percent), fertilizers (42 percent), and grains such as corn, wheat, and rice (40 percent).

Many of the high-technology industries — those that are critical to our future growth and strength — are highly dependent upon export markets. Aerospace, computers, semiconductors, and scientific instruments are the growth industries of the future. While they will not provide the bulk of the new jobs, they will have a major impact on maintaining our technological lead in global markets and modernizing our basic manufacturing and service industries. Without export markets, these industries would greatly shrink in size and importance.

Without imports, our economy could not operate. It is as simple as that. We import 20 percent of our total energy from abroad, and are dependent upon foreign sources for 52 percent of our crude oil. Over one-half of our radio and television sets are imported, as are one-third of our machine tools; one-half of our zinc and nearly a quarter of all the copper that we use comes from foreign sources.

It might be argued that if we did not import so much from abroad, we would have more jobs at home. Why should we buy television sets and automobiles from Japan? Why not manufacture these products at home? The answer is that American consumers like the lower prices and high quality that imports provide. To close the door to foreign products would greatly raise prices of nearly everything we consume. Furthermore, other countries would no longer be able to buy our exports, and so our aerospace, computer, and electronic firms, along with millions of farmers, would greatly suffer. We would simply be trading off increased jobs in automobile and television-set manufacturing for fewer jobs in computers and agriculture. And the net result would be an overall reduction in jobs — for as mentioned above, we gain far more jobs because of our exports than we lose because of imports.

All of these structural changes, from the shifting geographic centers of growth within the United States to our increasing dependence upon foreign markets, have not gone unnoticed by our politicians. It was a recognition that Americans were tired of an economy that was not performing well that led to the success of Ronald Reagan when he captured the White House in 1980. Promising a new economic program that would restore confidence and vitality, President Reagan quickly put into place a program of massive tax reductions. Given the name "supply-side economics," but dubbed by the press "Reaganomics," this new economic program was supposed to launch our economy on a path of stable and sustained growth. Democratic politicians have scurried to develop an alternative to Reaganomics, and appear to be stumbling toward some form of industrial policy. And the American public is left with an enormous uncertainty: Will Reaganomics eventually succeed, even though it produced a serious recession from 1981 to 1982, generated high interest rates (which continue to threaten the new investment that is critical to our economic future), and saddled us with unprecedented budget deficits? Or should we alter course and adopt a more aggressive industrial policy to strengthen our economic base, as suggested by many Democrats?

The interesting fact about all of these issues — the changing nature and location of our jobs, our adjustment to basic structural shifts in the economy, and our adoption of new and untried economic policies — is that we are not alone. It is not just Americans who are going through wrenching times. The Germans, the French, the British, and even the Japanese are confronting the same issues: In each of these countries, displaced workers are attempting to build new careers, many of them in the same high-technology industries as in the United States. A large postwar generation of young workers is having to be assimilated into the economy. The potential of each economy to grow has been reduced significantly. Incentives for new productive investment have been seriously eroded. And most important, each of these countries is experimenting with new economic policies, much the same as we are doing in the United States.

The Japanese, increasingly criticized for their great success in trade and envied for the accomplishments of their industrial policies, are engaged in an economic experiment designed to achieve economic security. They are not modern-day Vikings, as commonly portrayed in the Western press, ruthlessly pursuing foreign markets to plunder for the glory of Japanese economic power. Nor do they operate "Japan, Inc.," a mysterious consensus-management involving government, business, and finance, all shrouded in a mist of Asian inscrutability. Rather, the Japanese are operating a well-honed economic experiment designed to achieve a precious economic security. It is an experiment that is being broadened from a traditional concern with developing Japan's industrial base to providing more amenities to the Japanese people in the form of improved standards of living, creating an economic safety net to ensure continued economic development, and building a capability in basic research rather than relying upon imported technologies from the West.

The British are attempting to break past traditions of government support and instill their economy with renewed incentives and vitality. Many of the nationalized industries are slated to be sold back to private investors. Taxes on personal and corporate income are being reduced. Government spending is to be brought under control. But the unique characteristic of the British economic experiment is its strong faith in monetarism. Viewed throughout the world as the first major practical test of the economic policies advocated by Milton Friedman, the British have set out to determine whether a controlled and constant rate of growth of the money supply in the economy, preferably at a low rate, will lead to the sustained stability and growth that the monetarists have long promised.

"The French have a talent for doing things differently. And they are indulging it once again," commented a reporter in Paris after the election of François Mitterrand as president of France on May 10, 1981.[4] And Mitterrand wasted no time in announcing to the people of France, and to the world, that a major new economic experiment was about to be launched. "In today's world, there can be no loftier duty for our country than to achieve a new alliance between Socialism and liberty, a more noble ambition than to offer it to tomorrow's world," the new president stated at his inauguration.[5]

Although the most dramatic and publicized aspect of the French experiment in economic socialism has been the nationalization of much of French industry, there are many other very important elements to the program. Mitterrand was the first of the major world leaders to attempt to deal meaningfully with high unemployment. He implemented an industrial policy designed to launch France to the forefront in high-technology development. And he attempted to introduce more freedom and equality into the French economy.

The West Germans are assiduously avoiding any of the policy extremes of either the Americans or the French. Rather, they have adopted an economic experiment that former chancellor Helmut Schmidt called "the golden middle road."[6] In their economic policies they are seeking moderation and stability, unwilling to jeopardize the social partnership between government, business, and labor that was so carefully worked out during the postwar growth era. There are no plans to slash taxes or government spending, nor are the priorities of government being dramatically altered. The Germans have set out to determine if the strengths of past economic policies can be modified to meet the challenges of the future.

The five economic experiments being tried respectively by the United States, Japan, West Germany, Great Britain, and France represent a unique event in modern world history. Never before have the major countries of the free world undertaken such independent and individualistic attempts to deal with common economic problems. In the past the leaders of these countries would have gathered around the conference table knowing what to do when faced with unemployment and stagnant economies. They would have put into place traditional Keynesian solutions: Taxes would have been reduced, government spending increased, and the money supply loosened. The economy would have been stimulated to return to full employment. Today it is virtually impossible for two Western leaders — let alone a room full of them — to reach a consensus on the desired course of economic policy, for they are engaged in an unprecedented search for an economy that works.

This book is about that search, and what that search holds for our future. It concerns strong-willed and idealistic political leaders who came to power at a unique turning point in our history. It discusses their efforts to alter the basic direction of the global economy, as well as simply provide more jobs and economic security to the peoples of their individual countries. Some of these experimenters are implementing industrial policies that are highly successful, others are dismantling outdated industrial policies, while still others are ignoring the problem altogether. And all of their approaches are clashing, pitting longtime economic partners against each other. Their search is of historic importance, and its outcome will have a profound impact on our lives.

This book is for readers who want to understand this search — who are curious as to just how other countries, along with the United States, are attempting to deal with problems of unemployment and economic stagnation, lack of private incentives, and increased foreign competition. What is Reaganomics, and how does it differ from the economic policies tried in the United States in the past? How does the British attempt at monetarism differ from Reaganomics? Are the French really testing economic socialism, or is their program no more than a repeat of the social democratic policies that have been adopted by many European countries? Why are the Japanese so adamant in continuing their quest for economic security in the face of growing global criticism and the threat of trade restrictions? And what underlies Germany's attempt to maintain stability in its economic policies?

This book is also for readers who wonder: What can we learn from these experiments? Is one of them working so successfully that it will serve as a model for all of the industrialized countries in the future? Will Reaganomics or French socialism suddenly emerge as the new economic model, serving to guide and coordinate economic policies among the major countries? Do the Japanese hold some magic formula for making industrial policy work, a formula that could be applied in the United States? Are the Germans, with their middle-of-the-road economic policies, going to be the most successful?

Finally, this book is for readers who would like answers to the most important question: Can we build an economy that works? And here we find two quite different alternatives. To continue our current course will lead to even greater uncertainty, misunderstandings, and confrontations in the global economy. We will quickly turn to isolationism and protectionism. Political leaders of the future will attempt to insulate their own country's economy from the consequences of policies being pursued in other countries. Trade barriers will be erected, selected industries will be protected from foreign competition, and the world will begin to look much like it did in the 1920s and 1930s. The result could well be a repeat of global depression and military conflict. To continue our current course is to invite a disastrous repeat of history.

Fortunately, there is an alternative: the alternative of the Power Economy. *Power* is a most important word; in Latin the word is *posse,* meaning "to be able," and it implies the capacity to act, to be capable of performing, to affect strongly. And *economy,* of course, refers to jobs, economic growth, inflation, income — all of those things that are so important to our material well-being. When combined, the words give a strong image of an approach that is able to provide greater economic security and stability to all the peoples of the Western world than currently exists.

Rather than face a future of continued recessions, growing unemployment, lurking inflation, and protectionism; rather than risk a return to autarky and trade warfare — with the possibility of increased military conflict — we have the choice of altering course and adopting economic policies that would create the Power Economy.

Such an economy would be led by the five major countries that are now engaged in the individualistic and uncoordinated economic experiments described in this book. These countries have the combined economic power and wealth, along with the necessary leadership, to create such a global system. It would be an economy offering more rapid growth in the future than is likely to occur if each country continues along an independent path. It is an economy that holds out greater promise of putting millions of unemployed workers back on the job, and one that could ensure the continuation of free trade. Given the alternative, we really have no choice but to embrace the Power Economy.

The Power Economy

The Tumultuous Seventies

*A*s the 1960s drew to a close, the political leaders and people living in the industrialized countries of the world were eagerly anticipating the future. They were looking forward to a continuation of the rapid economic growth and low inflation that characterized the postwar era, when from 1950 through 1970 the industrialized countries averaged an impressive annual real growth rate (one adjusted for inflation) of 4.7 percent, and inflation grew at an average rate of only 3.7 percent.

It was a period of remarkable economic stability. France, Germany, and Japan had not experienced a serious recession in nearly a quarter of a century. In the United States the postwar recessions were mild and of short duration. Jobs were plentiful and taxes were kept low. Politicians were able to promise expanding public services, knowing that a strong and growing economy would provide the financing. The major industrialized countries seemed to have discovered economic utopia.

Unfortunately, this utopia came to an end during the tumultuous 1970s. The first evidence of the turmoil that was to plague the global economy throughout the decade appeared in the form of the breakdown of the international financial system. On August 15, 1971, President Richard Nixon shocked the world when he announced that he had directed Treasury Secretary John B. Connally, Jr., "to suspend temporarily the convertibility of the dollar into gold or other reserve assets except in amounts and conditions determined to be in the interest of monetary stability and in the best interests of the United States."[1]

This bombshell abruptly ended the international monetary system that had served the industrialized world for nearly thirty years. During that time the United States had performed the role of central banker to the entire noncommunist world. The dollar was the standard international currency in trade and financial circles, and the United States stood ready to convert dollars into gold at a fixed price of $35 per ounce — a price that had not varied since it was first set by President Franklin Roosevelt in 1934.

As long as the dollar remained strong and stable, and the United States stood by its pledge to sell gold at $35 an ounce, trade contracts could be agreed upon without fear of significant price changes; businessmen could invest abroad with reasonable certainty that hard-earned profits would not disappear overnight due to a currency devaluation; and government leaders could establish economic policies without undue concern for protecting the value of their currencies.

Such stability and certainty ceased with President Nixon's announcement. The international community was in shock. All of the major financial centers stopped currency dealing and foreign stock markets plunged. The Japanese watched the European reaction, while the Europeans feared that the United States would turn protectionist. There were strong rumors that foreign governments might retaliate by placing surcharges on American imports.

These events were soon followed by an even greater jolt to the global economy when, on October 17, 1973, the Organization of Petroleum Exporting Countries (OPEC) announced a 5-percent monthly reduction in oil exports to the United States and other pro-Israel nations. The oil producers in the Middle East acted quickly to shut down the flow of oil to the industrialized West. On October 18, Saudi Arabia cut production 10 percent, and Abu Dhabi stopped all oil exports to the United States. Libya followed this lead the next day. Then, on October 20, Saudi Arabia took the decisive step and imposed a total embargo on oil exports to their longtime friends and allies the Americans. The Saudis were immediately followed by Kuwait, Qatar, Bahrain, and Dubai.

Initially, the OPEC actions caused little concern in the United States. Newspapers reported that in Washington "the announcement by Saudi Arabia came as no surprise here, and [has been] taken with studied calm, as have several similar announcements from other countries earlier this week."[2] With our own massive internal supplies, along with large imports from Canada and Venezuela, the embargo was not expected to cause any serious impact on the American way of life.

It was quite a different matter in other parts of the world. The Japanese and the Europeans were not in the fortunate position of the Americans. They were vulnerable, and they knew it. The Japanese imported all of their petroleum from abroad, and 83 percent of this oil came from the Middle East. An oil embargo would quickly cripple the booming Japanese economy. In Europe the situation, while not quite so precarious as that in Japan, was still tenuous enough to cause great concern. France, Italy, Spain, Belgium, and the Netherlands imported all of their oil from the Middle East and North Africa. West Germany received almost three-quarters of its oil from these sources, and the British imported nearly two-thirds from the Arab producers.

The oil-dependent countries immediately began to implement energy-conservation policies. In Great Britain the government declared a state of national emergency as motorists clogged streets and jammed service stations, waiting in long queues for petrol. Panic buying and hoarding of oil products broke out in Germany, and emergency legislation was enacted that would enable the government to ban driving on Sundays and holidays, impose lower speed limits, and ration gasoline and heating oil. Japanese government officials stated at the outset of the oil embargo that they would move prudently in imposing conservation measures. The president of the United States called upon our nation to pull together, saying that while we faced an energy crisis, there was no crisis of the American spirit to deal with the problem. Only the French viewed themselves as possibly immune from the situation — thinking that the embargo would be less severe because of France's "privileged" place in the Arab world. But eventually even they were forced to impose a number of measures to conserve energy.

On March 19, 1974, the oil embargo against the United States came to an end, and with it the worst of the fears dissipated. The vast industrial base of Europe, the United States, and Japan would not be brought to a halt by a lack of oil. It was quickly becoming apparent, however, that the quadrupling of oil prices by OPEC had launched a new era of higher inflation and greater concern for energy conservation, and had revealed the vulnerability of industrialized economies to foreign sources of energy.

"The oil problem is the most urgent and baffling of those that governments are facing," stated the influential Organization for Economic Cooperation and Development (OECD).[3] The International Monetary Fund (IMF) described the situation as constituting "perhaps the most complex and serious set of economic problems to confront national governments and the international community since the end of World War II."[4] And even the United States began to realize the permanency of the change. "So far, the spurt of energy costs hasn't torn gaping holes in the fabric of American life," observed the *New York Times*. "But change has begun, and more is coming."[5]

Change soon came in the form of a recession unlike that experienced by the global economy since the Great Depression some forty years earlier. During 1974, real growth of the American economy declined continuously. Unemployment increased from 4.6 percent to 9.0 percent as an additional 4,214,000 workers lost their jobs. Nearly one-third of all manufacturing plant capacity was standing idle, and inflation was soaring, with consumer prices rising at an annual rate of 12.2 percent. Never before had the American economy suffered from stagflation — the malady of simultaneous relatively high unemployment and inflation during a recession — and the specter was frightening. Newspaper articles began to appear suggesting the possibility of a second great depression, and American policymakers were in a quandary over what to do about it.

The United States was not alone in suffering through the most serious recession in postwar history. Economic growth came to a virtual standstill in nearly all of the economies in the industrialized world. Inflation reached the highest level in more than twenty years. Massive deficits in trade balances occurred as the industrialized countries struggled to pay for their oil imports, placing great strains on international financial markets.

It was clear to political leaders throughout the world that the 1974–75 global recession was dramatically different from previous recessions in several significant aspects:

- It was deeper than any of the previous recessions.
- It took much longer for global recovery to occur.
- Inflation continued to rise as the level of economic activity fell (in the past, a recession always reduced inflationary pressures).
- The recession occurred simultaneously in nearly all industrialized

countries, suggesting far greater economic interdependence in the global economy than was previously true.
• Sharp price increases in energy, food, and other basic materials occurred, which greatly distorted price relationships and created new and large trade imbalances.

The first major political leader to recognize that the global economy had gone through something far more significant than a routine economic recession was Chancellor Helmut Schmidt of West Germany. "The Western economies have been profoundly shaken by the serious recession following worldwide inflation, the collapse of the international monetary system, and the oil crisis," stated Schmidt. "All this led to a structural upheaval in the global balances-of-payment network, to a structural upheaval in world trade, in world demand, and thereby in employment."[6]

To rebuild the economy for the future would require resolving these problems and adopting a set of economic policies that recognized the reality of a global economy far different from the one that had been operating during the postwar era. The "postwar era has ended," wrote Schmidt in *Foreign Affairs,* and our primary task "[is] to restabilize the economic foundations of the democratic state."[7]

Most of the industrialized countries set about the task of restabilizing their economic foundations as the recession of 1974–75 drew to a close. It was a tough period of structural adjustment, for there were formidable problems to be overcome. New investments had to be made, in more modern and energy-efficient plant and equipment. Resources had to be shifted from personal consumption and government social programs toward private and public investments. Stringent conservation measures needed to be imposed and alternative sources of energy secured. Export markets had to be developed and expanded in order to offset the higher cost of oil imports, and new technologies were needed to ensure that export-oriented industries remained competitive.

Politicians attempting to make these changes often confronted recalcitrant electorates, yet from 1976 to 1978 the global economy progressed toward equilibrium. The success of the adjustment process is revealed by the current-account balances of major groups of countries. (See table 1.) Current-account balances — the total exports minus total imports of a country, plus the net inflow of investment income — indicate the relative stability of the global economy. In 1973 the industrialized countries (OECD) earned a current-account surplus of $13 billion, the OPEC countries incurred a small surplus of $4 billion, while the developing countries were in deficit by only $7 billion. The quadrupling of oil prices dramatically altered this situation and led to a major transfer of resources from the industrialized and developing countries to the OPEC countries. Between 1974 and 1977 the OPEC countries earned astounding current-account surpluses, selling far more oil than they were spending on imports. And the industrialized and developing countries ended up with combined deficits during 1977 of $36 billion.

It took several years for the adjustments made by the industrialized countries to succeed. By 1978 their current-account balances were $11 billion in surplus while the OPEC surplus was zero, and the international banking system was readily able to finance the $21-billion deficit of the developing countries. The OECD noted: "The prospects . . . have changed considerably since the last economic outline . . . and in many respects for the better." Current policies seemed likely to "produce a more balanced international pattern of payments position" and "many factors seem[ed] to be running in favour of less turbulent conditions on exchange markets and better business confidence."[8]

Any return of confidence on the part of business or any feeling of relief by political leaders was destined to be short-lived, for the second major oil shock of the decade soon occurred. In December 1978, OPEC announced a staggered increase intended to raise the average price of crude oil 14.5 percent, from roughly $13.00 to about $14.50 per barrel, by October of 1979. But it did so during a period

TABLE 1. CURRENT-ACCOUNT BALANCES AMONG MAJOR GROUPS OF ECONOMIES (COMBINED TOTAL, IN BILLIONS OF U.S. DOLLARS)

	1973	1974	1975	1976	1977	1978	1979	1980
All industrialized countries (OECD)	+13	−26	+5	−15	−22	+11	−34	−72
Non-OPEC developing countries	−7	−23	−33	−21	−14	−21	−32	−54
OPEC countries	+4	+57	+29	+33	+23	+0	+49	+96

SOURCE: Economics-Policy Research Dept., Bank of America, San Francisco.

of strong demand created by the hoarding of inventories by producers and an interruption of Iranian supplies. As a result, oil prices shot up to about $28.00 per barrel by early January 1980, more than double the price a year earlier. The oil shock of 1979 was fully as large as that of 1974, and the specter of a repeat of the global recession of 1974–75 quickly became a concern. More important, all of the adjustment efforts to achieve a more stable and balanced global economy seemed to evaporate as the industrialized countries plunged again into a current-account deficit, this time reaching $72 billion in 1980.

As the 1970s drew to a close, it seemed to many of the weary and harassed political leaders of the industrialized countries that the economic deck of cards was stacked against them. No matter how diligently they worked, how creatively they imposed adjustments upon their people, or how responsible were consumers and business to changing conditions, external events would overwhelm their efforts. And reinforcing this frustration was a growing realization that far more basic problems were threatening the future of the global economy. These were problems of lower economic growth and rising unemployment.

The End of the Growth Era

With the end of the Second World War and the return to a peacetime economy, the world embarked upon a period of unusually high and sustained economic growth. This development was somewhat surprising, for most politicians and economists of the time were busy predicting a postwar recession, if not a depression. It was widely thought that the tremendous reduction in defense spending would so depress the United States economy that growth would plunge. Furthermore, the Western European and Japanese economies lay in ruin: people wandered the countryside in search of food, factories were piles of rubble, and transportation and communications systems were almost totally nonexistent.

Yet the United States economy did not go into recession. The American consumer, flush with large savings from wartime earnings and motivated by strong pent-up demands for new housing, automobiles, and other consumer durables, went on a spending spree. As a result, the economy quickly made the transition from wartime to peacetime production and began to boom.

The European economies also made a remarkably rapid recovery.

Aided in large part by massive infusions of capital and technology from the United States under the Marshall Plan, and possessing a well-educated and hardworking labor force, Western Europe rebuilt agricultural and industrial bases. Propelled by such rapid adjustment, the industrialized economies grew at an average real rate of 4.4 percent during the decade from 1950 to 1959. (See table 2.)

Once the postwar adjustment phase was completed, it was thought that economic growth would slow down. Again the experts were surprised, for the global economy entered a period known as the golden age of economic growth. All of the major industrialized economies averaged growth rates in excess of 3 percent, and the amazing Japanese economy was growing by over 10 percent annually. Sustained economic growth came surprisingly easy, and was soon accepted as the normal way of life. Such rapid economic growth was not a God-given right but was the result of several growth-inducing factors. In the first place, private investment was growing at a very high rate. Responding to low interest rates, rapidly expanding world markets, and plentiful investment opportunities, private business leaders throughout the industrialized world were investing heavily in new plant and equipment. Second, energy costs were very low. In fact, the price of energy did not even keep pace

TABLE 2. REAL GROWTH IN GROSS NATIONAL PRODUCT AMONG INDUSTRIALIZED ECONOMIES (ANNUAL AVERAGE)

	Decade of Postwar Adjustment (1950–1959)	Golden Age of Growth (1960–1973)	Phase of Oil Shocks and Stagflation (1974–1983)	Projected Era of Moderate Growth (1984–1992)
All industrialized countries (OECD)	4.4%	5.0%	2.2%	3.0%
United States	3.8	4.1	2.1	3.2
Japan	7.9	10.4	3.7	4.0
West Germany	8.7	4.7	1.7	2.5
Great Britain	2.8	3.1	1.0	2.0
France	5.1	5.8	2.2	2.2

SOURCE: Economics-Policy Research Dept., Bank of America, San Francisco.

with overall inflation, and the ready availability of low-cost energy provided a big boost to economic growth. Third, the United States was able to perform the role of peacekeeper, free trader, and capital exporter to the rest of the world. So dominant was the U.S. economy that it could absorb large trade and capital-account deficits while providing an open market for the exports of Europe and Japan. And finally, productivity was increasing throughout the world. The growth in output per hour worked meant low inflation and rising standards of living for workers.

The oil shocks and stagflation of the 1970s brought the golden age to an end. From 1974 through 1983 economic growth rates among the industrialized countries averaged only 2.2 percent. And for the major industrialized countries, the reduction in growth rates was most dramatic: Japan's annual growth declined from 10.4 percent to 3.7 percent; United States growth dropped from 4.1 percent to 2.1 percent; while that of West Germany fell from 4.7 percent to 1.7 percent.

Expectations among political leaders and economists are that the global economy is entering a period of slow growth. More important, political leaders firmly believe that unless dramatically different economic policies are adopted, low growth rates are inevitable. During the years from 1984 through 1992, economic growth among the industrialized countries is expected to average just 3.0 percent, and for Japan and the Western European countries the decline in growth potential is dramatic. While experts ultimately may be as surprised as they were in the past, they now see indications that higher growth rates are unattainable because the conditions that brought about rapid growth no longer exist.

The era of low-cost energy is over. Energy is expensive and its cost is expected to increase at least in line with overall prices. In the five major industrialized countries, private investment will remain sluggish owing to low rates of return for new capital investments, increasing competition from such newly industrialized countries as Brazil, South Korea, Hong Kong, Singapore, and Taiwan, and the continuation of efforts to protect many of the old "smokestack" industries. The labor force will be growing much more slowly in the United States and Japan. And in Europe productivity growth will be significantly lower. All of these conditions are difficult to reverse, for they are caused by basic structural changes in the industrialized economies.

The Problem of Unemployment

As if the end of the growth era was not enough to cause consternation among political leaders, the fear of rising unemployment was reverberating from the American Midwest to Western Europe. It was a problem of immediate attention, front-page news in London, Paris, and Bonn. It was a problem felt by workers who had lost their jobs during a recession and were not being hired back during the economic recovery; by students who graduated from the universities and could not find work; and by displaced coal miners and automobile workers who were suddenly faced with poverty.

The problem was hardly new. It had arisen in the 1930s as millions of workers wandered the streets and took to the rails in search of jobs that did not exist. But the economic growth of the 1950s and 1960s had, until then, buried such fears. The labor forces of Japan and the industrialized countries of northern Europe and North America came to expect employment as a normal state of affairs.

But by 1980, 25 million people were unemployed in these countries, and the total would soon rise to 35 million — more than double the 15 million out of work a decade earlier. Memories of the recession years surfaced, and provocative headlines began to appear: FOOTSORE, WEARY AND WORKLESS . . . DOWN AND OUT IN EUROPE . . . WHERE WILL THE JOBS COME FROM?[9]

Yet there was something quite strange about this period of rising unemployment compared to that of the Great Depression. Jobs were not disappearing from the economy because plants and offices were closing their doors and forcing employees onto the streets, as during the thirties. Quite the opposite was occurring. The industrialized economies were adding millions of new jobs each year. In fact, during the slow-growth decade of the 1970s the industrialized economies created a total of 28 million new jobs, only 1 million less than the increase during the fast-growth 1960s. Something far more basic — something unprecedented — was behind this new unemployment problem: there was a massive increase in those who wanted work, particularly young adults and women.

The postwar baby boom started in the United States with the end of the Second World War, when the men and women in the military forces returned home, married, and began to form families. The birth rate increased rapidly until the peak year of 1957, when 4,308,000 babies were born, 50 percent more than in 1945. And then the birth rate began to decline, slowly at first, and then more and more precipitously. By 1976, birth rates in the United States had declined to the lowest level in our entire history. Never before had the birth rate risen and dropped so fast in so short a time.

The result of this baby boom was a generation of Americans who descended upon the marketplace in the 1970s looking for work. And while the American economy was creating jobs nearly as rapidly as in the past, it still was not doing so fast enough. There were just too many young Americans wanting work. Compounding the problem for policymakers was the knowledge that this situation was not permanent, for the baby bust of the 1970s meant that in the 1990s there would be a large decline in the number of young adults wanting work, and the American economy faced the probability of an eventual shortage of workers. This is a major reason for the expected slower economic growth rate in the future.

The same baby-boom and baby-bust phenomenon also occurred in Western Europe, but about five years later than in the United States. Birth rates did not begin to increase until after the European economies had recovered from the devastation of the war. But once recovered, Europeans behaved much like their American counterparts. And young adults made their presence increasingly felt beginning in the mid-1970s. From 1975 to 1985, the population aged twenty to twenty-four expanded by 12.4 percent in Western Europe, ten times faster than the growth of the total population. Similar to that of the United States, the West European economies face the future problem of a lack of workers in the 1990s and the current problem of smoothly integrating a unique postwar generation into the work force.

The rapid increase in the number of women who wanted to work was the second major phenomenon that added to the unemployment problem of the industrialized countries. Women began to enter the labor force in increasing numbers during the 1970s, particularly in the United States. The proportion of American women aged fifteen to sixty-four who were either working or actively seeking employment increased from 48 percent in 1970 to 60 percent in 1980, leaving a greater proportion of American women active in the labor force than in any other major industrialized country. British women were the second-most-active, with a labor force participation rate that increased from 51 percent to 58 percent.

French women also joined the labor force in increasing numbers during the decade. Only the German and Japanese women did not significantly increase their participation rates; however, one-half of the working-age women in these countries were already active in the labor force. In these five large economies, a total of 32 million people were added to the labor force between 1970 and 1980, and 19 million were women. Nearly two out of every three new entrants into the labor force were women — a remarkable record of increased participation.

Along with the increase in the number of young adults and women who wanted work, other forces were operating to add to the unemployment problem. The recessions and OPEC oil shocks, spiraling inflation, and the decline in new investment that characterized the tumultuous 1970s all contributed. Furthermore, the industrialized countries were facing increasing competition from several newly emerging industrialized countries in such basic industries as steel, shipbuilding, textiles, and consumer appliances. As a result, many workers in Western Europe and the United States were being displaced in these industries.

The political leaders in the major industrialized countries were beginning to realize that unemployment, like slow economic growth, was largely the result of basic structural changes occurring in their countries. Unfortunately, they lacked any strong sense of direction in dealing with the problem, for the Keynesian economic model that had provided policy guidance in the past seemed to most of these leaders hopelessly out of touch with the new reality.

Keynes Loses Favor

During the postwar growth era the economic views of John Maynard Keynes dominated economic policy in the major industrialized countries, particularly in Great Britain and the United States. This great British economist, who in 1936 published his revolutionary economic treatise *The General Theory of Employment, Interest, and Money,* had a profound impact on a postwar generation of politicians, policy-makers, and economists in these two English-speaking countries. American presidents and British prime ministers openly referred to "Keynesianism" when discoursing on economic policies, the press frequently dubbed the postwar era the "Keynesian era," and economists spoke in awe of the "Keynesian Revolution." So great did Keynes's influence become that in late 1962 President John F. Kennedy, referring to a major policy speech he had just given to the Economic Club of New York, exuberantly commented: "I gave them straight Keynes and Heller, and they loved it."[10]

While the other major industrialized countries were not so open in their acceptance of Keynesian views, they followed many of the same principles. The French were reluctant to embrace the theories of an English-speaking economist, yet their own economists integrated many of the Keynesian policy prescriptions into French thinking. The Japanese did not need an economic theory to convince them of the importance of strong government leadership in the economy; they were well embarked upon such a course for their own unique reasons. And the Germans, while cautious to avoid the excesses of Keynesianism for fear of inciting inflation, nevertheless wrote Keynes's basic tenets into law in 1967 in their Stability and Growth Law for the Economy.

The importance of Keynes in the global economic arena of the postwar era lay not so much in whether his views were overtly embraced or not, but in the fact that the principles he first espoused served to establish a general framework for policy coordination among the major industrialized countries. His overall emphasis on a stronger role for government intervention in influencing the growth and stability of the economy was readily accepted by leaders of nearly every political persuasion in the major economies of the free world.

When the world leaders gathered at their summit meetings to discuss mutual economic problems, they were speaking to each other from a similar viewpoint. When their technical experts convened to iron out specific points of conflict, there was a common basis for negotiation and compromise. And when they imposed particular economic policies in their own countries, these policies were remarkably compatible with those being implemented in other countries. The great legacy of Keynes was that he provided the major economies of the free world with a policy framework that enhanced cooperation and coordination, and in the process added significantly to the stability of the postwar global economy. It is just such a consensus that is now missing and that makes current economic progress difficult — a vacuum that the Power Economy intends to fill.

What were these basic Keynesian principles that served to unify postwar economic policies among the major industrialized countries? In the first place, Keynes totally rejected the prevailing view that the market economy would automatically adjust to bring about full employment. The classical economist of his day held the belief that the laws of supply and demand in a free market economy would operate to provide jobs for all of those who wanted work. If the demand for labor exceeded the supply, wages would rise to equate the two. And if there were more people who wanted work than there were available jobs, wages would be bid down until full employment was attained.

Observing that millions of unemployed workers were seeking work in Great Britain, the United States, and Europe during the height of the depression, Keynes concluded that the markets were not capable of producing full employment. Wages were not flexible downward, but were rather rigidly fixed by union contracts, market imperfections, and government regulations. It was therefore impossible for them to decline sufficiently to bring about full employment, and the only solution was for government to provide the necessary stimulus to generate economic activity.

Such a conclusion led to the second basic Keynesian principle of the postwar era: A strong economy required active intervention on the part of government in the form of changing the level of public expenditures and taxes. The core of Keynesian policy prescriptions was a proactivist stance of government. When the economy was operating below par, the solution was for government to increase public expenditures or reduce taxes in order to stimulate greater total spending — or, as economists say, to increase aggregate demand. And if the economy was too strong — that is, if there was a danger of inflation and full employment prevailed — then government should reduce public expenditures, raise taxes, or do both.

The third basic Keynesian principle regards the process through which a change in government expenditures or taxation works through the economy to generate employment and investment. And here Keynes postulated his famous "consumption function." His function simply says that the amount of spending by individuals, households, and the economy as a whole is primarily determined by the level of income. As income increases, so does consumer spending, and, conversely, as income declines, so does the level of spending.

Thus, according to Keynes, an increase in government spending on welfare programs or Social Security adds directly to the income of the individual recipients and will lead to an increase in consumer spending. An increase in spending on defense or highway construction adds to the income of workers in those industries and hence boosts consumption. Alternatively, a reduction in taxes raises the after-tax income of the taxpayer, which generates more consumption. All of this increased consumption leads to a higher level of aggregate demand in the economy, stimulating business to hire additional workers, to expand investment in plant and equipment, and to implement new technology.

A fourth and final policy principle was added to the Keynesian troika: that there exists a trade-off between unemployment and inflation. The so-called Phillips curve — named for Professor A. W. Phillips of the London School of Economics, who first pointed out in 1958 what he thought was a stable relationship between levels of unemployment and rates of inflation — quickly became an integral part of the Keynesian policy package. It gained prominence because policymakers thought they could fine-tune the economy through appropriate changes in expenditures and taxes to achieve a "desired" level of unemployment and inflation. For instance, a choice could be made to position the economy at a point on the Phillips curve where unemployment was 3 percent and inflation 4 percent (an outcome commonly associated with Democrats) or, alternatively, at a point with a higher level of unemployment, at 5 percent, and lower inflation, at 2 percent (a result thought to be favored by Republicans). Numerous options existed along this curve, and the only task of the politicians was to select the desired point of trade-off between unemployment and inflation. Once the selection had been made, the economic technicians could determine the appropriate change in public expenditures and taxes to hit that point.

These four principles dominated economic policy in the major industrialized countries throughout the postwar growth era. To be sure, a few lonely voices pointed out that the Keynesian principles had given employment far greater weight in policy debates than inflation was given, that Keynesian principles were leading to an ever-expanding role of government in Western economies, and that these principles tended to ignore the so-called supply side of the economy (which involved such matters as increasing worker incentives, expanding savings, and encouraging investment), but they were voices without much following. The apparent success of the Keynesian technicians was such that the dissenters were treated with benign amusement, if not disdain. Their day was soon to arrive, however. During the turbulent decade of the 1970s, both unemployment *and* inflation soared. This was thought to be impossible in the Keynesian world, and it called into serious doubt the presumed trade-off of the Phillips curve. It had long been observed that the curve seemed to be shifting to the right, implying an ever higher level of inflation associated with a given level of unemployment.

Now it seemed that the curve had disappeared altogether — a

fact that Professor Milton Friedman of the University of Chicago lost no time in pointing out. In his presidential address to the American Economics Association in 1967, Friedman used his prestigious platform to state that while there may be "a temporary trade-off between inflation and unemployment, there is no permanent trade-off." Rather, there is a "natural rate of unemployment" that is determined by "the actual structural characteristics of the labor and commodity markets."[11] And if the Keynesian policymakers attempt to drive the unemployment below this natural rate by increasing government spending or expanding the money supply, the results will only be more inflation.

Professor Friedman was joined by other professional economists who began to chip away at the foundations of Keynesian thought. Professor Martin Feldstein of Harvard University pointed out that government emphasis on stimulating consumer spending — and particularly the high tax rates on investment income and the growth of Social Security — was greatly sapping the incentives of Americans to save and to invest. Professor Murray Weidenbaum of Washington University in Saint Louis estimated that the maze of federal regulations that had mushroomed with the increased role of government in our lives was costing $100 billion a year. Economic theorists Robert Lucas and Thomas Sargent, founders of the "rational expectations" school of thought, attacked the very core of Keynesian policy activism. They argued that efforts by government to stabilize the economy or increase economic activity would be completely ineffective.

What began as a trickle of criticism soon turned into a frontal assault. Keynes was blamed for the decline in savings in the United States, and for the low level of new investment. The tendency of governments to operate with large budget deficits year after year was laid on his doorstep. He was charged with leading the global economy down the path of stagflation.

Even well-known establishment Keynesians seemed to be deserting his cause. Nobel Prize–winning economist Lawrence Klein, who relied greatly on Keynesian concepts in building the econometric models that had made him world-famous, stated: "The conditions of the 1930s gave rise to the Keynesian Revolution. The conditions of the 1970s are different, and they should give rise to other policies. . . . We should have switched from demand management — of manipulating the overall economy — to supply analysis and management."[12]

Conclusion

As the 1970s drew to a close, the political leaders of the major industrialized countries were reeling. Oil prices had skyrocketed from $2 a barrel at the beginning of the decade to $31 a barrel at the end, bringing about raging inflation. The international monetary system constructed at Bretton Woods in 1944 had been destroyed and replaced by a new system that created great uncertainty in the financial markets. Large trade and current-account deficits were being incurred by the industrialized countries, as well as by the less developed countries. The number of unemployed had increased from 15 million to 25 million, and there was little hope in sight for a decline in these numbers.

The global economy appeared to be mired in a period of long-term stagnation — of low growth and high inflation — while the Keynesian economic policies that had worked so well in the past now seemed hopelessly out-of-date. It is hardly surprising that a new generation of political leaders would suddenly appear and embark upon a search for an economy that would operate under totally different concepts and policies than those of the past. The stage was set for a new era of economic experimentation.

The United States
Flirts with Reaganomics

*O*N FEBRUARY 18, 1981, President Ronald Reagan entered the packed chambers of the House of Representatives to a thunderous standing ovation. It was 9:00 PM in Washington and the members of Congress had gathered in joint session to hear the new president lay out the details of his economic program. Expectations were high, for rumors had been growing since his election that this new program would mean radical change for the country.

After first cautioning that "we can no longer procrastinate and hope that things will get better [for] they will not," the president went on to propose "a comprehensive four-point program . . . aimed at reducing the growth in Government spending and taxing, reforming and eliminating regulations which are unnecessary and unproductive, or counter-productive, and encouraging a consistent monetary policy aimed at maintaining the value of the currency." The proposal to reduce taxes provided the basis for what would become known as "supply-side economics," or "Reaganomics," and it was far from conservative. "Our proposal is for a 10 percent across-the-board cut every year for three years in the tax rates for all individual income taxpayers, making a total tax cut in tax rates of 30 percent," the president announced. Taxes were to be reduced by $44.2 billion in 1982 and the slashes would continue until they reached a massive $162.4 billion by 1986. This 30-percent reduction "will leave the taxpayers with $500 billion more in their pockets over the next five years," President Reagan declared.[1]

Never before in the history of the nation had a president proposed reducing taxes by so much for such a long period. Normally tax reductions were proposed for one year, never for as long as three. Nor were previous presidents ever so bold as to suggest that tax rates should be reduced by 30 percent and tax revenues by $500 billion.

In terms of its intended impact on the nation, supply-side economics was on par with the New Deal of President Franklin Roosevelt. The economic policies of postwar administrations, even those programs named to evoke a new era — the Fair Deal of President Harry Truman, the Great Society of President Lyndon Johnson, the New Federalism of President Richard Nixon — were built upon a common approach. Government spending and taxation policies were designed to stimulate aggregate demand — the sum of spending by consumers, investors, and government. For nearly half a century, ever since the New Deal programs of Roosevelt and the emergence of Keynesian economic thinking, demand had dominated economic policy.

In pursuing these policies, officials assumed that the supply side of the economy would take care of itself. The willingness of Americans to work and to save was treated rather benignly. Individuals would work because they wanted to earn money to pay for the goods and services they demanded. Savings were what remained from income after consumption. Business would automatically expand new investment in plant and equipment as it reacted to the impact of an increase in demand for its products. Little conscious thought or effort was given to direct stimulation of the supply of labor and capital in the economy.

This was to be changed with the economic program of President Reagan. Supply, rather than demand, was to become the driving force behind economic policies in the future. The supply of labor was to be increased. The supply of savings was to be expanded. The supply of capital for productive investments was to be encouraged. Government expenditures and regulations were to be reduced if they interfered with incentives to expand the supply-side capacity of the economy. It was supply-side economics that was to do the job of strengthening the American economy, not the old demand-driven policies of the past. And the engine that was to drive this new supply-side experiment was a massive reduction in taxes.

"The cut in tax rates will provide individuals greater incentives for productive employment and for savings," explained a White House background paper amplifying President Reagan's economic message. "Also, reduced tax rates will make tax shelters less attractive and productive investments more attractive. Thus, cuts in individual taxes are expected to contribute to increased investments that will expand the productive base of the economy and create more jobs."[2]

Given the importance of tax reduction to the supply-side experiment of the Reagan administration, it is not surprising that the president threw down the gauntlet to any potential opposition in his economic message of February 18, 1981: "I would direct a question to those who have indicated already an unwillingness to accept such a plan: Have they an alternative which offers a greater chance of balancing the budget, reducing and eliminating inflation, stimulating the creation of jobs and reducing the tax burden? And, if they haven't, are they suggesting we can continue on the present course without coming to a day of reckoning?"[3]

Few were willing to challenge the new president openly on his supply-side economics. One Democratic leader hesitatingly suggested that "locking this country into a 30 percent tax cut over a three-year period will obviously stimulate consumption dramatically" and "spur inflation."[4] A few businessmen expressed concern over the possibility of large budget deficits and high interest rates that such policies might produce. But the president was easily able to beat down such opposition. Drawing upon his prodigious abilities to communicate to the people, and demonstrating an unexpected flair for playing the rough-and-tumble game of political arm-twisting in Washington, Ronald Reagan moved quickly toward a showdown in Congress.

It wasn't much of a contest. Two days before the tax bill was to be voted upon in the Democratic-controlled House of Representatives, the president went on television to appeal to the American public for support. The response was overwhelming. House Speaker Thomas P. ("Tip") O'Neill, leader of the Democratic opposition to the White House, told reporters that the Monday-night speech "touched off a telephone blitz like this nation has never seen."[5] On Wednesday, July 29, 1981, the vote was taken in the House. After a mere seven hours of debate, Reagan won 238 to 195, as 48 Democrats joined 190 Republicans in giving the president a decisive victory.

Earlier in the day a similar bill passed easily in the Republican-controlled Senate. Following the House vote, a compromise bill was quickly agreed upon by both chambers. On August 13, 1981, President Reagan signed his historic package of tax reductions into law. In 190 days in office President Reagan "has not only wrought a dramatic conservative shift in the nation's economic policies and the role of the Federal Government in American life but has also swept to a political mastery of Congress not seen since Lyndon B. Johnson," reported the *New York Times*.[6]

The Laffer Curve

The intellectual and economic basis for the Reagan experiment is a rather simple concept known as "the Laffer curve." Named for Professor Arthur B. Laffer, a zealous supply-side advocate from the University of Southern California, the Laffer curve is commonly thought to have been born during a luncheon with a high-ranking White House official of the Gerald Ford administration. While deeply engaged in a discussion of the many problems confronting the American economy, and forcefully advancing his views that much of the fault lay with large government and high taxes, Professor Laffer reportedly drew on a table napkin a curve that resembled the one shown in figure 1.

The curve showed a presumed relationship between tax rates and

FIGURE 1

THE LAFFER CURVE

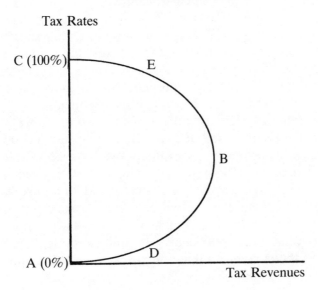

tax revenues that suggested that a reduction in taxes would lead to an increase in tax revenues. Such a view totally contradicted conventional wisdom. Most politicians assumed that in order to raise more government revenue — to finance increased defense spending, pay for Social Security, or fund other government programs — taxes would have to be increased. And if taxes were lowered, either government expenditures would have to be reduced or a budget deficit incurred. Not so, suggested Professor Laffer. And, needless to say, such a contrary viewpoint fell upon very receptive political ears.

The rationale behind Laffer's thinking is demonstrated by the Laffer curve. (See figure 1.) At point A on the curve, tax rates and tax revenues are both zero — if no taxes are levied, there will be no tax revenue. At the other extreme, point C, tax rates are 100 percent and tax revenues are zero. With totally confiscatory tax rates, no one will work, save, or invest. Admittedly, this is a hypothetical situation, for people have to live, and this implies some effort. But the extreme case has great relevance for economic policy: it suggests that once tax rates reach very high levels, the economic incentives to work and invest are dramatically diminished. For instance, if a worker is taxed at a 90-percent tax rate on additional earnings, there is little incentive to expand work effort.

The relevant concern for economic policy is not these extreme points, however, but the shape of the curve that connects the two points and where the economy is operating on that curve. And here Professor Laffer drew a smooth curve connecting points A, B, and C. In moving from point A to point B, an increase in tax rates will result in an increase in tax revenues. But at point B, tax rates begin to become confiscatory and any increase in taxes above point B will lead to such a reduction in work effort that tax revenues will actually decline. And the higher taxes are pushed, moving along the curve from B toward C, the greater the decline in revenues.

The conventional view was that the economy was operating along the AB part of the curve, say at point D, so that any increase in taxes would lead to increased government tax revenues. Professor Laffer argued that the economy was actually operating along the BC portion of the curve, maybe at point E, and so a decrease in tax rates would increase work incentives, and tax revenues would rise rather than fall. Using this simple curve, Professor Laffer and the many economists and politicians who quickly joined his cause greatly altered the current thinking regarding macroeconomic policy, and particularly tax policy.

Relative Prices and Economic Behavior

The primary emphasis when considering tax changes should be on relative prices rather than aggregate demand, according to the supply-side economists advising President Reagan — or, as they state the issue: "In the technical terminology, the distinction is between first-order income effects or first-order relative price effects."[7]

The supply-side economists mean that the first consideration (first order) in establishing economic policy should be relative price effects. And by relative price effects they mean the impact of taxes on important personal economic decisions such as work-versus-leisure and savings-versus-consumption. For instance, if the tax rate on earned income is increased from 25 percent to 50 percent, then leisure time becomes more valuable relative to the decreased economic reward from work. A worker making $10.00 an hour will receive an after-tax income of only $5.00 at the higher tax rate, compared to the previous $7.50 under the old tax rate. This decline in after-tax income provides a greater incentive to work less, for the loss of income from an additional hour of golf or watching television is now only $5.00 instead of $7.50. The same reasoning applies to savings-versus-consumption: a higher tax rate on interest earnings creates greater incentive to consume, for the return from savings has been reduced.

This is quite different from making income effects the top priority in setting economic policy. In this approach, the most important consideration is the effect of a tax change on the income of the taxpayer, not its effect on his or her incentives to work and save. A reduction in personal income taxes leaves the individual with a higher after-tax income, which enables that person to spend more. This increased spending will generate a greater demand for goods and services, leading to additional output in the economy and thus more jobs.

Note that the same end result is achieved in either approach — an increase in work effort in the economy. However, the supply-side economists argue that primary emphasis must be placed on stimulating work incentives directly, while the demand-side economists, as they are frequently called, suggest that additional work effort is the indirect result of increased aggregate demand. While such differences in view may seem rather arcane, they are of major significance in the setting of economic policy, for they involve such critical issues as what taxes and whose taxes should be reduced.

In addressing this question, the supply-side economists make a second major shift in the conventional wisdom: The emphasis in economic policy must be on marginal tax rates. In reaching this position, the economists point out the obvious. Individuals and economic institutions alter their behavior at the margin. We do not decide to work zero hours a week or fifty hours a week. Rather we make a choice on working forty or forty-five hours. Similarly, a corporation does not generally make a decision to terminate all planned investments in new equipment, but rather whether to increase or decrease such investment by 10 percent or 15 percent. Such decisions are referred to by policymakers as "marginal changes" in our economic behavior.

When applied to our reaction to tax changes, it is the amount of taxes that we pay on our additional earnings or savings that alters our behavior. For instance, if an individual earning $30,000 a year receives a raise of $3,000, the additional taxes on this income would have been $1,470 — 49 percent of the raise — under the old tax law. To increase the incentive to work, the Reagan administration reduced the marginal tax rate for such an individual to 38 percent in 1984, or $1,140 — a reduction in taxes of $330.

A third major change brought about by the supply-side economists shifts the emphasis in tax policy from a concern with equity to a focus on efficiency; that is, the overriding goal of tax policy should be to improve the efficiency of the economy by reducing barriers to the increased supply of labor and capital rather than to concentrate on achieving a "fair" or "equitable" distribution of the tax burden.

While "the effects of tax changes on the income level distribution of tax liabilities . . . are, to be sure, important concerns of tax policy," writes Norman B. Ture, a leading tax expert among the supply-side economists, the "current pressing concern of public economic policy is to identify the obstructions to growth in labor's productivity and, if feasible, to reduce these impediments." Dealing effectively with these barriers "will require policymakers to change sharply the focus of their concerns and priorities."[8] Professor Laffer is somewhat more direct in making the same point: "Taxing the rich is sometimes a good way to further impoverish the poor."[9]

These statements do not necessarily represent a pro-rich and anti-poor bias among the supply-side economists, but an acceptance of the fact that any reduction in marginal tax rates in order to encourage greater work effort and more savings will benefit those with higher incomes more than those with lower incomes. And since those with higher incomes are taxed at higher marginal rates, they are expected to show the greatest response to a reduction in tax rates. Doctors, lawyers, and other professionals are expected to work longer hours. Business executives will accept more challenging and higher-paying positions if they can retain more of what they earn. Entrepreneurs, investors, venture capitalists, and mortgage bankers will be willing to undertake more productive, and possibly more risky, investments since their after-tax returns will be greater. The benefits from the resurgence of economic activity among these groups of high-income and high-taxed individuals will "trickle down" to the poor in the form of more and better-paid jobs. And so Professor Laffer can make his point that reducing taxes on the rich will also benefit the poor and lower-income workers.[10]

A fourth major shift in policy thinking concentrates on making changes in taxes rather than altering the level of government expenditures. The supply-side economists totally reject the use of government expenditures as an appropriate policy tool. According to them, changes in expenditures do not alter marginal behavior, for they do not directly stimulate additional work effort or savings. Indeed, government expenditures represent little more than a shift of resources from the private sector of the economy to the public sector. The choice is whether society desires to spend more money on public welfare or education rather than on automobiles, housing, or clothing. It is a choice of spending priorities, not a choice of appropriate economic policy alternatives.

A fifth, and final, major shift in policy thinking introduced by the supply-side economists is one that has caught the imagination of a number of leading politicians, and for good reason. This is the suggestion that tax cuts will be self-financing; that is, reductions in marginal tax rates will so stimulate work effort and savings that the economy will expand sufficiently to provide the additional revenues to pay for the tax cut.

So confident were the supply-side economists in the efficacy of their analysis that they promised a budget balance within three years of President Reagan's historically large reduction in personal taxes. "It is reasonable to conclude that each of the proposed 10 percent reductions in tax rates would, in terms of overall tax revenues, be self-financing in less than two years. Thereafter, each installment would provide a positive contribution to overall tax receipts," wrote Professor Laffer. Nor would the largess be confined solely to the federal government, for "it should be noted that a significant portion of these revenues would accrue to state and local governments, relieving much if not all of the fiscal distress evident in these governmental units as well."[11]

In light of such promises, it is hardly surprising that the tax reduction program proposed by President Reagan in early 1981 won such an overwhelming victory in Congress. Few politicians could vote against a program that promised to restore the vitality of the American economy while leaving "the taxpayers with $500 billion more in their pockets over the next five years." To accomplish this economic miracle, the president adopted the entire package of policies advanced by the supply-side economists: The program was sold to the public as the appropriate means to restore the good old American values of work and savings. Marginal tax rates on personal income were the primary policy tool. Equity concerns gave way to efficiency considerations. And, above all, the program would be costless in terms of economic sacrifice. It would pay for itself in less than two years.

The Work-Leisure Choice

In making a massive reduction in marginal tax rates the heart of Reaganomics, the president and his economic advisors were not relying on brand-new economic theory. The Laffer curve is a somewhat simple statement of well-known and readily acceptable economic theory. The antecedents of the Laffer curve go way back in the history of economic thought, and include some of the most famous names in the economics profession, who began raising the issue of the disincentive effects of high taxes over two centuries ago. The work-versus-leisure-choice question, in particular, has been around for a long time.

In the mid-eighteenth century it was commonly thought that low wages were necessary to force people to work industriously. As income was driven lower, either through high taxes or low rates of pay, the worker would have a greater incentive to work harder, for only then could he or she earn enough to live on. This rather barbaric view was challenged by several economists in France, who postulated that high wages would enhance rather than inhibit innovative activity and productive work effort. David Hume introduced these ideas into England around 1750, writing that "exorbitant taxes, like extreme necessity, destroy industry, by producing despair."[12] His good friend Adam Smith picked up on this point and incorporated it into his famous treatise of 1776 on the *Wealth of Nations.*

According to Adam Smith, the basic wealth of a nation consists of the real goods and services it produces in proportion to its population. The growth of aggregate supply is the very nature and cause of wealth. And to ensure such growth, there must be positive incentives to encourage the supply of productive work effort. "The liberal reward for labour . . . increases the industry of the common people," wrote Smith. "The wages of labour are the encouragement of industry, which, like every other human quality, improves in proportion to the encouragement it receives."[13]

This is not the only theme from Adam Smith that runs through the Reagan experiment. The great Scottish economist also provided the ammunition for the supply-side argument that high taxes may well lead to a reduction rather than an increase in government revenues: "High taxes, sometimes by diminishing the consumption of the taxed commodities, and sometimes by encouraging smuggling, frequently afford a smaller revenue to government than what might be drawn from more moderate taxes."[14]

Other great names in economics developed these ideas and pushed them closer to becoming conventional wisdom. In 1803, Professor J. B. Say — a name revered among the supply-side economists — added to the arsenal of tax-disincentive literature: "Taxation, pushed to the extreme, has the lamentable effect of impoverishing the individual without enriching the state"; and John Stuart Mill reemphasized in 1848 that "over-taxation, carried to a sufficient extent, is quite capable of ruining the most industrious community."[15] By the turn of the twentieth century, these ideas had become the predominant view on taxation and the generation of government revenue.

Consequently, when economists in the Reagan administration turned to marginal tax reduction as the core of their economic experiment, they were treading on very familiar theoretical ground. Unfortunately, the ground is far less familiar when it comes to the practical impact of these changes. In assessing just exactly how the individual worker will respond to tax reductions, the economic theoreticians from the past and the Laffer curve from the present offer precious little guidance. The theory runs aground on a long-standing controversy known as "the substitution effect versus income effect" of such tax reductions.

As discussed earlier, the view adopted by the Reagan supply-side economists is that an increase in taxes will diminish work effort, while a reduction in taxes will make work more worthwhile and hence lead to an increase in the productive effort. Such a position is based on changing the price of work in relation to leisure, and is referred to as the substitution effect. With a reduction in taxes, the individual will substitute work for leisure.

It is quite possible, however, that a reduction in taxes will lead to a decline in a person's work effort. With the reduction, the after-tax income of the individual has been increased, and therefore the taxpayer may decide to work less — for the same standard of living can be maintained now with less work effort. This is referred to as the income effect.

Finally, it is not at all clear that the majority of individuals have much choice in how long they work. Most of us work full-time for institutions that require a set number of hours of work, somewhere between thirty-five and forty hours a week. We have very little latitude in altering these hours, and so the choice between work and leisure is more hypothetical than real.

These issues are of great importance in the Reagan economic experiment, for they raise basic questions about whether the program of work incentives will be effective or not. If individuals work less rather than more because of the reduction in marginal tax rates, then the program will produce results exactly opposite from those intended. Or if the individual has little flexibility in deciding how much to work, the experiment will fail. These are issues where there is very little practical evidence to guide the policymaker.

What evidence that does exist suggests that the primary worker in the household, either the head of the household or the sole wage earner, will respond very little to any change in tax rates. Most of the individuals in this position have little choice: they must continue working to support the household. The secondary worker does have greater choice and it is here that the incentives could be expected to operate. A secondary worker may decide that it is worthwhile to work, since he or she can retain a greater percentage of earnings. Or a relative or housemate may take a full-time position rather than continue working part-time. The supply-side economists argue that these secondary workers, along with older workers and high-income professionals, will increase their work effort with a reduction in tax rates. And since these workers make up about one-half of the total work force, the impact on the economy will be rather significant.

Savings and Tax Reduction

After noting that the savings rate of Americans had declined by nearly one-third since the 1950s and 1960s, the Reagan administration stated that it sought "to increase capital formation by both raising the level of output and reducing the fraction of output consumed." Reducing government spending was an important part of this effort, "but creating an environment where households choose to save a larger share of their income is of paramount importance."[16]

To increase savings, the Reagan economic planners proposed three changes: (1) reduce the tax rate on unearned income along with that on earned income; (2) make investments in tax shelters less attractive; and (3) extend the opportunity to use Individual Retirement Accounts (IRAs) to all working households.

Before Reaganomics, the tax rate on unearned income, such as interest, dividends, and the taxable fraction of capital gains, ranged from 14 percent to 70 percent, as compared to the tax rate on wages and salaries, which ranged from 14 percent to 50 percent. Reagan's advisors considered the higher marginal tax rate on unearned income to be not only unfair but highly disincentive to expanded savings. At a maximum rate of 70 percent, it was assumed, there was very little incentive to increase savings; rather, the individual was encouraged to spend and consume, thus reducing the amount of capital in the economy for financing productive investments. The upper rate of 70 percent was to be immediately reduced to 50 percent, and the differential tax rate between earned and capital income was eliminated. In the future they would be treated the same, so that the effective tax rate on income from savings would decline along with the planned reduction in tax rates on income from working.

Tax shelters were the second area where the Reagan administration hoped to achieve some reform. Many high-income taxpayers were reducing their tax burdens by investing in such tax shelters as real estate development, oil and gas exploration, art collections and cattle breeding — investments that were considered to be "unproductive" by the Reagan officials. The tax shelters were siphoning off capital from more productive investments in new plant and equipment and growth-oriented businesses. In lowering the overall marginal tax rates significantly, and particularly in eliminating the tax differential on capital income, it was hoped that these unproductive tax shelters would be less attractive.

And the third way the Reagan economists hoped to increase savings was through the Individual Retirement Accounts (IRAs). Under existing law, individuals who were self-employed could set aside part of their income in an IRA and delay paying taxes on these savings until retirement, but an individual working for a company that had a pension plan was not allowed to set up an IRA. Since the IRA funds generally were maintained in banks or other financial institutions, the money was available for productive investment in the economy. A simple way to expand this pool of savings was to extend the privilege of IRAs to all employed workers. Such a change also had the great advantage of decreasing the pressure on the Social Security system, for if private savings could be increased to provide for retirement, there would be less of a burden placed on the public pension program.

Under the new tax law, each worker would be allowed to contribute up to $2,000 to an IRA, regardless of whether he or she was already covered by an employer-sponsored pension plan. If only one spouse worked, a couple could set aside up to $2,250. "Given the sizable tax savings available from IRAs," the administration stated, "the total amount of money invested in them can be expected to rise sharply."[17]

The justification for these changes is the same as that advanced for increasing work effort discussed in the previous section. The supply-side economists argue that by changing the relative price of savings and consumption through reducing the effective taxes on savings, the individual will be encouraged to save more. And this increased savings will contribute to the strength and growth of the American economy.

Again this view is well grounded in economic theory. White House officials could quote from Adam Smith and say that "wherever capital predominates, industry prevails."[18] They could cite David Ricardo, who in 1821 argued that "it should be the policy of governments never to lay such taxes as will inevitably fall on capital, since by so doing, they impair the funds for the maintenance of labor, and thereby diminish the future production of the country."[19] Or they could refer to the work of more modern-day economists, and particularly the growth-oriented economists of the 1950s who pointed out that an economy can be moved to a higher potential growth path by increasing the savings rate. The Reagan economists did not have to worry much about the practicality of their savings incentives, for the evidence strongly suggested that the changes would bring about the desired result: Americans would begin to save more of what they earned.

Reordering Budget Priorities

Although reducing personal taxes was the core of the Reagan economic experiment, four other objectives were involved as well: (1) containing the growth of government spending, (2) reordering budget priorities, (3) reforming and eliminating unnecessary and unproductive regulations, and (4) encouraging a consistent monetary policy aimed at maintaining the value of the currency.

These objectives were not central to the supply-side economic program, and indeed they greatly interfered with the success of the program. Some were conflicting; others were mere rhetorical artifacts. Yet they formed an integral part of Reaganomics. As events were to unfold, the goal of limiting the growth of government spending was never realized. In fact, the Reagan administration became the greatest spender in American history, with budget outlays and deficits that far exceeded those of any previous administration.

Reforming and eliminating government regulations was relegated a rather minor role in the Reagan economic program, and was soon lost in the maze of debate over more important economic objectives. Monetary policy quickly moved to the forefront of debate, becoming the focal point of heated battles between the supply-side advocates and the monetarists within the administration. The monetarists argued that slowing down the growth in the amount of money in the economy was the only way to bring inflation down. But the supply-side economists were very concerned that this would lead to a recession, and therefore their experiment would appear unsuccessful.

The goal of reordering budget priorities was, however, successfully implemented, and may well be the only goal of the experiment that fully achieved what the Reagan administration intended. Yet even this goal was plagued with difficulties, for it was continually confounded with the goal of reducing the level of government spending.

The political rhetoric of Reaganomics emphasized the desire to reduce the overall level of federal government spending. So strong was this rhetoric that it took on an almost religious fervor, as if a dollar spent by government was morally and ethically wrong. In his inaugural address of January 20, 1981, President Reagan was most emphatic in his condemnation of government spending: "In this present crisis, government is not the solution; it is the problem. . . . It is time to check and reverse the growth of government which shows signs of having grown beyond the consent of the governed. . . . It is no coincidence that our present troubles parallel and are proportionate to the intervention and intrusion in our lives that have resulted from unnecessary and excessive growth of government."[20]

The rhetoric carried into the first Reagan budget, which was presented to Congress in February 1982. The major themes of this budget emphasized shifting program responsibility from the federal government to state and local governments, shrinking the government's share of total gross national product, and greatly reducing unnecessary discretionary spending.[21] Yet what was actually proposed was a significant reordering of budget priorities, not a massive reduction in total government spending.

When the Reagan administration assumed office and inherited a federal budget that had changed dramatically over the past two decades, it became a favorite exercise of White House officials to point out the nature of these changes. Selecting 1960 as the benchmark for comparisons, Reagan aides widely publicized their finding that defense spending accounted for 48.2 percent of total government expenditures during that year, while in 1981, the year before the Reagan ascendency, defense spending had declined to only 22.2 percent. (See table 3.) Furthermore, payments to individuals, which consisted mostly of Social Security, military and government retire-

TABLE 3. EXPENDITURES IN THE UNITED STATES BUDGET
(AS A PROPORTION OF TOTAL FEDERAL SPENDING)

Item	1960	1970	1981	1987[a]
Defense	48.2%	38.7%	22.2%	35.4%
Social Security, health, and other payments to individuals	26.4	33.7	50.2	49.0
Public investment	12.4	14.8	14.4	5.7
Other	13.0	12.8	13.2	9.9

SOURCE: *ERP*, Feb. 1982, 83.

[a]Projected by the Reagan administration in 1982.

ment programs, and Medicare, had mushroomed from 26.4 percent to 50.2 percent of the total. And public investment — expenditures on education, training, transportation, energy, natural resources, environment, and general science and technology — remained fairly constant at around 14 percent of the total.

The expenditures in this last category are important, for it was here that the Reagan administration looked for major reductions in what it attempted to sell to Congress and the American public as wasteful social spending by Democratic do-gooders. Yet social programs were not included in this category: most of the "wasteful" programs had long since disappeared under the budget-cutting knives of Presidents Nixon, Ford, and Carter. The programs to be cut represented critical public investment in America's future — but for the Reagan administration to identify them as such would only have highlighted their importance at a time when they were being targeted for massive reduction.

The shifts in the federal budget since 1960 were in response to some very basic changes in American society. By far the most significant change was the aging of the population. A far greater proportion of Americans were retired and more people were living longer in 1981 compared to 1960, when we were still in the postwar baby boom and had a youth-dominated population. By 1981 the birth rate had declined. Workers were retiring earlier and living longer, and this graying population, with its potential political power, had been the recipient of substantial increases in Social Security and health-care benefits.

In other categories also, Americans were asking more of government than had been true in 1960, particularly in such areas as cleaning up the environment, providing special education and training programs to certain disadvantaged groups in society, assisting state and local governments with their financial needs. The energy crisis had occurred, adding a further responsibility to government. The response of politicians to these structural changes in our society was to finance the expanding areas through reductions in defense spending. And even with such reductions, the share of the total output of the economy absorbed by the federal government grew from 18 percent in 1960 to 22 percent during 1981.

The Reagan administration wanted to alter this pattern:

This Administration has a different set of spending priorities than those reflected in the budgets of the recent past. This difference is expressed in the following guidelines used in developing the Administration's plans for restraining the growth of Federal spending:

- Strengthen the national defense.
- Maintain the integrity of social insurance programs while reforming entitlement programs to ensure that they serve those in greatest need.
- Reduce subsidies to middle- and upper-income groups.
- Apply sound economic criteria to programs where subsidies are justified.
- Recover costs that can clearly be allocated to users of services provided by Federal programs.
- Strengthen the Federal structure of government.[22]

When the Reagan administration completed the task of reordering budget priorities, the results were quite dramatic. As shown in table 3 for the target year 1987, the major "winners" were the defense establishment and those receiving Social Security and health-care payments. Spending on defense was slated to increase from 22.2 percent to 35.4 percent of total federal government expenditures, while payments to individuals would remain at around one-half of the total. Among the losers in this reordering were the poor and the middle class.

Yet the major loser was the economy itself, for the bulk of the budget reductions were concentrated in public investment. This is the category that contains nearly all of the federal government's investments in the growth potential of the economy — investments in such areas as education, research and development, energy, and natural resources. It is well known that such investments are essential to ensuring the continued strength of an economy, and in most industrialized countries they loom quite large in government budgets. The Reagan administration, however, planned to reduce public investment in the future from 14.4 percent of the budget in 1981 to just 5.7 percent in 1987.

The wrenching adjustments required to attain this reordering will be far greater than is implied by the data in table 3, for to increase defense spending from 22.2 percent to 35.4 percent of total federal outlays will entail a massive commitment of future budget dollars. And reducing public investment from 14.4 percent to 5.7 percent will actually mean significant reductions in existing programs. To appreciate how sharp such a change is, the allocation of the planned *increase* in total budget dollars must be examined. This is shown in table 4, where it is noted that in 1983 the Reagan administration was projecting federal government outlays in 1987 to be some $401 billion higher than they were in 1981. Of this planned increase in spending, roughly $195 billion, about one-half of the total, will be for defense. This means that nearly one out of every two dollars of increased federal government spending will go to defense. Nearly $163 billion, or roughly 41 percent of the total planned increase, will be used for Social Security, Medicare, and other payments to individuals. And when interest on the debt is included, there is very little left for any other program. In fact, public investment in education, energy, environment, transportation, and similar programs will actually be reduced to more than $14 billion below the level that existed in 1981.

The impact of these wrenching adjustments did not go unnoticed. In state capitals across the nation, it was reported that the once positive response to President Reagan's plan to create a "new federalism has turned sour as budget cuts squeeze many state treasuries." A coalition of seven national consumer groups issued a report strongly critical of the proposed budget reductions and warning of the "devastating policies in 14 areas, including food, health, energy, housing, credit and product safety." Congressional Democrats "assailed President Reagan's proposed budget as unfair and

TABLE 4. PLANNED EXPENDITURE SHIFTS IN THE UNITED STATES BUDGET, 1981–1987 (PROJECTED TOTALS)

Item	Amount in Billions of $	Amount as Proportion of Overall Increase
Defense	+ 194.6	+ 48.5%
Social Security, health, and other payments to individuals	+ 162.5	+ 40.5
Public investment	− 14.2	− 3.5
Interest on debt	+ 47.9	+ 11.9
Offsetting receipts	+ 10.4	+ 2.6
TOTAL	+ 401.2	+ 100.0%

SOURCE: *Budget of the United States Government: Fiscal Year 1983* (Washington, D.C.: GPO, 1983).

unworkable," while Republicans "predicted that the President would have trouble selling the budget to members of either party in an election year."[23]

Even business leaders were cautious when President Reagan turned to them for support, asking private industry to show a "spirit of shared sacrifice" by funding private substitutes for government welfare programs. A survey shortly after the presidential appeal found that many executives feared they had been "set up by the Federal government."[24]

Reforming Government Regulations

The federal government was deeply involved in regulating economic activity, spending over $7 billion annually through a number of different agencies. These agencies employed thousands of inspectors and analysts, who examined the safety of everything from food to nuclear power plants, assessed environmental impact statements, and issued tens of thousands of detailed rules governing economic behavior.

Much of this regulatory activity was anathema to the Reagan administration, and during the president's first year in office, 2,893 federal regulations were subjected to Executive Office review. The White House had two major criticisms of government regulatory activity: (1) there was simply too much regulation, which was stifling the growth and dynamics of the economy, and (2) the method of regulation was inefficient.

To solve the first problem, the administration quickly issued an executive order directing agencies to use benefit-cost analysis when promulgating new regulations, reviewing existing regulations, or developing legislative proposals concerning regulation. This was the first time that regulatory agencies had to quantify the expected impact of their activity by estimating such things as anticipated results in protecting lives, reducing accidents, and decreasing health problems. These benefits had to be measured against the possible negative effect on economic efficiency, including such repercussions as higher costs of regulated products and decline in output.

Furthermore, President Reagan set up a Task Force on Regulatory Relief, chaired by the vice-president, to review proposed regulations. The Office of Management and Budget greatly increased its role in assessing the need for new regulations. Yet of greater significance were moves by the administration to deregulate major industries and allow far greater competition than had existed in the past. Broad industry deregulation was already under way before the Reagan administration took office, particularly in the financial industry, and the new administration strongly supported efforts to make finance, trucking, airlines, and the energy and communications industries more open to competition.

To solve the second problem — the inefficient method of regulation — the administration began to introduce the concept of a marketable permit system for controlling air quality. Traditionally, government regulations have been quite specific in detailing how certain clean-air standards must be met. The standards of performance would prescribe the technology to be used, rather than allowing industry to develop its own solutions to the problem. Also, the same system of technology-based emissions standards was applied to all industries in a given geographical area — those who polluted and those who did not. Consequently, firms in an area where pollution was a minor or negligible problem were subjected to the same regulations as firms located in a densely populated and heavily polluted environment. The result of this standard, technology-based regulation approach was a significant loss in economic efficiency.

The administration encouraged the Environmental Protection Agency to move toward a transferable-permit system in which firms would be assigned separate emissions standards based on the type of industry. Individual allowances under this program would be designed to limit the total amount of pollution in the environment for a given area as part of a systematic approach to meeting air- and water-quality targets. A nonpolluting firm could sell its emissions permit to a polluting firm, and the overall environmental-quality targets would not be jeopardized. Or, alternatively, a polluting firm could design its own equipment to ensure that it met the requirements established by the emissions permit. This system of "pricing" government regulations was a major break with the past, and offered the potential for a far more effective regulatory system in the future.

Reforming government regulations never became a central part of the Reagan economic experiment, however, for the mission proved far more difficult than initially perceived. Many of the regulations that were to be eliminated served very legitimate social and safety concerns, and so it was a difficult task to assess the appropriate trade-off between economic efficiency and worker safety or environmental protection. Furthermore, the existing regulations had a well-established constituency, in both industry and the government bureaucracy, who did not necessarily attempt to block reform but who ensured that all of the complex issues were considered in the reform process.

Maintaining the Value of the Currency

The final goal of Reaganomics was that of encouraging a consistent monetary policy aimed at maintaining the value of the currency. What the administration meant by this was that it wanted a lower growth in the amount of money put into the economy over an extended period. This would lead to lower inflation rates, ending the double-digit ones then vexing the economy and causing consternation among consumers, investors, and business leaders. Lower inflation would restore confidence and bring about increased investment.

There was no doubt that the administration intended to take a firm position with respect to this economic goal. After observing that the federal government "bears the most direct responsibility for the increases in inflation and interest rates, which were due to excessive expansion of the money supply,"[25] and pointing out that the money supply had grown at an annual rate of 7.3 percent during 1979, officials announced that "the Administration assumes a gradual but steady reduction in the growth of money to one-half that rate by 1986."[26]

President Reagan did not have the power to enforce directly his goal of reducing the growth in the money supply from the 7.3-percent level during 1979 to 3.5 percent by 1986, for the Federal Reserve is independent of the White House. This fact was acknowledged by the president in his February 18, 1981, message on economic recovery: "Now we fully recognize the independence of the Federal Reserve System and will do nothing to interfere with or undermine that independence. We will consult regularly with the Federal Reserve Board on all aspects of our economic program and will vigorously pursue budget policies that will make their job easier in reducing monetary growth."[27]

His acknowledgment notwithstanding, few presidents in the past had taken such a firm and open stand on setting definitive targets for the conduct of monetary policy at the beginning of their administration. The setting of targets, and the conduct of policy to attain those targets, had generally been viewed as the sole prerogative of the central bank. It was rather unusual for the Reagan administration to be so direct and aggressive in its policy statements.

Fortunately, the administration was addressing a very sympathetic chairman of the Federal Reserve who also was strongly committed to tight monetary policy in order to reduce inflation. Several weeks before President Reagan announced his new economic program, the chairman of the Fed testified before Congress on the problem of inflation. "I have spoken often of the importance of breaking the inflationary momentum that grips our economy," he said. "That seems to me the preeminent objective of economic policy, partly because prospects for sustained growth rest on success in that effort." And shortly after the president delivered his initial economic message, Chairman Paul A. Volcker again testified: "I have the distinct impression that there is a broad consensus about the appropriate goals for economic policy."[28]

As part of this consensus, the chairman announced that monetary policy "must be — and must be seen to be — consistently directed toward curbing excessive growth in money and credit. Such restraint is inherent in the Federal Reserve's commitment to reduce the growth of money and credit over time until inflationary pressures subside." But Chairman Volcker gave warning that this task would not be an easy course to follow. "I might also note that our efforts to keep money growth within acceptable bounds will at times be associated with substantial variations in short-term interest rates in response to shifting credit demands, changes in economic activity, or other factors." Furthermore, the chairman noted that the success of monetary policy was critically dependent upon reducing the budget deficit: "In particular I cannot stress too strongly the need to change the strong upward trend in federal spending that has characterized recent years."[29]

These warnings were a precursor of problems that were to develop later during the experiment in Reaganomics, for volatile interest rates created great uncertainty in the financial markets and the Reagan administration produced massive budget deficits with its program of tax reductions and large increases in defense spending.

The Ghost of Adam Smith

Reaganomics was far more than an economic experiment. Like many of the experiments being tested in other major industrialized countries, it was a combination of economics and political philosophy.

In particular, President Reagan in the United States, Prime Minister Margaret Thatcher in Great Britain, and President Mitterrand of France strongly intermingled their economic policies with their political philosophies.

This is not to suggest that previous national leaders were not guilty of the same behavior — but previous leaders did not go to the extremes of those who more recently governed. The reason for their unique behavior is the extremely difficult times that these leaders have faced. Confronted with the numerous structural problems of a changing global economy, challenged by the demands of an aging population and massive unemployment, and left adrift without replacements for the social welfare state and Keynesian economics on which to base policy, these leaders have searched for new identities.

Reaganomics is an identity based on a political philosophy of a greatly limited role for government. And in developing this new identity, President Reagan rolled the clock back to 1776 and Adam Smith, who championed capitalism and laissez-faire economics. In enumerating the appropriate functions for government, Adam Smith was extremely cautious:

> The first duty of the sovereign, that of protecting the society from the violence and invasion of other independent societies, can be performed only by means of a military force. . . .
> The second duty of the sovereign [is] that of protecting, as far as possible, every member of the society from the injustice or oppression of every other member of it. . . .
> The third and last duty of the sovereign is that of erecting and maintaining those public works which the profit could never repay the expense to any individual or small number of individuals.[30]

Adam Smith's arguments for a powerful and permanent military force resound throughout Reaganomics. Such a force was necessary for the preservation of freedom and liberty. It was essential to protect the citizens from "invasion by a poor and barbarous neighbour." It is only by means of a strong defense "that the civilization of any country can be perpetuated, or even preserved for any considerable time."

Against those who might argue that a strong defense posed a threat to individual liberty, Adam Smith suggested that this would be true if the military leaders did not hold the broader social interests of the nation above self-interests for power and aggrandizement. "But where the sovereign is himself the general [and] where the military force is placed under the command of those who have the greatest interest in the support of the civil authority, a standing army can never be dangerous to liberty. On the contrary, it may in some cases be favourable to liberty."

President Reagan clearly viewed himself as the "civilian general" of whom Adam Smith wrote, whose greatest interest in expanding defense was the preservation of his nation's freedom. Throughout his speeches, messages to Congress, and official reports on the economy and the budget, there were numerous references to the need for a strong defense establishment in order to protect America's liberty.

The tone was set in the inaugural address on January 20, 1981. Speaking to "the enemies of freedom, to those who are potential adversaries," the newly sworn-in president stated that "peace is the highest aspiration of the American people." And he committed our nation to the defense of that freedom by promising that "we will negotiate for it, sacrifice for it; we will not surrender for it — now or ever."[31]

Within a matter of days, Reagan delivered his state-of-the-union message on economic recovery, in which the Department of Defense was singled out as the "only department in our entire program that will actually be increased over the present budgeted figure." Such an increase was necessary to counter what the president called the "massive military buildup" of the Soviet Union, which now had "a significant numerical advantage in strategic nuclear delivery systems, tactical aircraft, submarines, artillery and antiaircraft defense." To allow this imbalance to continue was, in the president's view, a "threat to our national security."[32]

And in his first economic report, President Reagan stated the primary function of government in language almost identical to that used by Adam Smith two centuries earlier. "I have made a conscious effort to ensure that the Federal government fully discharges its duty to provide all Americans with the needed services and protections that only a national government can provide," the president noted. "Chief among these is a strong national defense, a vital function which had been allowed to deteriorate dangerously in previous years."[33]

Our freedom and liberty are under an even greater threat than that from abroad, maintained the president, from the "unnecessary and excessive growth of government."[34] And here again President Reagan lifted pages from Adam Smith. In expanding upon his third role of government, Smith discussed at length several matters relevant to Reaganomics: what type of public works should be supported by government; what level of government should be responsible for providing these public works; and the regulation of economic activity.

"After the public institutions and public works necessary for the defense of the society, and for the administration of justice," wrote Smith, "the other works and institutions of this kind are chiefly those for facilitating the commerce of the society, and those for promoting the instruction of the people."

Adam Smith was very circumspect in his definition of what public works were needed for facilitating commerce. These were limited to "good roads, bridges, navigable canals, harbours, etc." Government should undertake to build the infrastructure that would enable national markets to develop and function — public works that facilitated the movement of goods from their site of production to market and that expanded local markets. Beyond these commercially related activities, there was little else for government to do.

And even these public works were not to be totally financed by government. The cost of building roads and other transportation systems was to be paid by tolls and fees. "The greater part of such public works may easily be so managed, as to afford a particular revenue sufficient for defraying their own expense, without bringing any burden upon the general revenue of the society." Such a system of private payment ensures that government will not become spendthrift on public works, for "their expense too, their grandeur and magnificence, must be suited to what that commerce can afford to pay."

Such a limited and privately financed role of government was also extended to education. "The institutions for the education of the youth may, in the same manner, furnish a revenue sufficient for defraying their own expense." And where private tuition was insufficient to cover education costs, or society desired to extend educational privileges to the masses, the appropriate source of revenue was from local governments. "Through the greater part of Europe, accordingly, the endowment of schools and colleges makes either no charge upon that general revenue, or but a very small one. It everywhere arises chiefly from some local or provincial revenue." The national government had no role either in establishing educational standards or in providing revenues for the provision of education. This public work clearly was a private and local government matter.

In general, Adam Smith suggested that all public works should be financed and managed by local governments, as he was very suspect of the ability of a national government to administer such programs. "The abuses which sometimes creep into the local and provincial administration of a local and provincial revenue, how enormous soever they may appear, are in reality, however, almost always very trifling, in comparison of those which commonly take place in the administration and expenditure of the revenue of a great empire. They are, besides, much more easily corrected."

Finally, Adam Smith argued against any regulation of economic activity, and referred to the large regulated trading companies that then existed in England as "certainly altogether useless." Regulations interfere with economic efficiency and good management, "which can never be universally established but in consequence of that free and universal competition which forces everyone to have recourse to it for the sake of self-defense."

The appropriate role of government as expounded by Adam Smith and that inherent in Reaganomics are remarkably similar. President Reagan, in both his policy statements and his budgetary actions, followed a course of significantly reducing federal government financing of all domestic public works, eliminating federal support for education (even to the point of recommending the abolishment of the Department of Education), shifting responsibility for providing most public works to state and local governments, and reducing government regulation of economic activity.

In his second economic report, the president stated that "for several decades, an ever-larger role for the Federal government [has] sapped the economic vitality of the Nation." He then enumerated some "common sense approaches" to making government more efficient and responsive:

We should leave to private initiative all the functions that individuals can perform privately.
We should use the level of government closest to the community involved for all the public functions it can handle.
Federal government action should be reserved for those needed functions that only the national government can undertake.[35]

In following these commonsense approaches, Reaganomics proposed the transfer of numerous activities to state and local governments. The administration developed a plan, called the New Federalism Initiative, for "a major reshaping of the fiscal relationship between the Federal government and the States."[36]

It was proposed that starting in fiscal year 1984 state governments assume full responsibility for financing and managing the entire welfare system of the nation. The existing Food Stamp Program and Aid to Families with Dependent Children (AFDC) would be transferred to the states. Furthermore, an additional forty-four federal programs were slated for transfer to state and local governments. These included nearly all of the education and training programs, most of the social, health, and nutrition services, and public works programs for airports, highways, mass transportation systems, and water and sewage development.

When the transfer was completed the federal government would be left with "primary responsibility for health insurance and the aged" and critical "national functions such as defense." Nearly all other federal programs would have been transferred in the "belief that State and local governments are more responsive to the needs of both benefit recipients and taxpayers."

For the few remaining federal programs, the administration proposed the imposition of user fees. Believing that the government provides many services that directly benefit clearly identifiable groups of business and private users, the president directed all agencies "to recover the cost of providing these benefits through specific fees instead of continuing the burden on the general taxpayer." Consequently, those who applied for patents and trademarks, used government-operated nuclear waste disposal facilities, camped in national parks, applied for nuclear regulatory licenses, used airports and coastal waterways, or were rescued by the Coast Guard would be billed for the service. Such fees were expected to generate an additional $3.5 billion in revenue during 1984, so this was no trivial effort.

With the efforts to reduce unnecessary and unproductive government regulations (as discussed earlier), the transformation of the American economy would be completed. Supply-side economic policies would restore needed strength and vitality to the private economy. The role of government in providing goods and services would be greatly restricted. Our freedom and liberty would be ensured through a massive buildup in national defense. The abuses of federal-government management of public works would be eliminated with the transfer of this responsibility to state and local governments.

More services would be financed with user fees, thus ensuring that government would not become profligate. But above all, the American economy would be operating under two basic premises that permeated Reaganomic thinking:

All nations which have broad-based representative government and civil liberties have most of their economic activity organized by the market.

Economic conditions in market economies are generally superior to those in nations [with a comparable culture and a comparable resource base] in which the government has the dominant economic role.[37]

Such strong faith in the ability of the market economy to function for the broader welfare of society would have pleased Adam Smith, for over two hundred years ago he wrote that "the invisible hand" of the private market will lead "the private interests and passions of man" in the direction "which is most agreeable to the interest of the whole society."

In advocating his economic experiment based on supply-side principles, President Reagan spoke with the fervor of a religious prophet. And it was not just economic issues that the president was addressing: a total change in the way in which America had been operating for the past half-century was the ultimate objective. In this regard his mission not only bore a great resemblance to the specific principles of Adam Smith, but also to the overall philosophy. For Adam Smith was writing for a new era in British economic policy, challenging decades of mercantile thought and policies. Smith sought to strip away the shackles of government regulation and constraining ideology, and replace it with the freedom of individual initiative and economic enterprise. Reagan was attempting to do the same. "This, then, is our proposal," he told an expectant American public during the early days of his first administration, " 'America's New Beginning: A Program for Economic Recovery.' "[38]

Japan Seeks Economic Security

URING JANUARY 1978, representatives of ninety-seven nations gathered in Geneva, Switzerland, to continue discussions on one of the most critical problems confronting the global economy: the rise of trade protectionism. The mood of the conference was foreboding. Everyone knew that the free flow of goods and capital between nations was essential for maintaining a strong global economy, yet there was the ominous knowledge that barriers to free trade were gradually being erected in one nation after another.

Nearly every nation was engaged in hammering out orderly marketing agreements with major trading partners. The industrialized nations had just won an agreement from the developing countries for more restraints on textile exports. A few months earlier, the United States and Europe had taken quick action to impose a special pricing system when cheaper Japanese steel imports began to threaten domestic steel production. In France officials referred to these developments as "organized free trade" while American policymakers spoke of "voluntary restraints."

Many reasons were being advanced to justify these efforts to organize trade and strike voluntary agreements in international markets. The actions of OPEC a few years earlier had greatly increased the cost of imported oil, and so nations scrambled to expand their exports to pay for this vital resource. Newly industrialized countries such as Brazil, South Korea, Singapore, and Taiwan were rapidly developing as major competitors for export markets. Unemployment was emerging as a major problem in the industrialized economies, and political leaders were becoming increasingly concerned about protecting jobs. In spite of these serious issues, the blame for the emerging trade difficulties began to focus on Japan — the nation most successful in expanding its export markets during these difficult times.

From $19.3 billion in 1970, Japanese exports grew to $98.3 billion by 1978 — a 5.1-fold increase that far exceeded the 3.8-fold increase in exports for the other industrialized countries. Japan's trade balance with the rest of the world (the amount by which Japanese exports exceeded imports) recovered from a low of $1.4 billion during 1974, when the nation reeled under the initial shock of the OPEC oil price increase, to a massive $24.6 billion in 1978. And $11.6 billion of this surplus of exports over imports was with the United States, which was beginning to feel the full impact of Japanese trading success.

By early 1978, the Japanese were being openly criticized throughout the world for their success in trading. "It is perhaps farfetched to compare Japan with King Midas, yet its international competitors can probably be forgiven for thinking in those terms. Despite a sharp increase in the value of the yen, Japanese exports are still soaring," observed the *New York Times*.[1]

The prime minister of New Zealand commented that it was time for Japan to be "dragged, kicking and screaming," into a more responsible role in the international community.[2] Senator Lloyd Bentsen, chairman of the Joint Economic Committee of Congress in 1979, "struck a truculent note in a Senate speech, arguing that free and fair trade is on the decline worldwide, in part because of Japan's 'siege mentality' approach to international trade."[3] Sir Roy Denman, a high trade official in the European Common Market, observed that "there is an atmosphere of August 1914 about world trade today."[4] By 1982 the news headlines were talking of a "U.S.-JAPANESE TRADE SHOWDOWN" and experts were speaking of an atmosphere that is far "uglier than in the past."[5]

The atmosphere was changing for the Japanese as well. Rather than promising to improve the trade balance and striving to appear conciliatory, they began to speak in far tougher terms. "Why is it that Britain only harps on the imbalance in British-Japanese trade despite the fact that its deficit in trade with Japan is smaller than its deficit in trade with West Germany?" wrote Yukio Matsuyama, one of Japan's most prominent journalists. "Why is it that no newspapers make a fuss when Canadians buy an American golf course but opposition is voiced when Japanese do the same thing?"[6]

"We prefer Japanese labor to American," a Toyota official curtly pointed out when asked why Japanese automobile manufacturers were not building their plants in the United States.[7] And when Japan's minister of foreign affairs, Yoshio Sakurauchi, left his country on a trip to Washington in 1982, the headline on the front page of the *Japan Times* announced: "SAKURAUCHI TO RUN GAUNTLET IN THE U.S."[8]

The source of these developments, from the growth in trade surpluses to the deterioration in relationships between Japan and the other industrialized nations, was the economic experiment being pursued by Japan. Undoubtedly the most difficult experiment to understand, particularly by other Western economic powers, and certainly the most criticized, the Japanese experiment was thought by many to be nothing more than the modernization of old-style mercantilism. The emphasis on maintaining favorable trade balances, subsidizing export growth, nurturing foreign sources of raw materials, and deliberately encouraging the development of certain industries all seemed closely akin to the mercantilistic principles of the past.

To unsophisticated observers, Japanese manufacturers and trading companies were "Asian Vikings," rampaging across the seas in pursuit of foreign markets to conquer for the continued aggrandizement of Japanese economic power. An equally naive interpretation envisioned "Japan, Inc.," an impenetrable combination of government, business, and finance — all shrouded in a mist of Asian cultural mystique — that operated to give a distinct trading advantage to the Japanese.

These attitudes are all misleading. The Japanese are not modern-day mercantilists. They are not an Asian rebirth of the seafaring Vikings, nor can they be appropriately characterized as Japan, Inc. It is not trade that they desire so much as economic security. And it is not some mysterious system that they have developed that defies Western logic, but rather a well-honed economic experiment designed to achieve security.

The Japanese experiment is composed of three main elements: (1) the development of priority industries that are on the forefront of global markets; (2) the practice of consensus planning and management that serves to coordinate the activities of government, industry, and research in the pursuit of common economic goals; and (3) the limited use of government incentives to guide the direction of private industrial development.

These three characteristics have long been present in the Japanese economic approach, and they are being refined as the experiment is adjusted for the future. Yet there are several new facets to the Japanese endeavor that represent dramatic departures from the past. It is in the creation of a leading technology, or what the Japanese call their miracle product — a "fifth generation" of computers — that they intend to maintain their global superiority in industry.

This new technology will go far beyond simply keeping Japan on the forefront of global markets in the future. It is expected to have large spillover effects on the remainder of the Japanese industrial base, permeating the country's traditional electronics, automobile, steel, and consumer-appliance industries to make them the most efficient mass-producers in the world. Furthermore, this new technology is being carefully integrated into plans for building a new welfare society and improving the quality of Japanese life. These new departures are what make the Japanese economic experiment so innovative, and they offer important lessons to the rest of the world.

The Search for Economic Security

Although achieving economic security became the dominant goal of the Japanese experiment during the 1970s, when that nation's economy faced its most serious challenges in recent history, the desire for such security has a long tradition that flows from the earliest days of postwar reconstruction through the evolution of Japan into a world power.

At the end of the Second World War — or the Pacific War, as it is called in Japan — the Japanese economy was in shambles. Millions of Japanese were homeless. Cities lay in ruins, with two of the largest smoldering from the holocaust of the atomic bomb. There was not enough food and much of the country was near starvation. Three-quarters of the industry had been destroyed, transportation had collapsed, and the black market was rampant. Adding to the problems was the return home of over six million Japanese who had been living in overseas possessions that were now the property of the Americans or had been reclaimed by the Chinese and others. "Japan in the summer of 1945 was a nation totally exhausted both physically and morally," writes Yale historian John Whitney Hall. The Japanese people were "emotionally and intellectually bewildered."[9]

Even at the end of the American occupation — April 28, 1952 — after nearly seven years of rebuilding with the assistance of American aid, Japan was still poor and weak. The per-capita gross national product was only $188, lower than that in Brazil, Chile, or Malaysia. Nearly one-half of the labor force was employed in agriculture. Labor productivity in manufacturing was extremely low, and technology lagged well behind that of other nations.

All of this was to change rather dramatically. Within twenty years Japan rose to become the second-most-powerful economy in the free world. With a GNP of $413 billion in 1973, the Japanese economy surpassed such economic giants as France, Great Britain, and even West Germany. Japan's economic growth rate was unprecedented in world history. Seemingly coming from nowhere, the Japanese suddenly had joined the vanguard of the premier economies of the world.

It would seem that the Japanese miracle would have instilled great self-confidence in the Japanese people. Such an economic recovery required hard work, perseverance, and talent — characteristics that the Japanese have in abundance. Yet self-confidence is not one of these characteristics. Even today, insecurity seems to pervade the Japanese psyche. As Professor G. C. Allen of the University of London, a leading expert on Japan, observed: "It is no exaggeration to say that Japan, by this time highly developed industrially, retained the outlook of an under-developed country."[10]

The search for economic security seems to dominate nearly all policy discussions in Japan, even in the best of economic times. And when threats to the economy do occur, such as the OPEC oil embargo and price increases of the early 1970s, the emphasis on security becomes almost paranoid. The oil situation "is the worst threat to Japan, the Japanese economy, and our way of life since the war," lamented Japanese politicians in late 1973 as OPEC curtailed oil supplies.[11] Finance Minister Takeo Fukuda predicted that the economic crisis touched off by OPEC actions would force Japan to abandon a two-decades-old policy of economic growth, while other officials warned that the "oil crisis and international inflation would bring Japan's economy to complete collapse."[12]

In the aftermath of the oil crisis, the Japanese became even more consumed with the need for economic security. In its *New Economic and Social Seven-Year Plan,* published in August 1979, Japan's Economic Planning Agency devoted the major portion of its proposal to "ensuring economic security and fostering the foundations of further development." The Japanese planners stated that the major goal of economic policy for the future was to ensure that "stable and sustained long-term growth of the economy is secured." To accomplish this goal, "foreign policies and domestic economic management that take into account economic security will be implemented so as to secure stable supplies of natural resources, energy, food, and other materials that are essential to Japan."[13]

The apparent preoccupation of Japanese policymakers with economic security is not idle paranoia. Geography dictates that Japan secure stable sources of raw materials from abroad — a fact of life clearly demonstrated by the oil crisis of the 1970s. Although Japan is the second-richest economic power in the free world, it is one of the poorest in terms of raw materials and arable land. With a land area of only 143,751 square miles (ranking fifty-fourth among all the countries of the world), Japan must support a population of 118 million people (the seventh-most-populated country in the world). To support this population, Japan must import nearly all of her raw materials.

Japan is totally dependent upon imports for lead ore, bauxite, wool, and cotton, and has only minimal internal sources for such other critical raw materials as crude petroleum, iron, copper, zinc, and manganese. Japan must also import massive quantities of food. Nearly all of the wheat, barley, soybeans, and feed cereals that the Japanese consume must be imported. (See table 5.)

This lack of raw materials and the dependence upon imports for economic survival permeates deeply into the Japanese psyche. It has given the Japanese a unique national psychology, a sense of economic precariousness that is difficult to appreciate in the resource-rich United States. It has made the Japanese very protective of their farmers and export-oriented manufacturers, and dominates their discussions in international economic forums. "Dependence on foreigners for the necessities of life is the economic basis for a pervasive sense of national insecurity at all levels of Japanese society," observed a study on Japan from the Brookings Institution. "This dependence of the whole economy on imports is so ingrained in the Japanese consciousness that there is a constant awareness of the foreign trade implications of both private and public actions. . . . Dependence on imported natural resources seems to provide a kind of unifying national challenge to the Japanese."[14]

A second major source of insecurity that drives the Japanese to seek economic security is a pervasive feeling that any period of strong economic performance is only a temporary phenomenon: Shocks will occur to set back growth potential; critical imports may be cut off; and current-account deficits will once again prove to be a serious constraint on economic growth. The future of the global economy is highly uncertain, and this means that the ability of the Japanese economy to continue growing at a rapid rate is quite precarious.

To a large extent, the Japanese leaders are only reflecting their past experience. The Japanese economy has not always enjoyed large trade balances, ready access to foreign markets, or shock-free growth. At the end of the Second World War, Japan lost traditional export markets, and it was a slow process to rebuild new ones. During the 1950s, the revival of Japanese exports was far slower than the revival of production. It was not until 1959 that the volume of exports equaled that of the prewar period, and by then industrial production was three times higher than before the war. Furthermore, the Japanese current-account balance was frequently in deficit, forcing Japanese policymakers on several occasions to put a brake on economic growth.

TABLE 5. MAJOR IMPORTS OF JAPAN
(AS A PROPORTION OF TOTAL DOMESTIC CONSUMPTION)

Raw Materials		Agriculture Products	
Lead ore	100.0%	Feed cereals	99.0%
Bauxite	100.0	Soybeans	96.4
Cotton	100.0	Wheat	94.7
Wool	100.0	Barley	85.4
Crude petroleum	99.7	Sugar	54.9
Iron ore	99.3	Meats	19.3
Copper ore	94.2	Fruits	18.4
Manganese ore	84.4		
Zinc ore	78.5		
Coal	58.4		

SOURCE: Patrick and Rosovsky, *Asia's New Giant*, 386–387.

The phenomenal growth record of the Japanese economy is of rather recent origin. At the time of independence in 1952 when the American occupation ended, Japan was viewed as an under-developed country. Both Japanese and Western experts were gloomy about the future. The economy was too small and too geographically removed to cause much concern in the West. The best that could be achieved, it was thought, was an annual growth rate in the neigh-borhood of 5 percent, and even such a modest projection was viewed as wildly optimistic. When the actual growth rate turned out to be twice as rapid, there was a certain incredulity about the performance.

Japanese reservations about the future were borne out during the 1970s when Japan's economy was hit with the shocks discussed in chapter 1. These shocks reduced the potential growth rate of the economy by nearly one-half, plunged the current-account balance into large deficits, and gave credence to the belief that economic growth was tenuous. It was during this time that the Japanese economic experiment became dominated by the search for economic security — a search that manifested itself in the aggressive pursuit of export markets in order to pay for critical imports and maintain the economy at a stable, but slower, growth path.

Priority Industries

In order to achieve economic security, the Japanese turned to the economic policy that had served them so well during their great postwar growth era: the nurturing of the industrial base. By the 1970s, the Japanese had developed an automobile industry that was the second-largest in the world and the leading exporter among all Western countries. Their consumer electronics industry was well established and had penetrated the massive markets in the United States and Western Europe. Japanese steel was among the lowest-cost and highest-quality in the world, and other Japanese products enjoyed well-deserved reputations and strong markets. These in-dustries provided the needed exports at a critical time, when the costs of oil and other natural resources were soaring.

Yet the Japanese policymakers did not rest on past laurels. They began to develop the industries of the future — those that would ensure economic security in the 1980s and 1990s. They launched a large-scale effort in research and development for Japan's computer electronics industry that emphasized the creation of an indigenous technology. New techniques for finding and processing natural resources were tested. All of these activities were carried forward using the strategies that had evolved over the past three decades — strategies that have become the Japanese industrial policy.

Industrial policy is nothing more than the application of government resources and influence to industrial affairs, and all nations practice such policy to some degree. In Western Europe, governments tend to nationalize those industries that are deemed critical to the future of the economy. In the United States, various industries are highly regulated, and others are supported with substantial government contracts. Yet it is the Japanese who have made industrial policy the core of their economic experiment, and who rely far more than any other modern nation on influencing industrial development as a means to achieve economic security.

Furthermore, the Japanese have done this while maintaining a highly competitive free-enterprise economic system. Japanese industrial leaders are among the most independent and aggressive in the world, but at the same time, they seem to follow the guidance of the Japanese government voluntarily. They vigorously compete among themselves, but offer a consolidated front to foreign competition. Slowly and carefully, they move out of their home markets to penetrate those of the third world, and then, from a base of incredible strength, they assault the markets of the United States and Western Europe.

Their success is readily evident, not only in trade statistics but in consumer markets from automobiles to television sets. Such success did not occur by happenstance. It was carefully planned and groomed. The industrial policy of Japan grew out of the pressure of shortages — shortages of natural resources, technology, and capital. At the end of the Second World War, all of these were in short supply. The only surplus that the Japanese economy enjoyed was labor. There was an excess of workers, and consequently wages were inordinately low when compared to the United States and Western Europe.

If the Japanese had followed the accepted doctrines of traditional economic development, they would have concentrated their industrial growth in areas in which they had a comparative advantage — that is, in the production of products that were labor intensive and required little capital and other resources. The Japanese would have produced much the same type of product that they did before the war: textiles, small appliances, toys, and similar products. These products did not require a sophisticated technology. They could be cheaply produced with a low-paid labor force. And they did not require large resource inputs. In other words, Japan would have rebuilt her postwar economy along the lines of a typical less-developed country.

Fortunately, there was little inclination on the part of Japanese policymakers to accept such a fate. "If the Japanese economy had adopted the simple doctrine of free trade and had chosen to specialize in this kind of industry," observed a high-ranking Japanese official, "it would almost permanently have been unable to break away from the Asian pattern of stagnation and poverty, and would have remained the weakest link in the free world."[15]

Instead, the Japanese adopted an aggressive industrial policy that required intensive employment of capital and technology. Industries were targeted in which labor productivity was expected to increase rapidly. Technology was selected that could be quickly adapted from abroad. And products were manufactured for markets that were expected to grow significantly.

Initially, most of the industries that were developed produced very basic goods that required prosaic technology. The products gradually were changed to those requiring more sophisticated technology and in which the value added by Japanese labor would be higher. Eventually, even these industries were supplanted by those higher on the technological scale, for the Japanese industrial planners pursued a course of sequencing their industrial development to ever more technologically advanced industries.

The first phase of the development was the immediate adjustment from a wartime economy that had been completely destroyed to a peacetime industrial economy. The emphasis was on building such basic industries as coal, iron, and steel, which were viewed as key feeder industries to shipbuilding, automobiles, domestic appliances, and other capital-intensive industries planned for the future. Exports were promoted in order to pay for the raw material inputs needed to fuel this new industrial economy. And efforts were taken to improve industrial technology by adapting the state of the art of the United States to Japanese conditions. It was also a period in which the Japanese policymakers felt it necessary to set up a system of economic controls, protecting the nation's new industries and restricting the outflow of scarce capital.

During Japan's second phase of industrial development, a period of consolidation of internal development that lasted from about 1950 to the mid-1960s, the Japanese continued to strengthen their basic industries. In particular, the steel industry received special tax and duty exemptions. The Japan Development Bank and the Long-Term Credit Bank provided low-cost loans. Under the guidance of the government, expansion plans among the various producers were carefully coordinated. Cartels were established to promote orderly markets. As a result of these industrial policies, Japanese crude steel production increased fourfold between 1951 and 1960, and the Japanese were operating the most technologically advanced and capital-intensive steel plants in the world.

In addition to consolidating the country's basic industries, the Japanese planners laid the foundation for an automobile industry and began to promote the development of petrochemicals, electronics, synthetic rubber, and various consumer products, such as cameras, binoculars, and sewing machines. Policies were adopted to coordinate the research-and-development activities of the companies that were beginning to produce these new products. Parts and accessories were standardized and their production was specialized, resulting in large cost reductions and major quality improvement, and export sales were coordinated in order to "restrain excessive competition."[16]

During the 1970s, the third phase of Japanese industrial development, "special sectoral programs," were launched for "a limited number of industries whose development or adaptation is of particular importance to the national economy."[17] The first of these programs was in the area of securing supplies of basic natural resources. In 1969 Japan's Ministry of International Trade and Industry (MITI) distributed a planning paper for discussion among government, business, and academic leaders that laid out the intent of this program. It also gave good insight into the nature of Japanese industrial planning.

"Since it is crucial for Japan's further economic development to secure, at low prices, the steady supply of basic natural resources such as oil, ferrous and non-ferrous metals, uranium and wood," MITI stated, "we will promote the development of natural resources overseas and petroleum resources in continental shelves. For this, we will actively take the most effective assistance measures to encourage the development of resources which will be diversified according to the riskiness of investment. Users of the resources are expected to take a positive part in the development ventures in view of the fact that they are vital to their operations."[18]

Other special programs were launched to modernize the machinery and electronics industries, adapt the textile industry to increasing global competition, and restructure the coal-mining industry to make it more efficient and alleviate "the social harm engendered by mine closings."[19] Special legislation was passed to facilitate the modernization of these industries. The Japan Development Bank provided low-cost loans to the machinery, electronics, and textile industries. Manufacturers were given special tax breaks. And subsidies were given to displaced workers in the coal-mining industry, while efforts were made to diversify the economic base of the coal regions by relocating new industries in those parts of the country.

All of these endeavors paid great dividends to the Japanese economy during the turbulent 1970s. When confronted with the dislocations created by energy-price increases and intense competition for export markets, the Japanese were in a strong position to compete. They could draw upon a well-developed industrial base to provide the high-quality and low-cost exports that would enable them to recoup from economic problems far more rapidly than did the United States and Western Europe.

It was not just luck that enabled the Japanese to be in the right place at the right time. Their industrial policy was developed only after lengthy and intense debate between government planners and private industrialists. It was a careful development plan that moved progressively from developing basic heavy industry to developing higher-technology industry. But more important, it was a development plan that looked to the long-term future growth of Japan. Through strong emphasis on growth, export promotion, plant-and-equipment investment, and industrial sequencing, the Japanese policymakers were able to guide their nation's economy through progressive stages of development and at the same time overcome numerous exogenous shocks. As many policymakers in both Japan and the West would agree, "Japan's industrial policy has been successful because of its logic and consistency."[20]

This same logic and consistency that worked so well in the past is being followed in the fourth, and current, phase of Japan's industrial program. The Japanese are building the industrial base that they think will be essential for their economic security during the rest of the 1980s and beyond. Government officials and business leaders have identified a dozen or so new strategic industries, which MITI is now nurturing as a knowledge-intensive industrial structure. All of these new industries involve high technology, and they encompass such areas as computers; semiconductors; telecommunications; numerically controlled machine tools; robots; advanced consumer-electronics goods such as videotape recorders; aircraft manufacturing; housing construction; and exploration and development of natural resources, including the remote-controlled mining of the seabed.[21]

While the Japanese clearly have been successful in sequencing their industrial development, moving to higher-technology products that provide for a greater value added by Japanese labor and hence more rapid economic growth, the questions still remain: How do they do it? What policies do the Japanese use to encourage the development of specific industries? Who determines what industries are to be nurtured? Why do Japanese industrialists, among the most competitive in the world, go along with such an industrial policy?

Consensus Management

The organization most directly responsible for implementing the industrial policy of Japan, and the one that has most formalized the procedure of consensus management, is the Ministry of International Trade and Industry. More commonly known by its acronym, MITI was established in 1949 as the successor to the postwar Ministry of Commerce and Industry. This change represented far more than a mere alteration of the agency's title. It symbolized a shift from "a domestically oriented industrial policy, whose main objective was the maximum production of basic commodities, to a policy oriented towards the international economy and aimed primarily at the promotion of trade and the restructuring and modernization of industry."[22]

Contrary to the popular view in many Western countries, MITI is not a centralized planning agency in the Japanese government that spends its time carefully choosing target industries and funneling massive government support to them, or even creating a master plan for the future development of the Japanese economy. The primary role of MITI in formulating Japan's industrial policy is fourfold: "(a) to provide forecasts of emerging industrial-structure trends in the form of a 'vision'; (b) to prime the economic pump if and when the market mechanism is in need of a complementary nudge (for example, acceleration of basic research and development); (c) to furnish information that will help industry adjust to the market environment; and (d) to coordinate industrial activity."[23]

MITI is a rather unusual government agency, for it attempts to coordinate bureaus concerned with broad issues of policy that affect all industry and other bureaus whose mandate is to develop specific priority industries. Of the seven major bureaus, two are involved with general trade policy, one is responsible for general industrial-policy matters, and another oversees industrial-location and environmental-protection policy. The remaining three bureaus have overlapping responsibility for developing the following specific industries: iron and steel, chemical products, industrial machinery, electronics and data processing, automobiles, aircraft, textiles, paper and pulp, housing, ceramics and construction materials, and household and recreation goods.

The range of MITI's activities in industrial affairs and, particularly, the agency's involvement in rather detailed business issues make its role quite different from that of government bureaus in the United States. Most American business leaders would view with great alarm a government agency in Washington that probed as deeply into industrial matters as do the bureaucrats in Japan. The professional staff of MITI analyzes such issues as corporate vitality — in particular, adequate profitability and investment rates, the desirable structure of various industries, and their optimal rates of growth. Specific companies are selected to be "rationalized" — that is, to be merged with stronger firms or encouraged to retrench. Businessmen are routinely summoned to discuss the desired intent of government policy, for a great deal of latitude is allowed for such official administrative guidance in Japan. The legislative statutes passed by the Diet, the Japanese national parliament, have quite broad mandates and rely on the ministries "to promote, regulate, and guide those industries under their jurisdiction."[24]

Yet MITI and the other ministries involved in implementing industrial policy do not dictate terms or impose a central plan. Corporate leaders maintain their independence, and sometimes the desires of MITI are frustrated by the intractableness of the businessmen. For instance, strong efforts by MITI to consolidate the automobile industry into fewer and larger producers during the 1950s and 1960s failed. Sumitomo Metals Company refused to delay all new investments in rolling facilities as suggested by MITI officials; instead, the company expanded capacity and challenged other steel producers for market share. In general, however, Japanese businessmen cooperate with government officials in implementing industrial policy, for they "understand that in the long term it is in their best interest, even though on particular occasions the issue being pressed by the industry is an unpopular one."[25]

Numerous organizations have been set up to help government officials and business leaders reach a consensus regarding industrial management. MITI has established various councils that act as advisory groups in forming policy. The councils include representatives from industry, trade unions, and universities, and they provide a continuous forum for an exchange of views between government and the private sector. Probably the most important of these is the Industrial Structure Council, which analyzes all basic MITI policy issues and submits to the minister of MITI recommendations and opinions.

Various specialized private-industry associations maintain a close working relationship with MITI's industry bureaus and divisions. These organizations advance suggestions for governmental policies that directly impact their particular industry, and they frequently implement the policies that are adopted by officials. In addition, there are three major business associations that cooperate with the government ministries in formulating broad-based industry policy: The Keidanren (Federation of Economic Organization) includes some seven hundred large corporations and is a powerful voice for big-business interests. The Keizai Doyukai (Committee for Economic Development) tends to advance more progressive policy suggestions regarding the role of business in broader issues. And the Skoko Kaigisho (Chamber of Commerce and Industry) represents the interests of the small businesses throughout Japan.

These private associations play a vital role not only in forming industrial policy but in preventing the government from moving toward more centralized planning. There is certainly no intent on the part of government to become the centralized planner for Japanese industry, but without the existence of strong private associations with highly skilled research staffs, the possibility of this occurring would be much greater. The associations represent an essential part of the consensus process that operates so effectively in Japan, helping maintain a balance between government and private enterprise. As Professor Ezra F. Vogel of Harvard University notes:

Perhaps the most important factor in influencing industrial policy is the framing of questions about a particular issue with Keidanren as well as MITI. The issues raised thus become the focus of official and unofficial concern and debate. Keidanren has a sizable staff doing research for committee sessions in which business leaders study, debate, and reach decisions about important issues. Government bureaucrats, scholars, and other knowledgeable persons frequently testify before these committees. Issues are mulled over in committee until widespread agreement emerges. Formal votes on important issues are almost never taken. Perhaps there is no better phrase to describe this process than consensus building.[26]

In Japan this process of give and take, interaction between industry and government, and joint involvement in the setting of industrial policy is taken quite seriously. Government officials are totally accustomed to working alongside their business counterparts in developing industrial policy, and vice versa. There is a sense of mutual respect, an attitude of working together for the common good. All of this is indicative of a relationship of trust.

Such a relationship of trust seems to be based on three factors: (1) continual contact between government and industry, (2) the existence of a mutual understanding between the two, and (3) a strong desire to achieve harmony between the various interest groups involved in developing Japanese industry.

The councils and other organizations established for interaction between government and industry are permanent. They do not change with election results. A new prime minister does not abolish the councils of the previous administration and establish his own. Nor do the Japanese follow the American practice of setting up temporary task forces or business advisory groups to address problems, and then tending to ignore the results of the efforts. Rather than serving as appendages to the policy process, the Japanese industrial organizations are totally integrated into that process itself.

Nearly everything about the Japanese style of industrial operation seems oriented toward maintaining long-term continuity. Government officials in MITI and other ministries involved in the setting of industrial policy occupy their positions for years — frequently for their entire career — and work with counterparts in industry who have the same stability and seniority. Many of them attended Tokyo University and draw upon "the old school tie network."[27] Many career government officials retire to politics and the Diet, or join private industry, further solidifying the continuity.

Not only do the industry organizations and the tenure of the policymakers provide a sense of permanency and continuity to industrial policy; more important is the long-run perspective of the participants in that process. This perspective begins with the role of government, and particularly its role in providing what is called "a vision of the future." MITI officials state that their major responsibility is "to arrive at a vision that may serve as a policy target and to persuade and guide industry towards that vision."[28]

In developing this vision, however, MITI obtains the opinions of industrial leaders, academics, and labor representatives. The various councils are drawn into the discussion, and considerable effort is exerted "to arrive at mutual understanding between business and government."[29] A vision is never imposed by MITI, for given Japan's "plan-oriented market economy,"[30] any centralized plan would be quietly and politely ignored.

There is a great willingness on the part of business and the general public to accept the role of government in setting future goals. Knowing that government has a long-run vision of how it would like to see Japan develop apparently provides a sense of security to the Japanese. This long-range perspective is strongly reinforced by the actions of private business. Corporate executives operate in their own self-interest to maximize long-term profits. If any particular business venture requires several years before a return is realized, Japanese management is not overly concerned. It is the long-run economic strength of the company that matters, not short-term returns.

This attitude is quite the opposite of that found among American businessmen, who tend to take a very short-run perspective. Growth targets, management incentives, salaries, and bonuses are all geared for immediate returns. As a result there is very little long-term planning. This difference in behavior is increasingly pointed out by the Japanese as one of the main reasons for their success, and they are quite perplexed as to how American business hopes to compete when it pays so little attention to long-term continuity.

Much of the continuity found in Japanese industrial policy is the result of a mutual understanding between government officials, politicians, and industrial leaders. There does not seem to be a split between public and private interests as in the United States. There are Japanese interests, and the task of government and industry is to enhance those interests mutually. Government officials respect the obligations and incentives of private industrialists to expand their markets, maximize profits, and make independent decisions regarding their businesses. At the same time, industrial leaders know that their best interests are being served by the Japanese government.

"The administrative leadership of MITI is not of an authoritarian nature," observes a former MITI official. "At the root of this leadership lie the relationship of trust between MITI and industry and the appreciation by industry of the role the Government has played for the past hundred years in protecting and encouraging industry, especially the contribution that the policies which MITI has followed since the war have made to industrial recovery and development."[31]

In large part this mutual understanding exists because of the Japanese conception of the origin and rationale for government authority. To the Japanese mind, "the whole nation is a family; what the house is to a biological family, the state is to the national family. The state is not merely a part of the system, but the very framework of it. . . . The state bureaucrats exercise authority not in the name of the people, but in the name of the House of Japan." In the Japanese way of thinking, the state does not interfere with the affairs of private business. It merely manages itself, exercising authority and control over its constituencies. One of these constituencies is private business, whose productive activity "is very much a part of the business of the whole nation-state."[32]

Finally, a relationship of trust exists because of the strong desire, on the part of all groups engaged in establishing industrial policy, to achieve harmony. This is one concept that is deeply embedded in Japanese policy discussions and day-to-day business activities. MITI officials speak of the need to achieve "harmony between nature, industrial activity and human life."[33] The current seven-year plan for economic development states that the proposed Industrial Relocation Plan will be implemented to "ensure harmony between industry and the regional community."[34] Even workers on the job daily recite the importance of achieving "harmony and cooperation."[35]

Ironically, it is harmony — the combination of parts or different views into an orderly whole — that gives rise to the misleading Western view of "Japan, Inc." The debate and clash of vested interests that is undertaken in the public arena in the United States is submerged in the closed councils of Japan. The participants in those discussions hold the same intense positions as do their counterparts in the United States. Yet they hammer out their differences and reach agreement behind closed doors, seemingly driven toward a consensus by an inherent acceptance of the desire to maintain harmony. Rather than seeing themselves as part of Japan, Inc., policymakers in Japan view the process as "much like the two wheels of a cart."[36] While each wheel is independent of the other, they move in the same direction with "a clear sense of common purpose," having been joined together through "a commonly accepted and extremely well-developed process to resolve conflict."[37]

Limited Government Assistance

The Japanese government does not provide massive assistance to industry, contrary to the popular conception in the United States and Europe. The view that private industry in Japan enjoys unfair advantages in international competition because of subsidized loans, large research-and-development grants from the government, preferential tax treatment, or protectionist import controls is more a holdover from the past than an accurate reflection of the present.

There is no doubt that the Japanese government was highly protectionist of its developing industry in the past. The government relied upon numerous grants, credits, loans, and tax incentives to implement industrial policy. When the effort was made to advance the technological capability of the electronics industry, the Japan Development Bank provided low-cost financing, and electronics firms were given special tax breaks. The Japan Petroleum Development Corporation, established in 1967, provided financial assistance to Japanese oil companies.

Government subsidies were made available for the rapid restructuring of the coal-mining industry. Small businesses had access to credit from such institutions as the Small Business Finance Corporation, the Central Bank for Commercial and Industrial Cooperatives, and the People's Finance Corporation. Firms that invested in research and development received preferential tax treatment and could obtain grants to cover one-half of the costs of equipment and facilities, or they could apply for a subsidized loan through the National Technology Promotion Fund.

Furthermore, Japan imposed high import duties and tight controls on capital flow. Beginning in 1950, when Japan was allowed to resume control of its economy as the period of American occupation was coming to a close, a foreign-exchange budget system was adopted that directly controlled trade and foreign exchange. Under this budget, priority was given to the purchase of essential materials from abroad that were needed for the reconstruction of Japanese industry. Only carefully selected imports were allowed to enter the country. This rigid system was gradually replaced by one of high tariffs and controls over the flow of capital out of the country in order to protect emerging industries and retain capital for domestic investment.

Today, nearly all of these duties and controls have been eliminated. Japan's average tariff level on industrial products is about the same as in the United States, and it is well below that of the

European countries. In addition, Japan has taken steps to reduce such nontariff barriers to trade as inspection standards, customs valuations, and government procurement practices. Government subsidies in support of industry are now among the lowest of any major country in the world.

This does not mean that the Japanese government is no longer involved in the development of specific industries or does not exert a major influence on them. The primary reason that Japan has been able to reduce greatly the level of trade protection and direct industry subsidies is the effectiveness with which the government can apply guidance and assistance in industrial policy. The well-functioning consensus-forming process gives the Japanese the advantage of being able to achieve remarkable results with minimal costs — far better results than in any other country.

Building upon their powerful system of consensus management, the Japanese have honed their limited government assistance in four significant ways: (1) by reinforcing consensus behavior, (2) by targeting assistance to trade-oriented industries, (3) by relying upon tax incentives rather than direct government support, and (4) by carefully phasing support during the development and declining stages of industrial growth.

MITI, as the primary agency in the Japanese government responsible for implementing industrial policy, makes effective use of certain inducements for reinforcing consensus behavior. The industrial leaders who participate in the myriad discussions and committee meetings run by MITI officials do not meekly acquiesce to government dictates. But they know that "when the time comes for them to request licenses, permits, choice locations, and tax breaks, MITI will respond more favorably to cooperative than to uncooperative companies. MITI's displeasure can be costly to a firm; it can use delaying tactics, raise difficult questions, take a very narrow view of depreciation allowances and deductions, and even influence the banks that lend to the firms. But all this is seldom necessary."[38]

It is seldom necessary because MITI carefully uses inducements as carrots rather than resorting to clubs. And the carrots are not used to influence the behavior of individual firms, but to achieve consensus within the broad guidelines and priorities established by the joint working groups of MITI. As Ezra Vogel, author of the best-selling book *Japan as Number One,* observed, MITI behaves similarly to the National Football League. The league establishes rules of play that produce relatively equally matched teams, of powerful competitive abilities. But it does not interfere in internal team activity or tell a coach how to do his job.

Nor does MITI dissipate limited government assistance among a number of different industries. As opposed to American politicians, who seem to have a fear of targeting support, the Japanese politicians accept industrial targeting. In the first place, the Japanese ensure that government assistance goes to industries that are trade-oriented and that offer the potential to expand markets abroad. And second, they funnel assistance to firms that produce consumer products. By comparison, much of American industrial aid is given to firms that produce military and space hardware, in the hope that such assistance will spin off to consumer-oriented firms. And if government assistance is provided to firms that produce consumer products, American politicians are careful to ensure that everyone is treated the same. In essence, the Japanese identify and assist those industries that are significant to their nation's economic-development priorities, while Americans attempt to create an economic environment that is conducive to overall industrial growth.

A major reason why the Japanese can effectively target limited government assistance is that they use tax incentives rather than direct government grants or contracts. The Japanese rely upon tax exemptions, for "a tax advantage is valuable only after an enterprise has done what the government wants it to do, whereas a subsidy is paid prior to performance and sometimes does not produce any improvement in performance."[39]

The Japanese view tax incentives as not only more efficient but also easier to achieve politically than subsidies, for the latter would open the process to more pressure from interest groups. While interest-group politics certainly enters into the process of granting tax exemptions, it is less of a problem in Japan than in the United States. The Japanese have developed a method to establish industrial tax exemptions that removes the process from the public arena.

Annual revisions in the tax system are made by the Tax System Deliberations Council, located in the office of the prime minister. The Ministry of Finance selects the members of the council, and all recommendations for tax revisions are rubber-stamped by the Diet. Furthermore, the deliberations of the council are not open to the public. This procedure for operating industrial tax policy is an attempt to keep the tax system free from politics. It also enables the council to target tax policy carefully in order to aid specific industries that have been designated as priority ones.

Finally, the Japanese carefully phase government support to assist targeted industries during two critical stages of the life cycle: the initial stage, when the industry is new and growing, and the mature and declining stage, when the industry faces increased competition from abroad and is losing its competitive advantage. Government support in the initial stage takes the form of granting subsidies for research-and-development activities, establishing joint development efforts among competing firms within an industry, and providing technical assistance and advice about financing, foreign exchange, and technology transfer.

Once the industry is well established, government assistance is withdrawn and the firms in that industry are left to fend for themselves in a highly competitive market. Then, when the industry enters the declining stage, government support is provided to encourage mergers, the closing of obsolete plants, and the development of new technology that might renew competitive capabilities. Such a phasing of government assistance ensures that no industry becomes dependent upon continued support, as is true of nationalized industries in Europe, and it maximizes the benefits of an industrial policy that carefully limits and targets government assistance.

Planning the Miracle Product

While the Japanese economic experiment builds upon a strong tradition of industrial sequencing, consensus planning and management, and targeted use of limited government assistance, these features are not what makes the experiment unique. It is the bold and daring move of the Japanese into planning a miracle product for the future that most warrants our attention.

The Japanese have named their miracle product "the Fifth Generation Computer System." It is to be a computer system that will greatly exceed anything being developed in any country, including the United States. Rather than following along in the footsteps of IBM and simply building larger and more efficient traditional information-processing computers, the Japanese intend to develop their own technology. They are attempting to leapfrog well beyond the existing state of technology of IBM and other advanced American computer firms to create a new computer-based-knowledge industry, or what is increasingly being called "artificial intelligence."

Their miracle product will be an information-processing system that has the capacity "to reason." It will do so by manipulating enormous amounts of information that will be constantly selected, updated, distilled, and interpreted as circumstances change. It will be, in effect, a thinking computer system. Users of these computers will be able to speak to them in everyday language, show them pictures and graphs, and give them handwritten messages. No longer will highly trained computer programmers be required to interact with the system. The computers will be readily accessible to the layperson, and since the Japanese intend to produce and market these new systems at a low cost, they will be available everywhere — in homes, offices, restaurants, farms, and small shops.

The Japanese planners have generated a great deal of skepticism with their plans for a miracle product, both at home and abroad. Some Japanese industrialists think the project is too risky, too daring. They worry that IBM is not undertaking a project with similar goals, and they see the most prudent course as doing what IBM does, only better and cheaper. Many American industrialists view the plan as "a lot of smoke." To think that Japan — well behind the United States and even Great Britain in the emerging field of knowledge processing — can capture the lead in world markets is incomprehensible.

Yet a leading American expert in this high-technology frontier, Professor Edward A. Feigenbaum of Stanford University, has written:

The Japanese have seen gold on distant hills and have begun to move out. Japanese planners view the computer industry as vital to their nation's economic future and have audaciously made it a national goal to become number one in this industry by the latter half of the 1990s. They aim not only to dominate the traditional forms of the computer industry but to establish a "knowledge industry" in which knowledge itself will be a salable commodity like food and oil. Knowledge itself is to become the new wealth of nations."[40]

And Ehud Y. Shapiro, a world authority in the field from the Weizmann Institute of Science in Israel, after spending several weeks exchanging scientific information with the Japanese experts working on this new project, reported:

There are thoughts and attempts throughout the world at responding to the Fifth Generation project, but as I see it, this battle is already won. The eventual success of the project will follow not from the amount of money invested in it, the number of people working on it, not even from the individual excellence of these people. It will follow from the coherent vision of its leaders, the genuine enthusiasm that they generate, and from the promising path of research they chose.[41]

In setting out to develop the Fifth Generation computer, the Japanese have followed rather traditional approaches. The Institute for New Generation Computer Technology was established in April 1982. The institute is a consortium of eight private firms that are leaders in the Japanese computer industry, two national government laboratories, and MITI. Forty of the brightest and most aggressive computer experts available in Japan are associated with the project. Many of them come from industrial firms that are backing the project, on loan for a period of three to five years. Others are from government research centers, and they are directed by a young leader who has smashed social stereotypes, tossed out social traditions, and is "capable of the kind of innovative thinking the Fifth Generation demands."[42]

The government has provided seed money of $450 million for a ten-year period and expects private industry at least to match or even double that amount. Elaborate plans have been drawn up, carefully outlining each step of progress and allowing for adjustments and revisions as progress is made.

The private companies who will manufacture and market the new computer system are totally integrated into the research activities so that no time will be lost in realizing the commercial opportunities from the project. The individual researchers who are on leave from the private industrial laboratories maintain close contact with their peers in the companies, weekly sharing technical reports and information. And after several years, they will be cycled back to their original firms and be replaced by others, so that once the project is completed, in ten or more years, a whole generation of young Japanese scientists and computer experts will have been involved.

The Fifth Generation project is a perfect example of the latest Japanese sequencing of industrial development, drawing upon consensus planning and management, and utilizing government resources to stimulate greater private participation. Yet the project breaks with the past in three unique ways: (1) the Japanese are attempting to develop a leading technology for the first time; (2) the new technology developed in the Fifth Generation computer industry is expected to permeate throughout the entire Japanese industrial structure, making the country's traditional industries far more efficient and competitive; and (3) the new technology is expected to improve greatly the overall quality of life for the Japanese people, not simply ensure their future economic security. In these regards, the project goes well beyond any previous industrial development undertaken in Japan.

Much of the success of Japanese industrial development has been in the ability to copy the existing technology in the United States and Europe and compete in world markets with less costly and better-quality products. Such a strategy has earned the Japanese a reputation as copycats in kimonos — masters at adopting technology imported from the West but incapable of producing original work. There is a great deal of truth to such a view, for the Japanese have built their economy by taking technology first developed elsewhere and improving upon it to the point that they have driven its originators out of business. They have certainly done this in cameras, watches, television sets, and consumer electronics, and they have come remarkably close in automobiles.

Yet duplicating technology developed elsewhere is not unusual. Professor Edwin Reischauer of Harvard University, former U.S. ambassador to Japan, observes: "These traits of relative weakness in theoretical innovation but great strength in practical application were characteristic of the United States too during its period of catching up with Europe. Americans have taken a leading place in science, scholarship, and thought only in recent decades. As Japan draws abreast of the West, the same change may occur there."[43]

For the Japanese planners, the change will occur with the Fifth Generation computer project. "Although we have mainly followed the lead of other countries in computer technology up to now, it's time for us to break with this outmoded tradition and center our efforts on the development of new computer technology based on our own conceptions, so that we can provide the world with new technology," stated Professor Tohru Moto-oka of Tokyo University in the opening address at the International Conference on Fifth Generation Computer Systems in October 1981.[44]

The second area in which the computer project breaks with past tradition is in its expected effect on the rest of Japanese industry and society. The industrial-sequencing developments of the past were undertaken to ensure that Japan remained competitive in international markets. Success in steel, automobiles, and consumer electronics was measured in terms of expanding export markets for the particular product. Such success, of course, contributed greatly to the overall strength of the Japanese economy. And the new computer project is expected to make the same contribution. Yet it also is destined to be widely used in all areas of economic development and social life. The success of the Fifth Generation project will be measured not only in expanded exports, but also in its impact "in all areas of social activity, [including] economics, industry, science, culture, daily life."[45]

More specifically, the Japanese planners are anticipating that the economy and society of Japan will move into a new era of knowledge processing made possible by their miracle computer systems. The products of Japan's traditional manufacturing industries will be far superior because of their higher quality, which will be based on all the knowledge that will be poured into their design and manufacture. Energy and other limited resources will be used much more efficiently through better design of manufacturing processes, as well as through methods of damage detection and automatic repair. Consensus management will be improved because of reductions in the time and costs required for making decisions and the access to better and more effective information.

Improving Quality of Life

Above all, the miracle product will greatly improve the quality of life in Japan. The Japanese economic experiment is heavily oriented toward developing an industrial economy. The major emphasis in establishing policy is on the nurturing of priority industries, which means that a highly select number of industries receive most of the attention. Thousands of small businesses and shops are left to fend for themselves, or receive only minimal assistance from government. Many of these small businesses are retailers, for Japanese distribution and retailing is dominated by neighborhood shops. Other small businesses are captive suppliers of the large conglomerates: they each manufacture a highly specialized product that is solely purchased by a single large industrial firm.

Employees in these small retail shops and captive suppliers receive far less pay than do their counterparts in the large industrial firms. Benefits are fewer, and job security is not guaranteed. Consequently, such employees and their families do not enjoy the higher standard of living that has come to those working for government, banks, and major industries in Japan. Nor do they have access to government social programs that would give them some security, such as those in most Western countries.

In addition, many of the social needs of the Japanese people have suffered as scarce resources have been allocated to private investment in priority industries. The Japanese have crowded into several large metropolitan areas where the industrial base is located. Little investment has been made in housing. Streets and highways are congested. Urban density, high levels of pollution, and low-quality housing have been the by-products of rapid growth and large investments in industrial development.

Compounding this relative lack of social investment are increasing pressures for social change. In the first place, the population is growing older, which requires that Japan begin to prepare the foundations for an economy and society that can meet the needs of a far older population than existed in the past. Second, population and industry are beginning to decentralize, dispersing to nonmetropolitan regions of the country. This trend seems to be a reaction against the overcrowding in the major cities and the resulting high cost of housing and industrial land. And third, there is an ongoing change in the national consciousness, from concern with quantitative expansion to improvement in the quality of life. These changes are bringing shifts in national priorities "from private consumption to social consumption, from material goods to spiritual abundance, from quantitative expansion to comfort and meaning in life, from economy to culture."[46]

The policymakers in Japan have consequently begun to emphasize a vision of the future called "A New Welfare Society." Many of the policies that the Japanese are proposing to use in building their new welfare society have a familiar ring. More resources will have to be set aside for social security. A full system of lifelong health care, covering everyone from mothers-to-be and infants right up to the elderly, is to be established. Improved educational facilities will be built. Efforts will be made to improve the variety of cultural facilities that are available to the Japanese people. Incentives will be given to the private housing industry to encourage the production of better-designed and higher-quality housing, and public-funded housing will be provided to those who cannot afford to purchase their own home. New highways, sewage systems, urban parks, and welfare facilities for the elderly are to be constructed. Needless to say, these programs will require a massive amount of capital, and public expenditures will be needed at a time when the growth rate of the economy is much lower than in the past.

In response, the Japanese policymakers call for the creation of a new Japanese-type welfare society that, by inference, will differ from the welfare society that was developed in the United States and Western Europe during the past several decades. It will be similar only in the nature of the social goods and services that are to be provided. Social security, health care, education, housing, and urban parks are not uniquely American, German, or Japanese. The Japanese welfare society will basically differ from that in the West in the planned emphasis on individual self-reliance, advance planning and consensus management, and maintaining the country's industrial base.

The Japanese policymakers speak of the importance of a "ring of solidarity based on individual self-reliance and stability of the household" that will be formed and "centered in neighborhood communities"; these will be "important conditions in building an environment where the individual members of the nation can lead full social lives." Apparently, the strong extended family unit that exists in Japan is expected to provide an essential source of stability and support in meeting future human needs. Such extended families, along with "the self-help efforts by the individual," will complement the social programs provided by the Japanese government.[47]

Furthermore, as they strive for their welfare society, the Japanese place a great deal of faith in their ability to plan for the future and obtain a consensus among different interest groups. Regarding social security, Japanese officials state that "in order to make an increase . . . possible under conditions of slower economic growth, it will be necessary to obtain national understanding and consensus concerning the extent of social security benefits and the size of cost burdens to meet these." In building the new communities of the future that are more energy-efficient and conservation-oriented, government will have to promote "greater national conservation consciousness" among the people. And in improving housing, "enlightenment will be promoted in order to ensure that the distribution of houses and residential land is conducted safely and smoothly."[48]

Finally, the Japanese are depending heavily upon a continuation of their strong and secure industrial base to provide the basis for their new welfare society. They recognize that "a stable and peaceful national life" requires stability of prices and employment. Inflation must be kept under control — clearly a major factor in building a sound social-security system — and jobs have to be ensured, which is the goal of their new knowledge-intensive industrial structure. The Japanese do not intend to be confronted with the economic and social instability of declining smokestack industries that is rupturing the social welfare system in the United States. Nor do they intend to diminish their search for economic security. "It should be noted that economic security is the basis of Japan's overall security," the Japanese planners succinctly note in their latest vision of the future.[49]

In summary, the Japanese have built a highly successful economic experiment that essentially relies upon an industrial policy to achieve economic security. Yet a major reason for the success of this industrial policy has been the rapid growth of Japan's economy. In such a situation, there are going to be far more winners than losers. If every industry is expanding — even though some are growing more rapidly than others — there will be little resistance from managers in industries that are being deemphasized for the sake of targeted ones. During the postwar era, Japan has not faced a situation in which a major industry had to be closed down or significantly diminished. (The closest call might be what happened to the coal industry during the 1960s; but that industry received substantial help from the government to minimize the economic and social impact, and the energy crisis of the 1970s gave coal a new lease on life.) It remains to be seen whether Japanese industrial policy can survive a serious threat, such as global protectionism or a prolonged period of stagnant growth. And it is too early to judge whether Japan can successfully broaden its industrial policy to incorporate the new welfare society envisioned by its leaders.

In the meantime, one would have to agree with MITI officials who suggest that Japan's economic experiment

is an inevitable result of the conditions in which the country finds itself. While drawing a great deal upon the economics of Western countries, this policy is also deeply rooted in the soil of Japan, and in the surrounding international environment. It is not an abstract objective system of logic to be found in a textbook, but, more appropriately, a green tree which is indeed bearing much fruit.[50]

West Germany and
the Golden Middle Road

*T*HE WEST GERMAN ECONOMIC EXPERIMENT was given official birth
on January 19, 1978, when Chancellor Helmut Schmidt delivered his annual policy address to the Bundestag, the lower house
of parliament. For the largest economy in Western Europe, it was
a far less dramatic and innovative undertaking than what the British
and Americans were to attempt. German economic policies followed
what Schmidt called "the golden middle road," a philosophy of
economic moderation that was steadfastly adhered to despite strong
international pressure to change.

In early 1978, West Germany was under pressure from the Carter
administration to adopt more stimulative economic policies. President Carter, worried about stagnation in Europe, was proposing
that the three strongest Western economies — those of the United
States, Japan, and West Germany — aggressively strive for high
growth rates. The higher growth rates of the "big three," he hoped,
would pull the rest of the world along.

The severe recession of 1974–75 was over and the American and
Japanese economies were flourishing. The European economies, in
contrast, emerged from the recession in rather anemic shape, and
the United States did not think that the Germans were pulling their
weight on the economic oars. Chancellor Schmidt, however, was of
a different opinion.

"It would mean overrating the economic potential of the Federal
Republic of Germany if some foreigners, politicians abroad, would
like to regard the Federal Republic of Germany as the locomotive

which is to pull all other states out of world recession," Mr. Schmidt told the Bundestag. Moreover, West Germany was "unable to follow the advice of those foreign advisers to whom our budget deficits . . . appear too small and who advised us to incur even greater budget deficits. We did not take this advice, because we do want to contribute to the expansion of the world economy but we do not want to become culpable for another round of inflation. That is why we are taking the 'golden middle road' between those who would have us be more stimulative and those who desire us to be more prudent."[1]

The Germans were not in the mood to engage in an economic experiment of extremes — such as the heavy reliance on tax reductions of the Reagan experiment or the avid faith in monetarism of the Thatcher government. Rather, they sought moderation and stability. "We want to wait until we can see its impact by next July," Count Otto Lambsdorff, West Germany's minister of economics, said in early 1978 concerning a modest tax-reduction program put in place a few months earlier. "We can't start one program before we've finished another. This stop, go, stop, go policy paralyzes decision-making in the business community," he told the press.[2] Besides, he said, "we cannot do more. . . . There are limits prescribed by our Constitution. . . . No German politician — unless he is bent on suicide — will adopt measures which would first of all and almost exclusively produce another burst of inflation."[3]

West Germany was trapped between the pressure for more economic growth and the fear of inflation. It was a psychological trap as well as an economic-policy dilemma. The economic dilemma existed because of the desire for more rapid growth to help balance the budget, to finance a heavily strained national pension system, and to increase employment. Yet to undertake more stimulative economic policies would only serve to raise the specter of inflation, a fear that has deep psychological roots in the German mentality. Given the monetary upheavals that the Germans had suffered through in the past, and which many believed led to the Nazi regime, German leaders felt that the psychological limit to a strong stimulation program would be reached long before the economic limits.[4]

Consequently, the German government sought to squeeze out gently any vestiges of inflation while maintaining modest goals of economic growth. At the same time, the Germans wanted to preserve their extensive system of social benefits. There were no plans to slash government spending, nor significantly to shift priorities in spending from social services to defense. New investments were to be made to help German industry adjust to high energy costs and increased trade competition. The social partnership between government, business, and labor that had been so carefully worked out during the postwar growth era was not to be jeopardized by any radical shift to new and untried economic policies. The Germans set out to determine if the strengths of past economic policies could be modified to meet the challenges of the future.

Although the German experiment was born under the leadership of Chancellor Helmut Schmidt and owes a great deal of its intellectual basis and pragmatic nature to him, the same theme has continued under the leadership of Chancellor Helmut Kohl. Upon taking office in October 1982, the new chancellor lost no time in informing the nation that "we live in a critical economic situation which calls for a difficult balancing act. We must pursue a convincing consolidation policy while simultaneously not curtailing demand too much. This calls for patience and sense of proportion."[5]

Germany's middle-of-the-road economic experiment is characterized by three major objectives: (1) to reduce the size of the government budget deficit gradually, (2) to maintain current budget priorities, and (3) to ensure an adequate but tight money supply. The backbone of the program, however, is Germany's industrial strength — a factor that the policymakers grew increasingly concerned about as their experiment in moderation evolved.

Reducing the Deficit

There were to be no extreme shifts in fiscal policy in the German experiment, nor any naive promises of immediate budget balances. The German course to reduce gradually the size of the public-sector deficit, in fact, began in 1975 with the Law to Improve the Structure of the Budget. At that time, the budget deficit was soaring upward and would represent 6.1 percent of Germany's gross national product by year end, compared to a 1.5-percent deficit-to-GNP ratio for the previous year. (By comparison, the deficit in the United States during 1975 was a much smaller 4.5 percent of GNP.)

For the cautious Germans, such a deficit was totally unacceptable. There was great concern that consumer and business confidence in the economy would be eroded, and that financial markets would panic. The answer was to increase government revenues and to reduce the growth of expenditures "resulting in a strengthening of private sector confidence."[6]

The Law to Improve the Structure of the Budget was not an ironclad economic law. It did not constrict the German government to following blindly a course of tax increases and budget slashing. Put forth as a "medium-term strategy" to reduce the deficit gradually, it was supplemented by other "Budget-Accompanying Laws" from 1980 to 1983. These laws have enabled the German government to expand expediently or pull back on government spending. This inherent flexibility was critical to the effective reduction of the German deficit that took place between 1975 and 1984.

In implementing its balanced fiscal policies, the German government clearly showed that it would expand government spending when the economy needed a slight boost but that it was prepared to pull back on the expenditure levers when inflation started to reappear. Furthermore, the Germans used their fiscal-policy tools very adroitly to achieve a balance between tax reform and needed public expenditure, and between their medium-term investment goals and short-term cyclical control. Above all, they never wavered from their objective of gradually reducing the size of the budget deficit.

The deficit was gradually reduced from a level of 60 billion deutsche marks in 1975 to DM 38 million in 1979. (See table 6.) As a proportion of GNP, the budget deficit declined from 6.1 percent to 2.7 percent, but during the recession years of 1981 and 1982, the deficit ballooned upward. A better way to assess the intent of German fiscal policy is to examine the budget deficit after the cyclical effects of the recession have been removed for statistical purposes. When the economy is in a recession, government expenditures in the form of unemployment benefits and other income-transfer programs increase, while government tax revenues decline. As a result, the actual budget deficit generally gives a misleading indication of the intent of government policy. Estimating a "no-recession budget deficit" is the standard method used to get around this problem. When the no-recession deficit is examined, it becomes even more obvious that the intent of the German policymakers was to reduce the budget. As a proportion of GNP, the cyclically neutral budget deficit of 2.7 percent in 1979 declined annually, reaching an estimated surplus of 1.7 percent in 1984.

Maintaining Budget Priorities

In pursuing their course of moderation in forming fiscal policy, the Germans did not attempt to alter public-expenditure priorities dramatically, as did the Americans. Instead, they made a gradual attempt to shift more emphasis to investment, particularly in the areas of energy and computer-communications technology.

In March 1977, the government adopted a medium-term public-investment program extending over a four-year period. In early 1978, measures were approved to stimulate research and development, particularly in small and medium-sized enterprises. In 1978 and 1979, programs were put in place to encourage greater conservation in the use of energy, to reequip public buildings with energy-saving technologies, and to provide bonuses and interest-rate subsidies to companies that increased their level of investment. And in 1984, a four-year program to increase the development of micro-electronics, computing, and communications technologies was

TABLE 6. BUDGET DEFICITS IN WEST GERMANY

Year	Amount in Billions of DM	Amount as Proportion of GNP	"No-Recession" Estimate[a]
1975	60	6.1%	+2.1%
1976	41	3.6	+2.2
1977	31	2.5	+2.1
1978	36	3.1	+1.3
1979	38	2.7	+2.7
1980	47	3.1	+2.5
1981	60	3.8	+2.4
1982	55	3.5	+0.9
1983	45	2.7	−0.5
1984	30	1.4	−1.7

SOURCES: OECD, *OECD Economic Surveys: Germany,* 1980, 30–33; ibid., 1983, 26–29; ibid., 1984, 26–29; idem, *OECD Economic Outlook,* 1984, 27.

NOTES: Data reflect public-sector deficits for all levels of government. Negative signs indicate budget surpluses.

[a] As proportion of GNP.

established. All of these changes reflected Chancellor Schmidt's firm belief that "progress in our country is the fruit not only of social policy but also of the continued modernization of our economy."[7]

Efforts to modernize the economy, however, did not greatly alter the overall budget priorities of the federal government. In fact, most of the incentives involved changes in the tax code and small grants designed to shift more private resources into productive investment. The federal budget was a remarkable example of stability and continuity, particularly when compared with the wrenching shifts in budget priorities in the American experiment.

During the years 1978 through 1981, when the German experiment was being formulated, budget priorities were altered very little. In 1978, for instance, 9.8 percent of the West German federal budget was allocated to defense, and in 1981 the defense share was still 9.2 percent. (See table 7.) Combined expenditures on income-security and health programs accounted for 70.0 percent of the budget in 1978 and 70.4 percent in 1981, while public investment declined moderately, from 9.5 percent to 7.4 percent.

In the American experiment, initiated in 1981 and designed to alter budget priorities dramatically over the next six years, defense expenditures were projected to increase from 22.2 percent of the total budget in 1981 to 35.4 percent in 1987, while public investment would decline from 14.4 percent to 5.7 percent. The only area of

TABLE 7. BUDGET EXPENDITURES IN WEST GERMANY AND THE UNITED STATES (AS A PROPORTION OF TOTAL FEDERAL SPENDING)

	West Germany		United States	
Item	*1978*	*1981*	*1981*	*1987*[a]
Defense	9.8%	9.2%	22.2%	35.4%
Social security, health, and other payments to individuals	70.0	70.4	50.2	49.0
Public investment	9.5	7.4	14.4	5.7
Other	10.7	13.0	13.2	9.9

SOURCES: IMF, *Government Finance Statistics Yearbook, 1983,* vol. 7, 305 (table B); *ERP,* Feb. 1982, 83.

[a]Projected by the Reagan administration in 1982.

budget stability in the American experiment was in anticipated expenditures on Social Security, health, and other payments to individuals. These were projected to remain constant at about 50 percent of total federal government expenditures.

An Adequate but Tight Money Supply

The West Germans have never trumpeted their monetarism. Nor have they engaged in strident debates over whether they should or should not pursue a monetarist course. Rather, they have quietly assumed that the growth rate of money should remain stable and constant, and that a lower growth rate of money is preferable to a higher one.

There has never been much doubt in the Germans' minds that monetary policy is important, but they have not gone overboard in stressing this policy to the detriment of fiscal policy. A balance between the two is what they hope to achieve, again striving for the middle road in economic policy. In the process, they have probably been the most ardent and successful practitioners of the "art of monetarism" in the Western world.

The Bundesbank, the central bank of Germany, is responsible for administering monetary policy and is largely independent of government control. It is similar to the Federal Reserve Bank in the United States, although there is greater coordination with government policy than exists in this country.

The immediate monetary target of the Bundesbank is the movement of a broad measure of monetary base called "central-bank money stock," or MCB. MCB is the sum of the total currency held by the public and required holdings of commercial bank reserves with the Bundesbank. At the end of each year, the Bundesbank announces an MCB-growth target for the coming year, and the bank attempts to operate monetary policy within this range.

Such a reserve-based monetary policy rests on four major assumptions: (1) that the central bank can control the growth rate of MCB; (2) that growth of the money supply in the economy parallels growth of MCB; (3) that the best measure of money in the economy is a broad-based indicator known as M3, which is primarily time and savings deposits, currency in circulation, and funds borrowed for less than four years; and (4) that GNP movement generally parallels M3.

If the monetary targets are not greatly altered from one year to the next, so that there is stability in the growth of the central-bank money stock, then the relationship of monetary policy to the performance of the economy is quite straightforward. For instance, if MCB grows at 7 percent during the year, the amount of money in the economy also expands at a 7-percent rate. Assuming that the full-employment potential growth rate of the economy is 4 percent, then inflation increases by 3 percent.[8] The central bank pumps enough money into the economy to support full employment and enable the economy to attain its potential growth rate. The money supply is not so tight as to cause a rise in interest rates that could possibly lead to a recession, nor is too much money being supplied so that inflation becomes a threat to the economy. There is very little interference with the financial markets, as interest rates are allowed to be determined by the interaction between supply and demand. (In some countries, including the United States in the past, the central bank attempts to stabilize or control the level of interest rates.)

The West German view of how monetary policy should operate is straightforward monetarism, and is nearly identical to the way such policy operates in the United States. The differences between the two countries involve the emphasis placed on monetary policy. In the supply-side experiment of President Reagan, monetary policy is of secondary importance to the supply-oriented tax reductions; monetary policy is given the task of supporting the tax incentives for more growth in business investment and in the supply of capital to the economy. In the middle-of-the-road experiment of Germany, monetary policy plays an equal role with that of fiscal policy, with government officials always seeking a balance between economic growth and inflation.

This role was made adamantly clear by Helmut Schmidt in his inaugural policy statement to the Bundestag. "Our monetary policy will, on the basis of flexible rates of exchange, and in concert with our partners' countries in the European 'snake,' continue to be oriented to safeguarding the economy as much as possible against external influences," stated the new chancellor. "While safeguarding our currency against external influences, our monetary and credit policy will ensure an adequate but tight money supply."[9]

The meaning of "adequate but tight money supply" was refined in policy terms during the crucial year 1978, when West Germany was under extreme international pressure to alter its economic policies, for it was this pressure that forced the German policymakers to define the nation's economic experiment clearly in their own minds. And not only did they define a course for fiscal policy as discussed above, they evolved a monetary policy that was compatible with their golden middle road.

In announcing its targets for 1978, the Bundesbank said that monetary policy must try to achieve several objectives. "On the one hand, it must seek to facilitate an increase in domestic demand in order to make up — as far as this is possible in the short run — for the losses sustained in export business; this makes a policy of cheap money appear desirable. On the other, it must prevent additional scope for price and cost increases from arising in Germany; this requires that the expansion of the money stock continue to be kept within bounds."[10]

The Bundesbank assiduously followed this middle-of-the-road path, tightening up on its monetary targets when the money stock appeared to be expanding too rapidly, and using other monetary tools when insufficient funds were not available to meet loan demand. In mid-1978, for instance, the Bundesbank raised the rediscount quota — the amount that commercial banks could borrow from the central bank when they needed to expand reserves to meet loan demand — by DM 3 billion. Furthermore, the central bank reactivated a policy under which it would buy public bonds in order to provide commercial banks with additional liquidity. These steps indicated that the Bundesbank was "abiding by its policy of trying to steady monetary development."[11]

On October 18, 1978, the central bank raised the minimum reserve requirements on commercial banks' domestic and foreign liabilities in order to contain the effects on the economy of massive inflows of foreign currency. But the Bundesbank was quite explicit in stating that this policy "did not constitute a switch to a restrictive course of monetary policy; on the contrary, care was taken to retain sufficient financial scope for the further recovery of the economy."[12]

And then, at a December 1978 meeting, the Central Bank Council of the Bundesbank set monetary targets for 1979 of 6-to-9-percent growth in the money stock — slightly more expansionary than during the previous year, but certainly not designed to rekindle inflation. "This should make it possible to continue the policy of monetary stabilization on the one hand and to ensure adequate financial scope for the expansion of the economy on the other," the Bundesbank announced.[13] Through the course of 1978, the Bundesbank evolved a monetary policy that sought to balance these goals of controlling inflation and enhancing modest growth — a policy of seeking the golden middle road.

This middle-of-the-road course characterized West Germany's monetary policy during the ensuing years. In 1980, the growth target was lowered to 5-to-8 percent, and the German monetary authorities operated just below the 5-percent figure in order to contain inflation, which was being fueled by a sharp increase in oil prices. For 1981 through 1983, the growth target was lowered again, to an operating range of 4-to-7 percent; and in 1984, the range became 4-to-6 percent. The central bank made it clear that it would move within this range as economic conditions required. And this it did.

During 1981, the Bundesbank maintained a tight monetary policy "to give a clear signal to strengthen confidence in the German currency and counteract the danger of importing inflation."[14] In 1982, "signs of progress in the field of domestic stabilization and the correction of the external disequilibrium" allowed the monetary policy to continue a gradual relaxation.[15] As for 1983, the Bundesbank indicated that "as long as the low level of economic activity remained among the foremost economic problems, and as price and cost movements and the external situation permitted, it intended to allow the central bank money stock to continue to expand in the upper half of the target range."[16] And in 1984, as West Germany's economy showed increasing signs of recovery, the central bank shifted to a somewhat tighter policy in order to contain the threat of the overvalued U.S. dollar on inflation.

Maintaining German Industrial Strength

The Germans take a great deal of pride in the strength of their industrial base — and well they might, for it has propelled West Germany's economy to the point that it is the third-largest in the free world and boasts the strongest manufacturing sector among all the industrialized countries. Nearly one out of every two workers is employed by an industrial firm. Manufacturing output accounts for 45 percent of the entire gross national product in Germany, greatly exceeding the 35-percent proportion in Japan and the 26-percent contribution in the United States. The Germans have become the most successful exporters of manufactured products and capital machinery in the world, earning trade surpluses that exceed those of any other country, including Japan.

Maintaining the industrial base is critical to the success of the entire German economic experiment. "Considering the large share of the Gross National Product accounted for by industry and the high percentage of the population of the Federal Republic of Germany employed in industry, it is the industrial sector which is particularly affected by the essential components of [economic] policy," observed OECD experts in a 1971 analysis of the German economy.[17]

Chancellor Helmut Schmidt totally agreed with this observation, telling the German people that "progress in our country is the fruit not only of social policy but also of the continued modernization of our economy. . . . We are faced with new tasks which we will lose no time in tackling. Industry, science and the state must act together to overcome the problems."[18]

To ensure that the industrial base continues to be the strong and secure foundation of their economic experiment, the Germans have relied on their industrial policy. It is a policy that lacks the drama of the attempt by the French to catapult themselves into high technology, and it is not enshrouded in the mystery of "Japan, Inc." In principle, the German policy is more akin to that of the United States: it is free-enterprise in nature and opposes nationalization or strong government intervention.

Yet a comparison between the results of the industrial policies of the two countries suggests vast differences. For while the Germans manage to earn tremendous trade surpluses, the United States operates with massive deficits. While the Germans maintain their market share in world trade, Americans are suffering through a rapid deterioration in their automobile, steel, and other basic industries. And while the Americans are engaged in a torturous debate on what type of industrial policy, if any, should be adopted in the country, the Germans have no such problems: their industrial policy is well established.

It is a policy that has three major characteristics: (1) it is dominated by the principles of the free-market economy while at the same time accepting limited intervention to ensure economic and social stability; (2) specific industries are targeted to receive special government assistance; and (3) strong centralization of economic and financial power is encouraged.

The Free-Market Economy

"The free market economic order constitutes the basis of all economic policy in the Federal Republic [of Germany]," the OECD noted in a major study of the industrial policies of member countries.[19] Nationalization is discouraged in German industrial policy, and when the government provides subsidies to industries, the grants are carefully defined to complement the private market rather than supplant it.

This does not mean that the government of West Germany refuses to influence industrial development, for government involvement with industry is far greater than is generally perceived. The Germans do not share the American predilection to let the ideology of free enterprise impede policy action. German policymakers are far too pragmatic to become trapped by their ideology. In West Germany, the principles of free enterprise serve to guide industrial policies, as well as to constrain policy when pressures develop that might lead to nationalization or protectionism. At the same time, the German policymakers do not hesitate to intervene to achieve selected objectives.

West Germany's general philosophy of free enterprise was most clearly enunciated by Ludwig Erhard, the nation's first minister for economic affairs following the Second World War. The free market "only has meaning as long as the economy is motivated and guided by free competition and free price formation," the former economics professor stated in a speech before the German parliament. "For competition is the most essential ingredient of a market economy system, and its elimination, limitation or prevention must inevitably lead to the collapse of the entire system."[20] This was far more than the personal view of an economics minister (and later chancellor) who was known as an aggressive free-enterprise advocate. Erhard's words reflected the underlying economic philosophy of the newly forming Federal Republic of Germany — a philosophy that was restated in almost identical words many years later by the moderate chancellor Helmut Schmidt.

"Competition calls forth the will to achievement," Schmidt told the Bundestag. "Competition has created in our country the foundations for social and economic progress. Embedded in the framework created by the state, the market economy solves the economic tasks better than other comparable systems. However, the market economy is at no point perfect. Rather, it must be constantly developed. In this context the federal government will continue . . . in the future to strengthen and promote the forces of competition."[21]

And this same theme has recently been sounded by Dr. Heinz Riesenhuber, minister for research and technology in the government of Chancellor Helmut Kohl. Writing in 1984 on the shift in German technology policy, the minister stated that "the reorientation of the German research and development policy is a result of consistently reminding ourselves again of the principles of free enterprise, characterized by a distinct separation between the areas of responsibility of the economy and the government. In the sphere of industrial research, the Government of the Federal Republic of Germany will accentuate its subsidiary role — more so than in recent past years."[22]

In developing their industrial policy, the Germans incorporated this free-enterprise philosophy into a set of broad guidelines called the Principles of Sectoral Structural Policy. These guidelines established the commitment to private management of industrial firms, ruled out the possibility of large-scale nationalization, limited the duration of government assistance, and promoted the forces of competition. Specifically, the principles state:

Primarily, it is the managers of industry who are responsible for the necessary structural adaptation in the context of a freely competitive economy;

Special governmental aids and other interventions can be considered only if the economic circumstances affecting individual [industrial] sectors are undergoing excessively rapid and sharp changes, and if the process, left to itself, would result in undesirable economic and social consequences;

Governmental aids must take the form of help for self-help, and can be granted only if they will durably strengthen the competitive ability of the enterprise;

The aids must be of a temporary nature and degressive in character, and must not restrict the functional viability of free competition.[23]

The second principle, which extends "permission" to policymakers to intervene in the economy, gives German industrial policy its dynamic character. Such intervention can occur if significant changes in the social and economic environment create undue hardship for German industry. Therefore, if there is a sudden rise in energy prices, or a rapid increase in international competition in an important market, government can provide assistance to ease the adjustment of German industry.

Social Intervention

While the German policymakers are strongly influenced by their free-enterprise philosophy, which tends to keep their assistance on the conservative side, they have never wavered about intervening when necessary. One of their most distinctive interventions has been to achieve a social objective — the humanization of the work environment.

The Germans have developed over the years one of the most progressive programs for integrating labor into management positions. Initiated by the British when they occupied the heavily industrialized Ruhr at the end of the war, a policy of codetermination in the management of the giant steel and coal industries was established. Codetermination called for equal representation by labor and stockholders on the boards of directors of these industries, as a compromise between the advocates of nationalization and those of free enterprise. And in 1952, codetermination was extended to all German industry, but with labor receiving only a one-third share of representation on the boards.

By the mid-1970s, improving the working environment had become a major issue in all industrialized countries. Workers were expressing their job frustration in greater absenteeism, drug use, high turnover rates, sloppy workmanship, and even occasional sabotage. The German response was to extend codetermination. "We see in a system of co-determination based on the principle of equal rights and equal representation for worker and shareholders an essential . . . item . . . in the field of social policy," stated Chancellor Helmut Schmidt. "A society wishing to move forward both economically and socially is inconceivable without co-determination and without the sharing of responsibility that goes with it."[24]

The Germans had long been lauded for their stable and strike-free labor-management relations, and much of the credit for this condition was attributed to the existence of codetermination. Also, much of the credit for Germany's phenomenal growth in productivity was attributed to codetermination, especially during the economic turbulence of the 1970s, when most countries, including the United States, struggled with low growth rates. And so it was natural that the Germans would turn to what had worked in the past. They proposed to increase labor representation to one-half of the supervisory boards of all companies with 2,000 or more employees. A total of 6 million workers in 670 companies would be affected, and labor leaders would achieve the parity that they had so long desired.

After intense debate, the labor representation was reduced to slightly less than one-half when German business leaders contested that parity would be an erosion of property rights and threatened court action to declare any legislation unconstitutional. Labor was unhappy with the compromise, for less than one-half membership on boards made "a joke of parity."[25] The legislation was enacted, however, and on July 1, 1976, large German corporations were required to increase substantially the membership of labor representatives on the supervisory boards of directors.

Intervention to achieve the social goal of humanizing the work environment is not alien to the German policymakers' overall commitment to free enterprise. Codetermination does not seek to alter the behavior of a firm in regard to economic incentives. The directors and managers of German industry are still expected to respond to market-determined prices, competition, and profit incentives.

There is no German version of the British view that the boards of major industries "must regard themselves as the high custodians of the public interest."[26] Codetermination attempts to humanize the working environment by ensuring that labor participates in management decisions; it does not alter the underlying free-enterprise basis of those decisions. The "functional viability of free competition" embodied in West Germany's principles of structural industrial policy is not restricted.

The same is not true for other forms of German intervention in industrial activity. The economic behavior of the firm is changed; the conditions of free competition are altered. Such intervention occurs in "industry targeting," a practice common among most countries, in which selected industries are singled out to receive special government assistance.

Industrial Targeting

As part of the postwar development program, West Germany targeted key industries for special government support and assistance. Such industries as iron, steel, and coal were viewed as essential to the postwar recovery of the German economy, and, in fact, they provided much of the strength of that recovery. But with the recovery accomplished, the Germans continued the practice of targeting growth industries, changing the goal of the policy from economic recovery to ensuring continued and rapid growth. The OECD noted in its study of German industrial policy that "the growth-conscious structural policy of the Federal Government is intended to facilitate the adaptation to new structures by deliberately easing the mobility of manpower and capital."[27]

Currently, the Germans target industries in four major categories: (1) basic industries, (2) mature growth industries, (3) potential growth industries, and (4) small and medium-sized firms. During 1983, a total of nearly DM 22,895 million (approximately $9.6 billion) was allocated to various companies in these categories. (See table 8.) This support represented 9 percent of the total federal government budget.

By far, the bulk of German industrial support is allocated to railroads, coal, shipping, and steel. The railroads, which receive more than one-half of all federal government support, are nationalized. And the German government provides them with massive support that ranges from research-and-development assistance to direct subsidies for below-market fares that are imposed by the government.

The other basic industries — coal, shipping, and steel — are mature and face declining markets. While they made tremendous con-

TABLE 8. FEDERAL SUPPORT OF INDUSTRY IN WEST GERMANY, 1983

	Amount in Millions of DM	Amount as Proportion of Total Allocation to Industry
1. Basic industries	**15,895**	**69.4%**
Railroads	13,564	
Coal	1,456	
Shipping	534	
Steel	341	
2. Mature growth industries	**4,979**	**21.7**
Energy	4,273	
Nuclear energy	*3,068*	
Coal development	*671*	
Other	*534*	
Aircraft	706	
3. Potential growth industries	**438**	**1.9**
Electronics	249	
Biotechnology	96	
Sea mining	93	
4. Small and medium-sized firms	**1,583**	**6.9**
TOTAL	**22,895**	—

SOURCE: Ministry of Finance, *Bundeshavshaltsplan für des Haushaltsjahr, 1983* (Bonn, 1983).

tributions to the growth of the German economy in the past, their day in the sun has long since disappeared. Lower-cost foreign competition has cut into their traditional markets. Coal deposits are deeper and more expensive to mine. The overall world demand for ships has declined significantly. In spite of such realities, the German policymakers view these industries as critical to the future independence and security of their country, and so they cannot be left to the normal adjustment process of the free market.

Not only would placing the future of these industries at the mercy of the market lead to "undesirable economic and social consequences" for the country as a whole, but there would also be tremendous impact on important — and politically powerful — local communities. Many of the companies in these industries are highly concentrated in certain geographic areas of the country, and German industrial policy therefore has a strong regional-development emphasis. Government support is provided to retrain and relocate workers in declining industries and to promote more diversified economic development on a regional basis.

The most difficult basic industry, both from a "rationalization" and a regional-development standpoint, is coal. It is also an industry that tests to their limit the German industrial-policy objectives, which are "to facilitate the processes of adaptation — but not, however, lead to the sheltering of obsolete structures."[28] To assist the coal industry in adjusting to a declining market and increased competition from lower-cost producers abroad, the German government has followed a course of protectionism, financial support, and stabilization of markets.

A duty on coal imports was imposed along with limitations on imports from countries outside the European Common Market. Subsidies are provided to reduce the cost of transporting coal. A tax has been imposed on fuel oil to increase the costs of competing energy products. Markets for coal use in the iron-and-steel, electrical, and heating-supply industries were stabilized. Tax incentives are given for the concentration or reorganization of coal-producing companies. Premiums are paid for mine closings. Guarantees and tax concessions are granted for other rationalization measures. And displaced workers in the coal industry receive severance pay for termination, adjustment and retraining support, and compensation for nonworked shifts in the mines.

The second major category of industrial support comprises the mature growth industries. These are industries that were targeted in the past for development and that are now mature and expanding. As opposed to the basic industries, whose time has passed, the mature growth industries still offer growth potential for the future. Not only are there opportunities for expanding export markets, but in addition these industries contribute to the general growth potential of the entire economy. For instance, the nuclear energy industry offers the opportunity to reduce German reliance upon imported sources of energy such as oil, as well as the possibility of expanding exports of nuclear power plants.

The mature growth industries are dominated by energy companies and research institutes, particularly those in nuclear development, although the coal industry receives a substantial amount of support for the development of new technology. This support differs from that provided as basic industry support in that it attempts to develop new products and markets, while the basic industry support discussed above eases the pain of adjustment to shrinking current markets. Other energy support is provided to improve efficiency in the use and distribution of energy. And finally, government support is provided to the civilian aircraft industry to develop new technology.

Interestingly, the Germans have invested very little public money in developing potential growth industries, although they have recently shown signs of altering this course. As indicated in table 8, the amount of federal government industrial support for industries that might provide the growing markets in the future is only 1.9 percent of the total. And most of this support is given to the electronics industry. Minor support is provided to biotechnology and sea mining, the only other potential growth industries identified in the German budget.

In early 1984, the German government announced a new program to develop microelectronics, computing, and communications technology. This is part of a concerted effort to reorient German research-and-development policy in hopes of nurturing new growth industries for the future. The overall program has five basic thrusts:

1. To invest in young talent in the area of science and technology (through improved cooperation between government and industry in the hiring of new talent, and through increased hiring in government research facilities)
2. To increase financial support of government research institutes,

while providing incentives that will restimulate competition of ideas and innovations

3. To subsidize part of the research-and-development costs of small and medium-sized firms (Such firms will be reimbursed for 40 percent of the gross wages paid to their research staffs)

4. To assist the start-up of new technology-oriented industries (This assistance will take the form of counseling for individuals founding a new enterprise, subsidies for development costs, and assumption of a portion of the risk of bank loans designated for financing new manufacturing facilities)

5. To improve the basic environment for research-and-development efforts in the economy

The fifth thrust is the most important one. "A climate must be created within the general public which will provide favorable preconditions for making use of existing creative abilities, bring about a positive assessment of the contributions by research and development toward economic progress and social security, reduce fears occasioned by technological developments, and eliminate any superfluous burden created by red tape," stated the minister for research and technology. This requires "a high degree of idealistic and financial freedom," he concluded.[29]

The Germans are not greatly altering either the course of their basic industrial policy or their overall reliance upon providing a stable and secure economy through balanced use of monetary and fiscal policies. Very little money is being allocated to these new-technology development programs. The microelectronics, computing, and communications programs will receive $1.1 billion (DM 3.3 billion) in funding during the next four years. The American computer industry, by comparison, spent $6.8 billion (DM 20.4 billion) on research and development during 1983 alone. Only $38 million (DM 114 million) is being earmarked for support of new enterprises. And just $15 million (DM 114 million) is available to subsidize the contracted research done by small and medium-sized firms. These are extremely small amounts of money for reorienting an industrial base as large as that of West Germany. Rather, the basis of the new direction seems to be "to strengthen the confidence of the economy in a stable economic development."[30]

The final category targeted for government support is small and medium-sized firms. And it is in this category that the German policymakers appear to be placing their hopes for the development of future high-growth industries. Innovative firms — those offering the potential of new products that can maintain German competitive strength in world markets — are favored with government subsidies and grants. Subsidies are given to promote new development. Technical advice and support is provided by government experts, and cooperative organizations are established to share technology and market information. The government operates a large institute in Munich devoted to applied research in product automatization, computer applications to production, managing information and data, and the like.

The German industrial planners are taking the position that given rapidly changing technology and markets in today's world, it is impossible to target specific new-growth industries. Rather, it is better to encourage small-scale entrepreneurship and innovation in hope that from a large pool of budding capitalists, several major industries will emerge that will be the large growth industries of the future.

Although German industrial policy is more extensive than is generally thought and more interventionist than the Germans might like to admit, it "is still at the noninterventionist end of the spectrum in Western Europe."[31] Among the major industrialized countries, only the United States intervenes in industrial policy to a lesser extent than does the German government.

Centralization of Economic and Financial Power

In early 1975, the Deutsche Bank, the largest commercial bank in West Germany, announced that it had purchased 19 percent of the stock of Daimler-Benz automobile company for approximately $1 billion in order to keep the stock from going to investors in Iran. Representing the largest stock purchase by a German bank in postwar history, it increased the total ownership by Deutsche Bank of the prestigious automobile company to a controlling 58 percent. But more important, it raised again in the public view the tremendous concentration of economic power among German banks, industries, and labor unions. It highlighted the significance of the third major characteristic of German industrial policy: the acceptance of strong centralization of economic and financial power.

This concentration starts with the big-three commercial banks: Deutsche Bank, Dresdner Bank, and Commerzbank. These three institutions are involved in a range of economic and financial activity that is unheard of in the United States. American banks are constrained by law from engaging in what are accepted as normal business practices for the German banks. Such normal activities include not only the usual banking functions of collecting deposits and making loans, but also owning and managing sizable shares of major German industries.

There is no separation in West Germany of the deposit-loan and investment-banking functions as in the United States. Nor are German banks limited in their geographic spread: they can operate freely throughout the country, while American banks are restricted in their activities outside their home state. Such latitude gives the German banks tremendous access to capital and the opportunity to invest this capital directly into German industry. And they have used their capital both to finance industry and to acquire very sizable industrial holdings.

German bankers have greatly diversified their holdings throughout the economy in order to minimize risk. The Commerzbank, for example, owns sizable shares in such diverse industries as breweries, department store chains, and construction companies. All of the banks are deeply invested in numerous manufacturing firms, as well as other financial institutions. Bankers sit together on the boards of these industries. In the mid-1970s, the Dresdner Bank increased its holdings to one-third in the same major engineering firm in Frankfurt in which the Deutsche Bank already held 25-percent ownership.

The banks are not alone in the centralization of economic power in West Germany. Both industries and unions are large and highly consolidated. The powerful Federation of German Labor Union contains over 7 million workers, accounting for 35 percent of all wage and salary workers. By comparison, the largest union in the United States, the Teamsters, has 1.9 million members, which is only 2 percent of American wage and salary workers. Furthermore, the German unions are themselves significant owners of industry. The Federation of German Labor Union, for example, owns banks, insurance companies, and the largest real estate concern in the country. And, as noted earlier, German labor occupies almost one-half of all the seats on the supervisory boards of industry.

The German industrial firms are among the largest in the world, having consolidated and merged themselves into "monolithic giants who have become important multinational players."[32] These German giants dominate the chemical, electrotechnical, and automobile industries. They operate plants worldwide, have captured international markets that frequently exceed their domestic markets, and export more than 40 percent of their entire production. Economic concentration is so great among the German industries that the largest 100 companies account for an amazing 25 percent of the entire business turnover in the economy.

Such economic and financial concentration is an integral part of the industrial policy of Germany. Consolidations and mergers have been encouraged by the government. And when an actual combination of industrial firms has not occurred, the government has initiated cooperation. As the director of the Center for European Studies at Harvard University has succinctly noted: "Concentration is a central feature of the West German system."[33]

To accomplish the desired concentration, the German policymakers have relied upon a variety of tax incentives, verbal encouragement, and technical assistance. Tax advantages are given for the merger of corporations and the transformation of personally owned enterprises into corporations. Government experts provide technical assistance in market analysis, comparison of industrial operations, and the exchange of experience. Joint research programs are encouraged. Cooperation among the small and medium-sized firms is promoted. The interaction between government officials and business and union leaders is extensive. In essence, "reorganizations and mergers are significant to structural policy wherever it is a question of adapting the organizational form and the size of an enterprise to a changing competitive situation."[34]

Although the Germans have an antitrust law similar to that which exists in the United States, they are not nearly so opposed to concentration per se as are the American regulators. The Germans attempt to balance the advantages of size and concentration against the disadvantages of monopoly power. German policymakers are not ignorant of the dangers of monopoly power, but in the trade-off between economic concentration and antitrust regulations, the Germans have leaned more toward concentration, while their American counterparts have opted more toward antitrust. The difference in their perspective is largely the result of how each defines the relevant market for judging competition. The Germans view the global economy as the relevant market, and so compare the size of German firms against their American and Japanese competitors. The Americans consider the relevant market to be the United States, and so compare the size of General Motors Corporation with Ford Motor Company.

Mistrust of Policy Extremes

The main reason that the Germans have so strongly adhered to their "golden middle road" economic experiment, at a time when other countries are attempting far more radical and innovative experiments, is their great mistrust of policy extremes. Conservative by nature, resolute by tradition, and tempered by experience, German economic policy simply reflects the character of the people.

So great is this conservative nature that the Germans never adopted the Keynesian prescription of strong government intervention in the macroeconomy until many years after it had become standard practice in the United States and other Western countries. And by the time the Germans did get around to accepting Keynesian principles of taxation and public expenditures as tools for stabilizing the growth of the economy, events had cast the Keynesian model into suspicion.[35]

It was not until 1964 that the German government became bold enough to use the term "deficit spending" in official policy discussions. And not until 1967 did the Germans finally accept Keynesian policy objectives, when they approved a Stability and Growth Law for the Economy. (The United States, by contrast, had adopted a similar law many years earlier, in 1946.) The German law states that "in their economic and budgetary policies, the federal and state governments must take into account the requirements of macroeconomic equilibrium. Within the boundaries of the free enterprise system, these policies must contribute equally to a stable price level, full employment, and foreign balance with steady, moderate economic growth."[36]

The German policymakers, however, never really accepted these broad policy principles, for their stimulation programs in the late 1960s were not general in nature but highly concentrated on certain industries and regions. In 1967, for instance, government stimulus was targeted on the coal industry in North Rhine–Westphalia. There was some effort to stimulate the economy using Keynesian principles following the OPEC oil crisis of 1973–74, but this was totally rejected in the oil crisis of 1978–80. By then, stagflation — the combination of inflation and high unemployment — had overtaken the German economy.

Such conditions were not supposed to occur in the Keynesian world, and their existence made Keynesian policy-solutions difficult. To stimulate the economy through expenditure increases or tax reductions in order to reduce unemployment would add to inflation.

Or, alternatively, to reduce inflationary pressures through tax increases would add to the unemployment problem. Such a policy dilemma is hardly the favorite fare of politicians, especially in Germany. Consequently, the Keynesian policies embodied in the German Stability and Growth Law were never fully accepted.

The German leaders also were constrained by the original constitution of the Federal Republic — the Basic Law, as it is called — which required that the central government balance its normal, or "operating," budget each year. The investment budget, what the Germans call their "extraordinary budget," could be financed with public borrowing. In 1968 the two budgets were combined, but the revenue obtained by borrowing could not exceed the total of expenditures for investment provided in the budget, unless deficits could be justified in order to avert economic disequilibrium. In practice, this means that the Germans must balance their budget over the economic cycle and cannot operate with long-term structural deficits as the United States currently is doing.

Furthermore, there is a great fear of inflation in West Germany — a fear fostered by the memory of the hyperinflation years of the 1920s and diligently passed on to subsequent generations until it has become deeply embedded in the German psyche. Germans recall the days when people hauled a wheelbarrel of money around to pay for a loaf of bread; when a lifetime of savings disappeared overnight; when Germany lay destitute as inflation destroyed the economy. Many even attribute the rise of Hitler and Naziism to hyperinflation. And so it is hardly surprising that a tradition of tight money is strongly reflected in the German economic experiment.

The West Germans, confronted with the need to develop an economic experiment, did not come from a strong tradition of activist government intervention in the macroeconomy. They did not have a history of continued growth in government spending and expanding government deficits to react against as did Ronald Reagan in the United States or Margaret Thatcher in Great Britain. The German chancellor could not launch his experiment as a bold and new break with the past. Nor could he use mistakes of previous big-spending governments as the foil in generating political support for significant policy change.

German leaders were left with no choice but to build upon their past and attempt to weld an economic experiment that drew upon the strengths of economic policies that had been developed during the postwar growth era. These policies and traditions from the past clearly were not Keynesian in nature, nor broadly interventionist in principle.

The Worldly View of Helmut Schmidt

A most important force shaping the German economic experiment was the economic and political philosophy of Chancellor Helmut Schmidt. No other experiment was set in place by a political figure with such a broad range of experience; and Schmidt's perspective and intellectual grasp of global forces were unsurpassed.

President Ronald Reagan came to the presidency of the United States almost totally devoid of any practical experience in international economics and finance. He had minimal exposure to the problems of other nations, and he lacked any deep intellectual, or even pragmatic, understanding of international issues. As a result, the American experiment was completely consumed with domestic economic issues, and policies were set in place that served to frustrate the efforts of other countries.

Prime Minister Thatcher, while bringing to her office far more political experience and probably a keener mind than that of her philosophical counterpart in Washington, was also consumed with domestic issues. The British experiment lacks a broad international perspective and, like that in the United States, does not seem to grasp the reality of a global economy that is now highly interdependent.

The experiments in France and Japan are also rather narrow in their focus, primarily designed to serve the immediately perceived needs of those particular countries, without much forethought being given to their feasibility in the global context. The Germans stand uniquely alone in their international perspective.

At the core of the West German experiment is a concept of global partnership: a mutual understanding of the problems common to all nations and a willingness to cooperate in dealing with those problems. While the Germans are not so naive as to think that all countries will put aside their nationalistic concerns for a utopian dream of global governance (and, indeed, Schmidt argued against such a dream), there is a deep understanding that there must be a "search for stability, or at the least calculability or dependability." Schmidt called this search "A Policy of Reliable Partnership."[37]

The search for a reliable partnership ranges across a broad spectrum of policies. Western Europe needs to maintain a strong defensive posture to counter the arms buildup of the Soviet Union. At the same time, according to Chancellor Schmidt, it must be recognized that the Russians want "to keep the door to talks and negotiation open"; regional structures for economic cooperation and security must be developed, he said, such as a growing relationship between the European Economic Community (the Common Market) and the Association of Southeast Asian Nations (ASEAN). In addition, development aid must be provided to the countries of Africa so that "steady economic and social development on a basis of political stability" can evolve; such aid does not stem from charity but "from sober self-interest: we want to help the nations of Africa to become strong economic partners with whom we can trade to our mutual advantage."[38]

In summary, the Germans hold a view of the world and their role in it that demands of political leaders the ability "[to avoid] provocations, clearly explaining to the other side the choices and options open to us, defusing dangerous situations through willingness to compromise, and enabling those involved to save face."[39] Such a view greatly constrained the range of policies that could be undertaken in West Germany's economic experiment. There was no way that the Germans could attempt the radical course of domestic action pursued in the experiments in the United States, Great Britain, and France when confronted with the realities of establishing a reliable international partnership. An overly stimulative fiscal policy as in the United States or the tight monetary policies of the British experiment would set off the possibility of high interest rates and great uncertainty in foreign-exchange markets. Clearly, this would not avoid provocations. Firmly adopting a given set of policies and dogmatically adhering to them, as did President Reagan, would not demonstrate a readiness for compromise.

It is not surprising that the Germans adopted the golden middle road in their experiment. Believing, as they did, that such a course of moderation was essential in a world facing the "dual threat of nuclear catastrophe on the one hand, and economic and ecological catastrophe on the other," they could pursue no other course. Such a course was seen as essential to restabilizing the economic foundations of the Western world. Moreover, as Chancellor Schmidt said in cautioning against radical detours, "it will be of vital importance that nations and governments do not allow themselves to be swayed from a steady and moderate course by conflicts and tensions which are often of only artificial topicality."[40]

Great Britain: The Iron Lady Imposes Monetary Discipline

*I*N THE PRE-ELECTION SPRING OF 1979, Prime Minister James Callaghan of Great Britain was being challenged by Margaret Thatcher, leader of the Conservative party. The troubled British economy was the election issue. Manufacturing output in 1978 had been lower than in 1973, and during this five-year period the average growth in productivity had slowed to a miniscule 0.6 percent per year. Britain's "slippage in the international-league table of economic performance" had begun to "penetrate the British mind."[1]

Although the economy was showing improvement under Callaghan's leadership — inflation had been reduced from a rate of 24 percent in 1975 to 8 percent in 1978 — 1979 began with a spate of economic problems. Britain's 1.5 million low-paid municipal workers were demanding 40-percent wage increases and truckers wanted 20-percent increases. The Labour government was trying to hold raises to 5 percent. The stalemate sent the truckers out on strike and tied up the British economy during the bitterly cold weeks of January. Wildcat strikes among municipal workers left mountains of uncollected garbage in some communities and threatened to close hospitals and cut off essential services in others.

The deteriorating labor situation played right into the hands of the Conservatives. A public-opinion poll in early 1979 showed the Conservatives with a 19-percent lead over Labour. "Caesar had one Brutus, but Prime Minister James Callaghan is beset by thousands of traditional allies of his Labour Party — Britain's trade unionists," reported the press. And they "may be delivering a death blow to his Government."[2]

Yet even if the Conservatives took over the leadership of government, few observers expected any significant change in economic policies. Even though Margaret Thatcher campaigned for a renewal of free enterprise, promised tax reductions and increased incentives, and said that she would curb the power of the unions, strong historical forces were operating in Britain to prohibit any major restructuring of the economy.

British government officials, civil servants, and politicians were accustomed to high levels of public spending, not lower ones. The British "remain a very cautious people, wary of the unfamiliar."[3] They do not want to discard the "ideals of social democracy in favor of a competitive society in which only the thrusting will inherit the earth."[4] Real change was thought to be extremely difficult to accomplish in England, especially when the government attempting such change ran into the reality of union power.

People still remembered the disastrous attempt of the last Conservative government — that of Edward Heath in the early 1970s — to stimulate growth and renew flagging British industry. The result was inflation, a huge balance-of-payments deficit, and overall economic problems so bad that the British economy finally ended up in "the arms of the International Monetary Fund."[5] As an influential British journalist summed up, "the time [had] come for a correction . . . rather than any imperious demand for a sharp change of course."[6]

On May 3, 1979, Margaret Thatcher won a decisive victory in Britain's general election, sweeping Conservative members of Parliament into office with her. When the final votes were tallied, she emerged with a 43-seat majority in the House of Commons. James Callaghan submitted his resignation to Queen Elizabeth, and Mrs. Thatcher agreed to the queen's request that she form a new government.

The new prime minister was in no mood for cautionary corrections in the direction of British economic affairs. This was not to be a "pretty gentle time," as suggested by a leading British banker.[7] She quickly went to work on a speech for Queen Elizabeth to deliver that would launch her new economic experiment.

"My Lords and Members of the House of Commons," began the queen in opening Parliament on May 15, 1979.

My government will give priority in economic policy to controlling inflation through the pursuit of firm monetary and fiscal policies. By reducing the burden of direct taxation and restricting the claims of the public sector on the nation's resources they will start to restore incentives, encourage efficiency and create a climate in which commerce and industry can flourish. In this way they will lay a secure basis for investment, productivity and increased employment in all parts of the United Kingdom.[8]

A sharp change of course was obviously what the prime minister had in mind. And this sharp change was soon forthcoming. On June 12, 1979, a little over a month after taking office, the Thatcher government announced the basic policies of an economic plan that was to be "a new beginning" that "can pull our own economy round, even in a world of slow growth."[9]

The first and most important goal of this new economic program was to impose a strong monetary policy. "Given the continuing surge in bank lending, I have concluded that there is no option but to act directly to reduce that growth," announced Sir Geoffrey Howe, chancellor of the exchequer, in introducing the economic policies to the House of Commons. "It is not enough to speak of the importance of monetary policy, unless one is prepared to carry one's words into practice." The British experiment was to be a test of Professor Milton Friedman's famous tenet that a strong and stable economy required that the money supply grow at some stated and known rate, preferably a low one, in order to contain inflation.

The second goal was to reverse the "actions and interventions by Government itself: laws that stand in the way of change and stifle enterprise." Stagnation was a particular problem in British industry, much of which had become dependent upon government support and subsidies. And so the new government set as a major goal that of unshackling British industry.

And the third goal was to encourage greater enterprise by the individual. This was to be achieved by shifting "some of the tax burden from taxes on earnings to taxes on spending," which was the only way "that we can restore incentives and make it more worthwhile to work." To make this tax change without greatly increasing the budget deficit would require substantial reductions in government spending, a change in policy that further would increase the incentives for expanded private initiative.

Such a dramatic change in the course of economic policies was destined to encounter tremendous opposition, for the British had long been accustomed to large government. Taxes on personal income were among the highest of the major industrialized countries, but such taxes were necessary to finance a massive social welfare system. British labor frequently demanded and received wage adjustments from government that far exceeded the growth in inflation and productivity. And much of British industry had been nationalized, and, as mentioned, was dependent upon government subsidies and support. Such a legacy of nationalized industry was deeply embedded in the British economy, and would not be easy to dislodge.

Imposing Monetary Discipline

"In deciding their spending plans for 1980–81 the Government has had in mind three central objectives," stated the Conservative leaders in their first budget. "First, to bring down the rate of inflation. To achieve this it is essential to contain and reduce progressively the growth of the money supply. This means that Government borrowing must in turn be firmly controlled. It is the main determinant of monetary growth."[10]

Controlling the money supply — or monetarism, as it is commonly referred to — became the central feature of the British experiment. All other economic goals were subordinated to this objective. Government spending was reduced to minimize borrowing needs. Income-tax reductions were offset with other tax increases to keep the budget more in balance. Public-sector borrowing requirements were reduced so that the money supply could be better controlled. Nothing was more important than reducing the money supply as the primary means for bringing down the rate of inflation.

As a leading British bank economist observed, "what probably distinguishes the present Government of the United Kingdom from its forerunners in the post-war period is the wholehearted and uneclectic way in which it embraced monetarism."[11] And this embracement seemed to intensify as the Thatcher government moved through the trying early years of the British experiment. Even when the economy went into a deep recession, which many observers attributed to the impact of stringent monetary policies, the government leaders clung tenaciously to their faith in monetarism.

In a special report on monetary control presented to Parliament by the chancellor of the exchequer in March 1980, the government stated emphatically that "a progressive reduction in the rate of growth of the money stock is essential to achieving a permanent reduction in inflation. It is a prerequisite to a sustained revival of the British economy. Other Government policies, such as those to restore incentives, support this objective. But control of inflation, and thus control over monetary growth, is indispensable."[12]

In July 1980, in a report on economic progress published by the Treasury, the government strongly reinforced this position: "Monetary policy is central to the Government's economic strategy. By maintaining strict control over the money stock, and ensuring that there is a progressive reduction in the rate of monetary growth in the years ahead, the Government intends to reduce substantially the rate of inflation and so help create the conditions necessary for sustained economic growth."[13]

In March 1981, in its official financial statement and budget report for 1981–82, the government stated that it was "committed to a progressive reduction in the growth of the money stock and to pursuing the fiscal policies necessary to achieve this."[14] And finally, in April 1982, the Treasury again reiterated the commitment to monetarism: "The present Government's economic strategy, aimed at reducing inflation as a precondition of sustainable economic growth, centres upon controlling the rate of monetary growth. The role of fiscal policy is to be consistent with the financial framework designed to achieve that."[15]

No other economic experiment was as closely identified with a single economic policy as that of the British. The Thatcher experiment became equated with monetarism, and it was largely viewed throughout the world as the first major practical test of those economic policies proposed by Milton Friedman, the world's best-known advocate of monetary-control policies. The writings and public statements of this eminent American professor from the University of Chicago found a highly receptive audience among the new economic policymakers in Whitehall. Indeed, one might say that Milton Friedman was the intellectual guru of the British experiment. To understand the role of monetarism in influencing the course of the British experiment, we therefore must review some of Professor Friedman's thoughts on monetary policy, and particularly his thoughts on what such policy could hope to accomplish.

"The first and most important lesson that history teaches about what monetary policy can do — and it is a lesson of the most profound importance," writes Friedman, "is that monetary policy can prevent money itself from being a major source of economic disturbance."[16] As Friedman notes, money has frequently been a source of disruption in the economy. Throughout its early history, the United States suffered from financial panics caused, in large part, by monetary disorders. The Great Depression of the 1930s was greatly intensified by inappropriate monetary actions on the part of the Federal Reserve Bank. And in recent years, drastic and erratic changes in the supply of money to the economy have exacerbated our economic difficulties. Thus, according to Friedman, a major task of the monetary authority is to prevent our "extraordinarily efficient money machine" from getting out of order.[17]

A second thing that Friedman says monetary policy can do is provide a stable background for the economy — ensuring that "the average level of prices will behave in a known way in the future [and] preferably that it will be highly stable." An economy does not function very well when the consumer or investor is never certain whether the rate of inflation will continue at 5 percent or suddenly increase to 10 percent, or vice versa. Such volatility in inflation makes it difficult to plan for the future, to assess the merits of a particular investment opportunity, or even to purchase an automobile. Consumption and saving patterns are disrupted. Investment is curtailed. And general economic malaise permeates the society.

And finally, writes Friedman, "monetary policy can contribute to offsetting major disturbances in the economic system arising from other sources." Such disturbances might come from a sudden increase in the price of OPEC oil, for instance, in which case the monetary authorities could tighten policy in order to offset the inflationary impact from the unexpected rise in energy costs. Or if an "explosive federal budget threatens unprecedented deficits, monetary policy can hold any inflationary dangers in check by a slower rate of monetary growth than would otherwise be desirable."

This does not mean that monetary policy can be effective in fine-tuning the economy — that is, in offsetting disturbances that are of a short-term nature or occur as a normal part of the business cycle. The disturbances must be major and structural, for if the monetary authorities attempt to expand and contract the money supply as an *active* policy tool during the business cycle, then the stability that is desired will be lost. Indeed, Friedman is quite emphatic that given the lags with which monetary policy operates on economic behavior, any attempt to stabilize the economy in the short run will do more damage than if no policy action is taken.

The monetary authority should adopt publicly the policy of achieving a steady rate of growth in a specified monetary total. "The precise rate of growth, like the precise monetary total, is less important than the adoption of some stated and known rate," Friedman writes. "I myself have argued for a rate that would, on the average, achieve rough stability in the level of prices of final products, which I have estimated would call for something like a three to five percent per year rate of growth in currency plus all commercial bank deposits."

In summary, what Professor Friedman was recommending was that the British — or any other government, for that matter — should stabilize the growth of money at some fixed and constant rate. There should be no attempts to make adjustments in monetary policy to stabilize interest rates or foreign-exchange rates; let those rates be determined by free-market conditions. Furthermore, the fixed rate of growth of money had to be maintained for a long period — say, for several years. To change direction every few months would only destabilize the economy. And finally, the growth of money should be around 3 percent to 5 percent, so that prices would stabilize at some low and constant rate of increase.

This was a tough prescription given the economic ills of the British economy during the spring of 1979. The money supply (sterling M3) was expanding at an annual rate of 12 percent, largely because of strong demand for bank credit and high government borrowing. During the first six months of 1979, sterling bank lending to the private sector grew at an annual rate of 28 percent. To control this growth, the government had instituted limits and penalty rates — called "the corset" — on bank lending. The corset, however, proved ineffective and was only distorting the financial markets. Further distortions were being caused by exchange controls on the outward flow of capital that were "more restrictive than that of any other major industrialized country."[18]

The Bank of England had been intervening to keep the exchange rate stable, but appeared, for the moment, to have abandoned that policy, although the central bankers still were attempting to hold domestic interest rates steady and were intervening to moderate bank lending when market pressures threatened to raise interest rates. To adopt a course of monetarism along the lines suggested by Milton Friedman required some tough decisions on the part of the British officials, particularly given the erratic and disparate policies that were being followed at the time.

Soon after the Conservatives assumed control of the government, they announced that the target range for the growth of money supply would immediately be reduced from an annual rate of 8-to-12 percent to a lower target of 7-to-11 percent, and that the target would be gradually lowered to 6 percent by 1983–84. Furthermore, and far more basic, they attempted to reduce the government deficit, by cutting spending and raising indirect taxes, and lowered the public-sector borrowing requirements. Fiscal policy was to be supportive and subordinate to monetary policy.

Finally, the British authorities had to confront one of the most difficult problems in implementing their monetary experiment: how to moderate short-term fluctuations in the money supply as the trend was being reduced. They well recognized that excessive short-term fluctuations might cause uncertainty about the government's resolve and its ability to control monetary growth. Such fluctuations, it was believed, through their "effect on expectations in the financial markets and in the economy generally, can set up conditions which both make the medium-term objective for the money supply harder to achieve, and delay its effectiveness in reducing the rate of inflation."[19]

To overcome this problem — which was perplexing monetary authorities in the United States as well as in Great Britain — the British adopted longer-term growth targets, avoiding month-to-month controls of the monetary aggregates. This is difficult to do, for the public pressure is intense for a change in course when the reported money supply begins to move outside the targeted range.

When the weekly and monthly aggregates move higher than the official target, participants in the financial markets become very nervous about excessive growth in the money supply and the possibility of renewed inflation. And as interest rates begin to move up in response to these concerns, the monetary authorities have a difficult task in remaining committed to their long-term perspective.

Or, alternatively, if the reported money supply dips below the target range, politicians and the general public begin to accuse the authorities of operating too tight a monetary policy and of threatening the economy with a recession and growing unemployment. Under such accusation, the British authorities were adamant that "it is almost certainly unrealistic to think in terms of a smooth path [in money supply] from month to month. . . . The monetary authorities can achieve the first requisite of control of the money supply over a year or more."[20]

There was no doubt that the Thatcher government had adopted a monetary experiment as prescribed by Milton Friedman. The Conservatives had fixed their target on an appropriate star — the monetary aggregate M3 — and had ceased targeting inappropriate stars.

They set long-range goals of reducing the growth rate at "some stated and known rate" that was close to the 3-to-5 percent suggested by Friedman. They stated their intent to stabilize the long-term growth of the money supply and not attempt to alter policies in the short run in a way that might destabilize the financial markets and the economy.

The experiment was heartily approved by Professor Friedman, who wrote:

> I salute Margaret Thatcher and her government for their courage and wisdom in moving firmly and promptly to cut Britain's bureaucratic strait-jacket. Britain has enormous latent strength — in human capacities, industrial traditions, financial institutions, social stability. If these can be released from bondage, if incentive can be restored, Britain could once again become a vibrant, dynamic, increasingly productive economy.[21]

Unshackling British Industry

Prime Minister Thatcher quickly set out to dismantle much of the nationalized industry that she had inherited. On July 17, 1979, the government announced that aid to companies in depressed areas was to be reduced by 38 percent during the next three years. On July 20, the decision to sell a major share of the government-owned British Airways to private investors was announced. On July 23, the government disclosed plans to sell about one-half of its ownership in British Aerospace, the largest plane and missile manufacturer in the nation. At the same time, more subsidies were pumped into state-owned British Shipbuilders in hopes of making the corporation more profitable so that it could be sold in the future. On July 26, the activities of the British National Oil Corporation were curtailed and some of its assets were to be sold to private investors.

In ten days, the new government had taken significant steps to overcome "the fossilized condition of Britain's economy."[22] The reaction to the prime minister's moves was stunning. Her opponents were furious. Her supporters stood in awe, a little overwhelmed by the audacity of their new leader. The press reported that the public attitude toward Mrs. Thatcher's changes was "one of some amazement. She is actually doing what she said she would, seemingly oblivious to Labour's opposition and to the reservations of many of her own supporters."[23]

Yet the government was not expecting miracles with its new industrial policies. The Conservative leaders cautioned that "it will take years to unshackle an economy whose legions of inept managers and highly organized and often disruptive labor force produced four percent less in manufactured goods last year than in 1973."[24] The government was well aware that it was dealing with a strongly organized and entrenched labor force, and with a business-management force who had come to depend upon government to bail them out of economic difficulty. But of even greater consequence, the new government confronted the legacy of an industrial policy that suffered from three well-entrenched characteristics: (1) the politicization of British industrial policy, (2) the diversified economic goals, and (3) the dominance of labor concerns.

Since the very beginning, when the basic concepts of industrial policy were being formulated in Great Britain, there has been an overriding emphasis on political objectives. Economic and management considerations were subordinated to political orthodoxy — an orthodoxy clearly stated in 1933 by Herbert Morrison, the author of British nationalization:

> The Public Corporation must be no mere capitalist business, the be-all and end-all of which is profit and dividends, even though it will, quite properly, be expected to pay its way. It must have a different atmosphere at its board table from that of a shareholders' meeting; its Board and its officers must regard themselves as the high custodians of the public interest.[25]

In all of the major British nationalizations, the dominance of political considerations is clearly evident. The coal industry was nationalized largely because a generation of British labor leaders had listened to the party speakers advocating state ownership and control of the mines. The electricity and transport industries were taken under government control because they were viewed as public monopolies, and if the transit lines were operated on a strictly commercial basis to maximize profit, management "would probably shut all of the commuter services into London, and that would clearly be nonsense."[26] The steel industry was nationalized because there was a strong element of concentrated economic power in the industry and "in an industry of such importance, monopoly must be public and not private."[27] Rolls-Royce was saved because its bankruptcy would have done "irreparable harm to British prestige."[28]

The politicization of industrial policy in Great Britain follows party lines. British industry is nationalized or denationalized depending on whether the Labour or the Conservative party is in power. The ritual seems to be carried out regardless of the needs of the economy.

Unfortunately, this political ritual has prevented Britain from developing an industrial policy identified with broad national economic goals, as is the situation in Japan. There is little sense of an industrial policy that is core to the future economic strength of the country, or essential to the phased progression of British industry into the more technologically advanced industries. Industrial policy, whether Conservative or Labour, lacks economic cohesion and stability. Rather, the policy represents ad hoc responses to a political orthodoxy that dictates that public control is essential to ensure that industry serves the public interest.

What is the public interest? There is no clear understanding — only a vague notion that private interests mean obscene profits, while the public interest is identified with everything that is good. This could be lower prices to the consumer, greater participation of labor in the management of an industry, more equality in wages and salaries, or maintaining jobs. Such a vague understanding leads to the many political conflicts that have continuously plagued British industrial policy and affected the management of the nationalized industries.

The contentious relationship that exists between the politicians and the managers of the government-controlled industries in Britain frequently breaks out into public diatribes. "The performance of certain of our existing publicly-owned industries leaves very much to be desired," complained a member of Parliament at the Labour Party Conference in 1975. "I have a constituency interest in steel. It is, perhaps, the most bureaucratic of all our publicly-owned industries, with the most inept management it is possible to imagine."[29]

In typical response to similar attacks, the chairman of the Central Electricity Generating Board resigned with the following retort:

Flagrant attempts have been made, for short-term political ends, to pull the rug from under our feet. But we are not lap-dogs to be turned this way and that way. We have stood firm. This has not increased our popularity in Whitehall, but no one has succeeded in making us take a single step which, in my view, was against the interests of the industry and its consumers.[30]

The crux of the problem is the lack of consensus about how British industry should be managed. There is a lack of trust between those who run the nationalized industries and those in government concerned with industrial affairs. There is confusion about the respective roles of the boards of nationalized industries, of the ministers, and of Parliament, with the result that accountability is seriously blurred. There is no systematic framework for reaching agreement on long-term objectives and strategy, nor is there assurance of continuity when decisions are reached. And there is no effective system for measuring the performance of nationalized industries and assessing managerial competence.[31]

The second major characteristic of British industrial policy is its diversified economic goals. The British saddle their industries with a multitude of economic objectives, many of them incompatible. Industries are "expected to provide a high level of service, keep down prices and make a profit, though not an embarrassingly large one — even if it is needed to finance a major investment programme."[32] Public ownership "makes possible a great extension of the part that workers can play in the running of the industries in which they are employed,"[33] but nationalized industries "are not doing a very good job in providing value for money . . . and consumers have a right to be consulted about how they should operate."[34]

It is hardly surprising that the managers of British public companies frequently resign in frustration. When they request an increase in prices in order to make a profit or undertake a needed investment, they are frequently turned down by government officials and given subsidies in lieu of price increases. Then they are chastised for not making a profit and thus reducing the drain on the public budget. The managers must balance the various demands of the workers and the consumers along with the traditional goal of running an efficient and profitable enterprise. At the same time, they are expected to comply with government objectives that vary from using the public companies to implement national economic planning to consolidating firms into larger and presumably more efficient units.

These conflicting economic goals are not unique to British industry; the same issues confront all industrialized countries. Whether one is talking about the United States, Japan, or Britain, the issue arises: How can appropriate prices be established in markets in which monopoly conditions exist and there are external costs and benefits? For instance, electricity and transportation are natural monopolies; that is, the capital requirements in these industries are so large and the markets served are sufficiently limited that only a small number of firms are able to provide the necessary service. There is no competition from numerous firms to ensure that prices are appropriate. Without some form of government regulation, the natural-monopoly firm could charge a much higher price than would be warranted for a normal profit. History is replete with examples of price gouging by railroads, oil and steel trusts, and utilities. Furthermore, it is difficult to force industrial firms to pay back the public for the pollution they generate in production without some government intervention in the pricing policy.

Most industrialized countries attempt to deal with these issues by regulating prices of monopolists and adopting regulations and taxes to force the firms to incorporate environmental and other social costs into their pricing structure. The intent is to maintain the essence of normal market conditions in determining the appropriate pricing behavior for the regulated firm.

The British, however, go much further along these lines and require their public companies to consider what economists have called social (or merit) wants. These social wants bear little relationship to the normal preferences of consumers for a particular product. For instance, to force a steel firm to introduce worker democracy into management has little to do with the preferences of consumers for steel products, and the costs inherent in doing this go beyond normal product-pricing conditions. The introduction of worker democracy satisfies a social or merit want that is viewed as important for nonmarket reasons. Consequently, normal pricing policies that serve as effective guides to determine consumer preferences, management efficiency, and adequate profits lose much of their potency in the British system. The result is that there is a sense of confusion and a general lack of clarity about purposes, policies, and responsibilities in the operation of British industrial policy.

The third, and final, major characteristic of British industrial policy is the dominance of labor concerns. As early as 1919, the Coal Industry Commission stated that the worker "must have a share of the management of the industry in which he is engaged, and understand all about the purpose and destination of the product he is producing; he must know both the productive and the commercial side of the industry."[35] The Trades Union Congress reiterated in 1953 that "public ownership makes possible a great extension of the part that workers can play in the running of the industries in which they are employed."[36]

British politicians and government officials who favor nationalization agree that the main purpose of industrial policy is to improve the lot of the worker. Disagreement exists, however, over the role of the worker in nationalized firms, and just how those firms ought to improve working conditions. The gap between vague political and economic generalities and specific operational guidelines regarding the worker has never been breached. It is one thing to state that "the elimination of the profit motive from the management of industry [will] lead to a more democratic system of management appointments, improved wages, better opportunities for trade unions to organize, and less likelihood of redundancy,"[37] and quite another to define exactly how these conditions will be achieved.

Four separate and distinct views have evolved on how nationalization will improve the role of the worker:

1. Nationalization will lead to higher wages and benefits for the worker.
2. Employment will be guaranteed, since the nationalized firm will be more efficient and competitive in the long run.
3. The workers will be able to participate more directly in the decisions affecting themselves and the future of the firm.
4. Labor democracy will be achieved, with the workers actually running the firms.

The first two issues are rather straightforward. Many British politicians appear to believe that private firms make inordinately high profits whose benefits flow to the stockholders and highly paid senior managers. If only those profits are socialized by bringing the firm under public ownership, then there will be substantially more resources available to distribute to the workers in the form of wages and benefits. Also, the public firm will be more competitive and stronger, so that employment can be "guaranteed" and the worker will not be subjected to the vagaries of private markets and threatened with the loss of work when recessions occur.

The excess-profits issue, and who receives those profits, is a matter of income distribution, which most countries deal with through personal income taxes and transfers. Dividends received by stockholders should appropriately be included as income and taxed accordingly. The wages received by workers in the industry should reflect the value of their work. It is quite inefficient to attempt to redistribute income and set wages through nationalization.

Nor is it at all clear that a nationalized industry is any less susceptible to economic recessions than a private firm. Both must produce and sell in the same market. This is not to say that public companies may not offer more employment guarantees than private ones — and, in fact, they probably do. But this is the result of the continuation of employment long after the market has determined the worker to be redundant, which is a form of worker subsidy, and does not represent a basically stronger firm. Only so long as the British taxpayer is willing to subsidize the worker in a nationalized firm that maintains redundant employees will the nationalized firm offer better job guarantees than a similar private firm.

The second two issues, those of labor participation and labor democracy, are somewhat more complex, for they concern the degree to which labor participates in the direct management of the industry. One approach — the least threatening to existing management-labor relationships — is to set up mechanisms to attain better working conditions and improve communications between labor and management. And nearly all sophisticated firms, whether private or publicly owned, attempt to do this. It is an accepted fact of advanced management techniques.

The next level of participation is one in which formal councils or committees are established for labor to offer suggestions and consultation to management. The issues may include working conditions, management style, measures of performance, and other topics that have traditionally been the sole prerogative of management. Usually, management is not bound to accept the suggestions, nor abdicate any of their executive powers.

At a higher level of labor participation, workers become directly involved in the management of the firm. This represents a sharing of the executive power, and might take the form of joint decision-making between management boards and workers' councils, or worker representation on the managing boards.

The highest level of participation is that of total worker democracy, in which the workers themselves run the firm. Not only are they the producers but also the managers. Such worker democracy was the ultimate goal of many of the early British socialists, and created great tensions in the development of industrial policy in the 1920s and 1930s. Today the issue is far from resolved, for in the Aircraft and Shipbuilding Industries Bill of 1974, Parliament required that "each corporation shall have full regard to the need to promote industrial democracy in its undertakings and the undertakings of its subsidiaries" and the Industry Act of 1975 stated that the National Enterprise Board should promote "industrial democracy in undertakings which the Board controls."[38] Yet, true to the British style of industrial policy, no precise form of industrial democracy was prescribed, so the issue of what form and to what degree workers should participate in management remains an open question.

When Margaret Thatcher came to power, she inherited this legacy of politicization of industrial policy, diversity and conflict of economic goals, and the dominance of labor concerns. And despite the aggressive rhetoric and strong actions of her government in her early days in power, it appears that this entrenched legacy of British industrial policy has held strong.

Was nothing done to reduce the role of nationalized industry in Britain? Were the free-enterprise statements of Prime Minister Thatcher mere political rhetoric? To be fair to the prime minister and her government, there were some important changes: The National Freight Company was sold to private investors in the budget year 1981–82. Exploration and production interests in the British National Oil Corporation (BNOC) were transferred to a new company, Britoil, and 51 percent of the shares in this new company were sold to the public in late 1982. The British Transport Docks Board was sold during the 1982–83 budget year. The controlling interest of British Aerospace was sold in February 1981. The government announced that it intended to sell a controlling share of British Airways "to the private sector when practicable."[39] And in late 1984, one-half of British Telecom, the fourth-largest telephone company in the world and the crown jewel of Britain's nationalized industries, was sold to private interests for £3,940 million ($4.7 billion).

So far, the impact of these changes on the budget has been minimal. When Prime Minister Thatcher assumed office, government budgetary support of industries was concentrated in five major areas: (1) regional and general industrial subsidies, which consisted primarily of regional development grants, selective assistance to industries to promote employment, and investment grants; (2) subsidies for the aerospace, shipbuilding, steel, and automotive industries; (3) subsidies for the coal industry; (4) subsidies for the transport industry; and (5) scientific and technical assistance.

During the budget year 1979–80, which reflected Labour-government policies, a total of £1,795 million was allocated to these five areas. (See table 9.) By the 1983–84 budget year, after the Conservative government had had four years in which to change the direction of industrial policy, the budget for these five areas had grown to £2,898 million. But plans for the budget year 1985–86 indicated that the government intended to reduce significantly its support of the aerospace, shipbuilding, steel, automotive, and coal industries. British industrial policy would thus concentrate on assisting depressed regional areas, providing subsidies to the national rail system, and supporting scientific and technical development.

Restoring Private Initiatives

The third goal of the British economic experiment — that of restoring private initiatives to the economy and society in general — is purer Thatcherism than any other aspect of her approach. It reflects the personality and individualistic philosophy of the prime minister to a far greater extent than do denationalization and monetarism, the other major goals.

Mrs. Thatcher strongly espouses the virtues of self-discipline, hard work, and personal responsibility. She calls for a return to the values of the nineteenth century, when the philosophical underpinnings of policy were provided by David Hume and Adam Smith. Her personal philosophy is that of a Victorian pragmatist, and she expounds this philosophy with all the verve and righteousness of a British public-school headmaster of a century ago: The problem with England is that the people have become too lax. They rely upon government to guarantee them jobs . . . to provide for their social needs . . . to coddle them from cradle to grave. The solution is for government to withdraw from the lives of the British people, and

TABLE 9. FEDERAL SUPPORT OF INDUSTRY IN GREAT BRITAIN (IN MILLIONS OF POUNDS)

	1979–80	1983–84	1985–86
1. Regional and general industries	532	667	640
2. Aerospace, shipbuilding, steel, and automotive industries	338	341	10
3. Coal industry	266	691	310
4. Transport industry	517	875	870
5. Scientific and technical assistance	142	324	390
TOTAL	1,795	2,898	2,220

SOURCES: *The Government's Expenditure Plans, 1983–84 to 1985–86,* Cmnd. 8789, vol. 2 (Feb. 1983), 15, 27; *The Government's Expenditure Plans, 1984–85 to 1986–87,* Cmnd. 9143, vol. 2 (Feb. 1984), 27, 42.

to allow the incentives of private enterprise and individual initiative to come to the fore.

Her speeches and public statements ring with these views. Policies "aimed at restoring morale of management and skilled workers will be the top priority of an incoming Conservative government," Mrs. Thatcher told Parliament in the spring of 1979.[40] "Tilt the balance toward freedom of choice and the wealth-producing process begins again" was a favorite statement on the campaign trail.[41] Her goal, she announced in a major policy speech early in her administration, was to re-create the spirit of those days when "Britain turned her face to the world and prospered" because people "had a supreme confidence in their own ability to create new enterprise and to prosper."[42]

In order to restore such private initiatives to the British economy, Prime Minister Thatcher and her policymakers turned to major reforms of the tax structure and the government budget: the level of direct taxation would be lowered in order to strengthen private incentives, and government spending would be reduced.

The Thatcher government set out to alter the structure of the British tax system by shifting from direct to indirect taxes. This was to be accomplished by reducing the marginal tax rates on income, increasing personal allowances in the tax code to exclude low-income workers from any income-tax burden, and raising the value-added tax. (A value-added tax is a tax on the incremental value added in the production of consumer goods and services. As such, it has the same economic effect as a general retail sales tax.)

Specifically, the basic tax rate was reduced from 33 percent to 30 percent, and the rate of tax on higher incomes was lowered from 83 percent to 60 percent. About 1.3 million individuals were excluded from paying any income taxes as a result of the increase in personal allowances. And the value-added tax was raised to an across-the-board 15.0 percent from a previous dual rate-structure of 8.0 percent and 12.5 percent.

These changes were expected to reduce revenue from taxes on income from £29,154 million to £25,089 million for the budget year 1979–80. Taxes on expenditures were to be increased from £28,765 million to £32,427 million. The proportion of general revenue to be collected from expenditure-based taxes was increased from about 37 percent to roughly 42 percent, while that from income taxes was reduced from nearly 38 percent to approximately 33 percent. (See table 10.)

The total amount of revenue to be collected by the British government was not changed significantly in the Thatcher experiment, unlike the American experiment of President Reagan a few years later. The new prime minister kept total government revenues at £76,608 million, nearly identical to the £77,011 million that the Labour government had projected a year before. It was not a reduction in overall taxes that Mrs. Thatcher hoped to achieve, but a shifting of the tax burden from taxes on income to taxes on expenditures.

Such a shift in tax policy represented a dramatic departure from the past. On June 13, 1979, the *New York Times* reported: "Britain's new Conservative Government laid out its plans today for the most radical change in the country's economic direction since the Labour Party's quiet revolution of the early postwar years. The Tories, surprising many of their own supporters with the boldness of their 'new beginning' budget, slashed personal income taxes and state spending in hopes of reviving incentives."[43]

"We need to strengthen incentives, by allowing people to keep more of what they earn," stated Sir Geoffrey Howe when he presented the new budget to the House of Commons. "This budget is designed to give the British people a greater opportunity than they have had for years to win a higher standard of living for their country,

TABLE 10. GENERAL REVENUE IN THE BRITISH BUDGET, 1979–80

	Amount in Millions of £		Amount as Proportion of Total	
Source	Labour Budget	Conservative Budget	Labour Budget	Conservative Budget
Taxes on income	29,154	25,089	37.8%	32.8%
Taxes on expenditures	28,765	32,427	37.4	42.3
National insurance	11,630	11,630	15.1	15.2
Other[a]	7,462	7,462	9.7	9.7
TOTAL	77,011	76,608	100.0%	100.0%

SOURCE: Ministry of the Treasury, *Financial Statement and Budget Report, 1979–80* (London: HMSO, 1979), 14.

NOTE: The Conservative budget reflects changes made on 12 June 1979, when the Thatcher government announced adjustments in the expenditure plans inherited from the preceding Labour government.

[a]Rent, capital consumption, and interest and dividends from public corporations.

their families as well as for themselves. I dare to believe that they will respond to the opportunity offered to them today."[44]

The economic rationale for these tax changes is identical to that discussed in the previous chapter on Reaganomics. If workers are allowed to retain more of what they earn, as they would with lower marginal tax rates, they will be encouraged to work longer. And if they can keep more of their earnings from savings, while having to pay higher taxes on consumption (through the increased value-added tax), they will be encouraged to save more and consume less. Greater work effort and increased savings will strengthen the supply side of the economy, resulting in greater investment, expanding productivity, and faster economic growth.

The British experiment of balancing income-tax reductions with expenditure-tax increases strengthened such economic incentives to a greater degree than in the Reagan experiment. This balancing relates to the troublesome trade-off, discussed earlier, between what economists call the substitution effect and the income effect of tax change. The substitution effect suggests that when marginal income-tax rates are reduced, there is a greater incentive to work longer and save more. Consequently, the supply of labor and capital inputs to the economy increases. The income effect dictates that quite the opposite result will occur — that with lower taxes on income, individuals will work and save less. Since they can maintain their income constant with less effort, the tax reduction encourages them to pursue leisure activities.

Which effect dominates economic behavior has long been a source of intense controversy among economists, and numerous studies have failed to clarify the issue. But the fact that the British experiment offset income-tax reductions with expenditure-tax increases meant that the income effect was largely nullified. Individuals would be far more likely to respond to the substitution effect.

Controlling Government Spending

To make their tax-incentive program work, the British felt that they also had to contain the growth of government spending. Unless public spending was stabilized, the government stated, "there can be no possibility of lower taxes, lower borrowing or lower interest rates." Furthermore, public expenditures had to be based on a "realistic assessment of the prospects for economic growth."[45]

The new Tory government immediately set about to lower planned public spending for the budget year 1980–81. Reductions were made in the amounts allocated for roads and transport, housing, education and science, and assistance to nationalized industries. The number of teachers was to decline from 526,000 to 505,000. Building programs for schools were reduced by one-half. Public spending on housing was cut by 5.6 percent, and local governments would be forced to implement staff reductions.

Speaking at the Guildhall in London, Prime Minister Thatcher was quite emphatic that one of her major economic goals was to "reduce public spending as a proportion of national income. There is nothing sound or moral in spending money we haven't got: Pennies don't fall from heaven, they have to be earned here on earth."[46]

The level of real government expenditures for 1980–81 (those after taking inflation into account) was to be about 5.5 percent below that planned by the previous Labour government, and a budget was proposed that would curtail expenditures another 3.5 percent by 1983–84. The number of government employees was to be reduced by 60,000, or 8 percent of the total. The total borrowing by the public sector, including public-corporation borrowing, was expected to decline from 4.8 percent of gross national product during 1979–80 to just 1.5 percent by 1983–84.[47]

The justification for these expenditure reductions was not simply an antigovernment posture or a desire to bring an abrupt end to the welfare state of Great Britain. While there were numerous references to public expenditures being "at the heart of Britain's present economic difficulties,"[48] the Thatcher government's attitude did not seem to be that public expenditures are inherently unproductive, while private spending is healthy for the economy. Rather, there was a realization that the past trend of growth in public expenditures could no longer be maintained, for the economy was not growing sufficiently fast to support an expanding public sector. To continue to spend at such a rate on public goods and services would require increased taxes, larger government deficits, and higher interest rates. All of these would reduce the potential growth rate of the economy even further and lead to higher inflation.

"To limit severely the resources devoted to our public services for the time being is not to deny that many of them need improvement," the new government stated in its first budget. "It is rather to recognize that the only way in which that improvement can be secured is to earn the money and resources by higher output."[49]

The growth of government spending was to be gradually slowed down with a minimal negative effect on the British people and existing government programs. This is clearly evident in the extent of proposed program reductions and increases. Changes were made at the margin. Priorities were shifted, but few government programs were eliminated or drastically reduced.

The major increase in spending was for defense: the proportion of the total budget spent was expected to increase from 10.8 percent during 1979–80 to 13.2 percent by 1983–84. (See table 11.) While this increase "reflects the Government's determination to give priority to strengthening the nation's defenses," such increases were at the same time designed to "achieve maximum value for money within the resources available."[50] There was not to be a massive buildup of the military at the expense of domestic programs. Social security and health programs were expected to increase somewhat as a proportion of the overall budget, reflecting the aging of the British population and the political potency of these programs. Public-investment expenditures in such areas as education and science, roads, and employment-training programs were budgeted for only slight decreases.

The only exception to this process of budgetary gradualism was in government subsidies to industry. General government support was projected to decline from £1,688 million during 1979–80 to zero in 1983–84. (As noted earlier, however, these reduction plans were never fully implemented and government support of nationalized industries actually was increased.)

TABLE 11. EXPENDITURES IN THE BRITISH BUDGET
(AS A PROPORTION OF TOTAL FEDERAL SPENDING)

Item	1979–80	1983–84[a]
Defense	10.8%	13.2%
Social security, health, and other payments to individuals	46.4	48.0
Public investment	25.7	24.6
Other	17.1	14.2

SOURCE: *The Government's Expenditure Plans, 1980–81 to 1983–84*, Cmnd. 7841 (1980), 16.
[a]Projected by the Thatcher government in 1980.

Thatcher and Reagan: Partners in Spirit Only

The economic experiment of Margaret Thatcher and that of Ronald Reagan are linked in the public mind and in the popular press. Numerous references have been made to the "Thatcherization of America" under President Reagan. Upon her election as prime minister, the *New York Times* editorialized that "her victory will give heart to such kindred American spirits as Ronald Reagan."[51] Milton Friedman wrote that "what happens in Britain is of great importance to us. . . . If Britain's change of direction succeeds, it will surely reinforce the pressures in the United States to cut our own government down to size."[52]

The two Western leaders are linked for many reasons. They both are conservatives in their political philosophy. They both ran on platforms that called for reducing the role of government and advocated significant changes in the direction of economic behavior. They both view themselves as the last hope to restore their faltering respective economies to renewed strength and more rapid growth. Prime Minister Thatcher has talked of rejuvenating the spirit of those days in the past when people "had a supreme confidence in their own ability to create new enterprise and to prosper."[53] President Reagan has spoken of creating "a climate that encourages the development of private institutions conducive to individual responsibility and initiative."[54]

Yet Prime Minister Thatcher and President Reagan are partners in spirit only, for there are significant differences in the two economic experiments. In the first place, the major policy emphasis in the British experiment is monetary control, while that of the American experiment is tax reductions. These are not just quantitative differences in policy stress, but substantive differences in policy essence. And second, the two experiments differ greatly in their degree of internal policy consistency. The British experiment adopted a set of policy objectives that are consistent with one another, while the American experiment is confronted with internal conflict.

Although the British economic experiment has three publicly avowed major objectives, one of them dominates and is the essence of the experiment: bringing down the rate of inflation. Inflation is the most important symbol of what is wrong with the British economy, and for good reason. The British people have long been suffering from the highest rate of inflation among all industrialized countries. During the decade from 1967 to 1977, consumer prices increased an average of 11.3 percent annually — well above the average for other Western European economies (7.2 percent) and the United States (6.1 percent). In 1979, the year of the election and the beginning of the British experiment, inflation was expected to increase 13.4 percent — also well above the expected performance of other industrialized countries.

This higher rate of inflation created tremendous economic and social problems. The standard of living of the British people had declined from being the highest among the larger countries of Europe to being one of the lowest. British labor unions were becoming increasingly militant in their wage demands, attempting to keep up with the inflationary spiral and, in the process, threatening the cohesion of the British economic and political structure. British products were being priced out of international markets, leading to a deteriorating trade balance and pressures on the currency.

It was hardly surprising that after detailing the tax changes that would be instituted in its new economic experiment, the Thatcher government stated that such changes "will not themselves be enough unless we also squeeze inflation out of the system. It is crucially important to re-establish sound money. We intend to achieve this through firm monetary discipline and fiscal policies consistent with it, including strict control over public expenditure."[55]

The effort to establish sound money, or monetary control, quickly moved to the forefront of policy changes in the British experiment. The new government immediately reduced the monetary targets, increased the lending rate, and established ceilings for total public borrowing. When money growth did not subside as rapidly as planned, the minimum lending rate was raised to a record level of 17 percent on November 15, 1979, a much larger increase than had been anticipated by the financial market. And then, on March 26, 1980, in presenting its budget for the next fiscal year, the government announced even tighter controls that, it said, "will involve a substantial further slowdown in underlying monetary growth," for if inflation was not controlled, "stability and prosperity will continue to elude us."[56]

The American experiment is dominated by the tax cut. Tighter monetary controls are only secondary to the primary policy of relying upon massive and long-term tax reductions to stimulate renewed economic incentives and restore more rapid economic growth. From day one of the new administration, there was no doubt that reducing taxes would be paramount in the Reagan economic experiment.

In his first inaugural address, President Reagan set the tone that would continue throughout the development of his experiment. "It is no coincidence that our present troubles parallel and are proportionate to the intervention and intrusion in our lives that have resulted from unnecessary and excessive growth of government," the president stated. "It will be my intention to curb the size and influence of the federal establishment."[57]

How was the growth of government to be curbed? Very simple: Just reduce taxes to such an extent that Congress would have no choice but to reduce the federal budget. Without sufficient revenues to finance the excessive growth of government, there would be no alternative but to dismantle many of the programs that had grown over the years.

The second major difference between the British and the American economic experiments involves their internal consistency. The British experiment is a carefully constructed program whose major policy objectives of tax reform, government-expenditure reductions, and gradual imposition of tighter monetary reins are all compatible. It entails few of the policy conflicts that plague the American experiment. Monetary policy does not confront an overly expansionary fiscal policy. Efforts at tax reform are not extreme. Reductions in government spending are well balanced, and no wrenching adjustments in budget priorities have been imposed.

The British experiment is internally consistent for several reasons. In the first place, the tax reductions on income have been offset with tax increases on expenditures. This means that the revenue side of the budget is being kept fairly well in balance, so that there are no extreme pressures to slash government spending in order to minimize potential budget deficits.

Second, changes in budget priorities are moderate. As mentioned, increases in spending on defense, social security, and health care are temperate, with the proportion of the total budget allocated to defense increasing from 10.8 percent to 13.2 percent over a four-year period, while that allocated to social security, health care, and other payments to individuals grows from 46.4 percent to 48.0 percent. These increases are offset by gradual reductions in relative spending on such public investments as education, roads, and job training.

Third, the ability to achieve a more balanced budget does not require extreme, and highly uncertain, changes in economic behavior. A budget balance is not overly dependent upon significant increases in personal savings and business investment, nor upon a sudden and dramatic increase in economic growth. Balancing the budget is built into policies over which government has some control — that is, balancing tax reductions with tax increases, and offsetting budgetary increases with budgetary reductions. This means that fiscal policy is not too expansionary, which would create undue pressures upon monetary policy.

And fourth, the objective of bringing down the rate of inflation through monetarism is clearly the most important economic goal of the entire experiment. There has never been any doubt about where the British policymakers are placing their priorities: all other government objectives are secondary to the effort to reduce inflation.

The American economic experiment, on the other hand, is replete with internal inconsistencies. It is characterized by policy extremes and conflicting objectives. The first major inconsistency is between massive tax reductions and the effort to attain a balanced budget. Taxes were reduced by $750 billion at the same time that a budget balance was projected to occur by fiscal year 1984. With such large tax cuts, the only way to balance the budget is to reduce government spending greatly and to assume an inordinately rapid increase in economic growth. Only a rapidly growing economy will produce the needed additional tax revenue, yet such growth is dependent upon changes in economic behavior that would be highly unusual in the American economy.

The second inconsistency arises from conflicting budget priorities — from the contradictory goals of an unprecedented increase in defense spending and a simultaneous reduction in total government spending. This conflict creates ever increasing pressure to reduce social and domestic programs, but there simply are not enough such programs that can be slashed. The result is further additions to the budget deficits resulting from the tax cuts.

The third inconsistency is the conflict between tight monetary policy and the desire to stimulate business investment. Tight money — particularly, monetary policy sufficient to prevent a resurgence of inflationary expectations fueled by large budget deficits — has led to high interest rates. These high interest rates are curtailing business investment, which is a critical part of the Reagan experiment.

The fourth, and most serious, inconsistency involves the failure to rank economic objectives. Priorities have never been established. Nor is there any sign of recognition on the part of the Reagan administration that priorities need to be established and compromises made. Even when conflicts between tight monetary policy, increases in defense spending, and massive budget deficits surfaced and drove the economy deep into a recession, priorities were not established. There seems to be an attitude of blind faith that the supply-side program will eventually work without adjustments in policies or compromises in conflicting goals — an attitude that approaches dogmatism.

While Prime Minister Thatcher and President Reagan may be philosophical colleagues, they differ greatly in how they chose to put into practice their views on restoring private initiatives and limiting the intrusion of government in our lives. The British economic experiment is uniquely different from that in the United States. It differs in policy essence as well as in policy structure. The British are pursuing monetarism and the policymakers at Number 1 Downing Street have designed a set of economic policies that are internally consistent in their effort to bring down the rate of inflation. The Americans are pursuing supply-side economics driven by a massive tax reduction. But the policymakers in the White House have never established priorities between their conflicting goals of stronger defense, smaller government, and a strengthened economy.

France Does Things Differently

"THE FRENCH have a talent for doing things differently. And they are indulging it once again," commented a reporter in Paris after the election of François Mitterrand as president of France.[1] On May 10, 1981, after nearly a quarter of a century of conservative rule, the French people selected a socialist to lead their country — a man who had joined the Socialist party just ten years earlier, when the party commanded only a miniscule 5 percent of the vote.

At a time when the electorates in other Western nations were selecting conservative leaders, the French people gave Mitterrand a 52-percent vote, a surprisingly strong mandate by French standards. The supporters of the defeated Valéry Giscard d'Estaing were stunned and in shock as they witnessed the "biggest political shift in a generation" for France.[2]

Apparently, French politicians were not the only ones to be shocked. There was a long delay before a message of congratulations arrived from President Reagan — a delay that commentators ascribed to "the surprise in Washington that Mr. Giscard d'Estaing had not won."[3] The French franc immediately plunged to its lowest level in nine years, capital began to flood out of the country, and the Paris stock exchange was thrown into a frenzy of manic selling. "So you've come to see the death of French capitalism," a broker on the floor remarked as he clutched a handful of sell orders.[4]

François Mitterrand was the first avowed socialist to rise to the leadership of a major Western power. Social democrats had ruled at various times in the past in Scandinavia, Austria, West Germany,

Great Britain, the Netherlands, Israel, and Australia, but these leaders were not of the same ilk as Mitterrand. They did not really strive for fundamental change of the society and the economic system, but "simply tried to run the established order in the spirit of socialism."[5] The new president of France, on the other hand, won on a purely socialist platform with the necessary electoral mandate to effect substantial change.

President Mitterrand wasted no time in letting the French people, as well as the rest of the world, know that change was in the wind. "In today's world, can there be no loftier duty for our country than to achieve a new alliance between Socialism and liberty, a more noble ambition than to offer it to tomorrow's world," the new president stated at his inauguration.[6] And a major part of this loftier duty was to launch France on an economic experiment that would differ dramatically from that being pursued in the United States, Great Britain, West Germany, or Japan.

Many of the specifics of this economic experiment had been laid out during the campaign. Running on a platform that was a somewhat milder version of the official Socialist party program, Mitterrand spoke of raising taxes on the wealthy, and increasing minimum wages and family allowances. Several major industries, along with the remaining private banks, were to be nationalized. The economy would be stimulated to reduce unemployment, and 250,000 public-service jobs would be created.

Yet there was no clear design to the economic experiment. What were to be the major thrusts? How was the economy to be stimulated without setting off an inflationary spiral? How did the new government intend to foster productivity and encourage greater business investment? It was futile to search among the campaign speeches of Mr. Mitterrand for answers to these broader economic questions, or to examine his rather short inaugural address for clues, for "the Socialists, caught off balance by their own victory, had no detailed plan of action on taking office."[7] Rather, the economic experiment would evolve over the next several months as President Mitterrand and his economic team wrestled with the problems of rising unemployment, high inflation, and a currency that was under attack.

President Mitterrand quickly set economic change in motion. At the first meeting of his cabinet, over $1 billion was allocated to build low-cost housing in an effort to give an immediate boost to the economy. Agreement was reached on raising the minimum wage by

10 percent, adopting substantial increases in family and housing allowances and pensions, reducing the retirement age for men from sixty-five to sixty, decreasing the workweek, and increasing the minimum paid vacation from four to five weeks. These changes were "the keynote of the new regime, which has promised to reduce the great inequalities in living standards that have persisted in spite of the country's fast-growing prosperity."[8]

On June 3, 1981, the cabinet announced that banks, oil companies, and the wealthy would be faced with higher taxes in the future. Furthermore, the government announced that it had halted construction of the Plogoff nuclear power plant in Brittany and that a new energy program, designed to place less reliance on nuclear power and more on energy conservation and the development of alternative energy sources, would be developed. Requiring the spending of about $71 billion over a ten-year period, this program would also add a substantial number of new jobs to the economy.

Continuing its massive restructuring of the French economy and society, the Mitterrand government approved, in mid-July, a historic decentralization plan that would be presented to the National Assembly for approval. The plan would greatly reduce the powers of the *préfet,* the local administrator who acted as the government viceroy in the provinces, and would transfer this power to locally elected councils and officials.

While the French people were away on their traditional August vacation, the new government was quietly going about its work. When the vacationers returned to their offices and homes in September, they were greeted by another round of massive alterations to their economy. On September 9, a sweeping nationalization law was approved that would provide for the takeover of thirty-six privately owned French banks, and eleven of the nation's largest industrial groups. Representing what was thought to be the biggest nationalization plan ever carried out by a Western democracy, and estimated to cost billions of francs, the plan would bring under government direction companies that were dominant in steel, computers, electrical equipment, electronics, chemicals, and military arms manufacturing. The nationalized banks would only complete the process, as France's four major banking houses, which controlled about 60 percent of all deposits in the country, had been taken over in 1945.

The Mitterrand government stoutly contended that this nationalization plan was essential in order to stimulate the economy to faster growth. "By taking control of industries with 750,000 employees, $35 billion in sales and the ability to produce everything from microprocessors to steel, the planners say, the government gains the means to stimulate growth, create jobs, increase investment and develop high-technology industries. And with 90 percent of the nation's banking resources under its control, the government can provide any financing that is needed."[9]

On September 15, Prime Minister Pierre Mauroy went before the National Assembly to deliver an economic state-of-the-union speech that represented the most significant policy statement to date of the Mitterrand government. Speaking from a position of political power — the prime minister reminded the deputies that the socialist government had "the means, the time, and the will" to put into place its reforms[10] — he outlined a series of programs designed to revive the economy and provide jobs. The retirement age was to be lowered from sixty-five to sixty, with some workers encouraged to retire at age fifty-five. The workweek would be reduced to thirty-five hours by 1985. Unemployed youths would be offered six- to twelve-month-long public-service jobs, along with job-training programs. Some sixty-one thousand new public-service posts were to be established. Industry was asked to curb overtime in an effort to spread the existing work among more people. A fund of $500 million would be set up to provide economic assistance to new enterprises that were established. Tax incentives were to be used to encourage small and medium-sized firms to expand. The message of government, as the prime minister stated, was "we must get France working again."[11]

Within a few short months, the French people had been presented with a mélange of new economic programs and plans for change. From centralization to decentralization, from radical reform to moderate alteration, from socialism mingled freely with capitalism to entrepreneurship coexisting with state control, the Mitterrand government had fashioned an economic experiment that was unique among those of the industrialized nations.

The French experiment had three major goals: (1) to immediately stimulate the economy to foster growth and greater employment, (2) to restructure the labor market to increase employment opportunities in the long run, and (3) to strengthen the industrial base of the economy through nationalization of key industries and promoting greater entrepreneurship.

From Stimulation to Restraint

When Mitterrand assumed office in May 1981, the French economy was stagnant. Prices were rising at an annual rate of around 13 percent, and the output of the economy was growing at a miniscule 0.2 percent. There was very little strength to be found anywhere in the economy. The growth of consumer spending had been steadily declining since 1980 owing to weakness of disposable income. The depressive impact of higher oil prices and the constraining economic policies of the Giscard government had sapped much of the vitality from the French consumer. Yet the situation was even worse for investment. Public-sector investment, long a source of strength in the French economy, was declining. Private business investment was even more depressed. Faced with high interest rates, a depressed economy, and political uncertainty, businessmen were in no mood to undertake new investments.

These were not auspicious conditions under which to begin a new regime, and Mitterrand set out at once to stimulate the economy. The new socialist government hoped to solve the growth and unemployment problems by quickly increasing government spending, using the public sector to "pull the rest of the economy toward success."[12] His plan was not an ill-conceived effort simply to unleash the public coffers, nor was it solely Keynesian demand-stimulation. Mitterrand hoped to stimulate the economy toward higher employment in the short run, using traditional Keynesian approaches, while at the same time restructuring the economy in the long run, relying upon new supply-side policies. The long-run policies involved creating new job opportunities and rebuilding the industrial base. The short-run policies attempted to increase the disposable income of the consumer as a means of stimulating spending.

Several actions were taken to increase disposable income. Family and housing allowances were raised by 25 percent, while the allowance for the handicapped was increased by 20 percent. The minimum old-age pension was boosted 20 percent. An assistance program for families in financial difficulty was introduced. Unemployment benefits were increased 6.8 percent. The minimum wage was raised 10 percent in June 1981, followed by a 5.4-percent increase implemented in September and November. These actions were effective, for private consumption grew at a rate of 2.4 percent during the second half of 1981 and 2.0 percent throughout 1982, compared to an anemic growth rate of only 0.9 percent during the first half of 1981.

The Mitterrand government was well aware that these policy changes would add to inflationary pressures. And with prices already rising at a rate of 13 percent annually, there was little room for error. The dilemma was how to stimulate the economy while at the same time reducing inflation. It was a dilemma because the standard approach — and that being followed in all other major industrialized countries — was to reduce aggregate demand, primarily through curtailing government expenditures. Obviously, this option was not available to the French, and so Mitterrand chose to impose an incomes policy and to raise selected taxes that would not overly curtail aggregate demand. The president's combination of economic policies was so delicately balanced that *Business Week* commented that "the Mitterrand government appears to have reasoned its economic strategy with Cartesian logic."[13]

The incomes policy was not imposed until the fall of 1981, after it became clear that inflation was continuing: prices were then rising at a yearly rate of nearly 16 percent. A three-month price freeze was imposed on essential goods such as bread, milk, sugar, coffee, and butter. Service charges were frozen at their October-3 level for six months. Profit margins on imported goods were held at October levels for three months, and industrial firms were asked to keep price increases below 8 percent. Only energy prices and wages were excluded from the new policies — energy prices, because the government was pursuing a conservation strategy and higher prices would curtail use of energy; and wages, because the government would not have been able to get agreement with the unions on freezing wages.

To keep the budget deficit within bounds, selected taxes were imposed. The government did not want to increase general taxes on either the consumer or business, for this would only decrease consumer spending and business investment, two areas critical to more rapid growth of the economy. Thus, the new taxes were carefully selected to minimize their impact on aggregate demand. Luxury taxes were increased, particularly those on deluxe hotels and on business-related entertainment expenses. A supertax was imposed on very-high-income individuals, along with the introduction of a wealth tax. And a windfall-profits tax was levied on banks and oil companies.

These economic policies were no sooner launched than they began to encounter rough seas. The storm was centered in the international markets, and it first struck the value of the French franc. When Mitterrand assumed office the franc immediately came under pressure. With new socialist leadership, and confronting an economy faced with high inflation and rising interest rates, most international financiers thought that the franc had only one direction to go: down. Yet Mitterrand fought back tenaciously. Tough exchange controls were imposed. French residents were restricted in their ability to buy foreign stocks and bonds. Companies exporting goods from France were required to repatriate the foreign currency they received within one month. "These measures are necessary at a time of rising international interest rates to protect our currency from temporary upheavals which are in no way justified by the fundamental elements of our economy or by the economic and financial policies proposed by the new Government," announced Prime Minister Mauroy.[14]

But the forces allied against the franc did not abate. Consumer prices continued to rise at an annual rate of 15 percent throughout the remainder of 1981. Interest rates were extremely high. The central bank of France, forced to intervene in the markets to defend the franc, was using up billions of its own reserves. The dollar was exhibiting unexpected strength against the franc and other major currencies, and rumors were widespread that France might leave the European Monetary System.

In October 1981, a long-expected realignment of the currencies in the European Monetary System (EMS) was made. The French franc and the Italian lira were devalued by 3.5 percent, while the German mark and the Dutch guilder were increased by 5.5 percent. This realignment, along with the price freezes imposed by Mitterrand, was expected to stabilize the franc. Unfortunately, this was not to be the case. The franc continued to deteriorate against the dollar and the German mark, and the French trade deficit began to rise to alarming proportions.

The Mitterrand government was forced to alter course: it could no longer maintain its initial stimulation policies. In mid-1982, the changes began. The franc was devalued by 10 percent against the deutsche mark and the Dutch guilder. A wage-and-price freeze was imposed, and when the freeze came to an end, in November 1982, it was followed by a more permanent price-and-incomes policy. The intent was to reduce inflation to 8 percent for 1983, which would be achieved through "anti-inflation agreements" between the government and individual sectors of the economy. Companies that did not sign these agreements, or violated the guidelines, would have their prices blocked. Also, the government ended the automatic indexation of wages, and pay increases were expected to be below the inflation target of 8 percent. "We want to have wages rise more slowly than prices in order to curb consumer purchasing power and increase profitability," explained Finance Minister Jacques Delors.[15]

Furthermore, government spending plans were scaled back, particularly general operating expenditures. The budget proposals for 1983 recommended an increase of 12 percent, compared to a growth of 28 percent during 1982. Taxes were also to be raised in order to reduce the budget deficit. These increases fell most heavily on professionals, who faced an 18-percent increase in social-security charges for the self-employed. Needless to say, these new taxes were not popular, and thousands of doctors, dentists, lawyers, architects, and other professionals protested in the streets of Paris in early October 1982.

Monetary policy also was tightened. More stringent lending quotas were set for the banks during the second half of 1982, and this was followed by a reduced target for the growth of money supply during 1983. The new target was 9.0-to-11.0 percent, compared to a range of 12.5-to-13.5 percent for 1982.

French officials were quite candid in admitting that they had dramatically altered course.[16] "We have paid a high price to learn the realities of living in a highly interdependent world economy," observed Planning Minister Michel Rocard. "We will hold spending down in 1983 by cutting many social programs. And in coming years, we plan to cut government spending from 46 percent of gross domestic [national] product to 42 percent by further cutting spending on social programs and aid to municipalities," stated Budget Minister Laurent Fabius. And when asked by reporters, What are the goals of French economic policy today? President Mitterrand responded, "Very traditional goals. We have to control inflation."

Such a reversal raised a number of questions about the viability of the French socialist experiment. *Business Week* concluded that "MITTERRAND'S PROGRAM LOOKS LIKE A LOST CAUSE,"[17] while the *Financial Times* of London summed up: "SOCIALISM, MORE OR LESS."[18] Had Mitterrand's economic experiment crash-landed? Was this the end of the great socialist attempt to reform a major Western capitalistic economy? What was left of the experiment?

Clearly the initial goal of rapidly stimulating the economy to faster growth was no longer a central part of the experiment. This goal was quickly abandoned when it confronted the dual realities of a stagnant global economy and other Western economies that were moving in quite the opposite direction. In retrospect, the French had little choice, for the pressures against them were simply too great. Furthermore, the French were never as committed to a policy of aggregate-demand stimulation as was commonly interpreted in the American and European press.

Their stimulation policies were not overly extreme, and in more normal economic times they might have been successful. Even with the significant increase in government spending programmed for 1982, the planned budget deficit was only 2.6 percent of gross national product, and the actual deficit ended up remarkably close to that which was planned. When compared to the massive budget deficits of the American experiment, projected to average 5.6 percent of gross national product for the years 1982 through 1985, the French were far more realistic about the capacity of their economy to finance increased government spending than was President Reagan. President Mitterrand appropriately observed: "We have maintained a good fiscal situation. Our budget deficit is less than three percent of GDP [gross domestic product]. Along with that of Great Britain, it is the smallest among industrialized countries."[19]

What the French policymakers did was to adjust their stimulation policies in order to provide a more stable economic environment in which to execute the far more important objective of their socialist experiment: that of rebuilding the French economy for the long-term future through restructuring the labor market and strengthening the industrial base.

Facing Up to Unemployment

The primary reason for the immediate reflation policies of the new government was to combat unemployment, a problem that was rapidly becoming worse. When Mitterrand was sworn in to office, the number of unemployed was 1.7 million, a postwar high for France, and the prospects were even dimmer, as unemployment was expected to top 2.0 million by the end of the year.

The French economy is confronted with a massive demographic problem resulting from the low birthrate during the war years 1914 to 1918 and the boom in birthrates in the early 1960s. The low birthrate during the First World War means that there are relatively few workers who are retiring, opening up jobs to the baby-boom generation that followed the Second World War. An estimated 750,000 young people are entering the labor market each year, while only 500,000 older workers will be retiring. This means the economy has to provide 250,000 new jobs every year just to keep unemployment from rising.

To deal with the unemployment problem, Mitterrand set out to restructure the labor market. His initial efforts at stimulating more rapid economic growth were only an attempt to stabilize the unemployment situation — and deliver on his campaign promises for immediate action — while he developed strategies for dealing with more basic employment problems.

The new socialist president was the first of the Western leaders to face up to the unemployment problem in a meaningful way. President Reagan in the United States seemed to accept high levels of unemployment as a necessary cost of his supply-side experiment. Prime Minister Thatcher stuck to her monetarism while unemployment soared around her. Chancellor Schmidt in Germany hoped that his middle-of-the-road approach would create sufficient jobs to employ the influx of new workers, while the Japanese economy was growing sufficiently rapidly to ameliorate the problem. Only President Mitterrand sought to deal with structural unemployment problems — firmly, directly, and with the active involvement of government.

The overall strategy that the French followed in restructuring the labor market was to share the work among more employees. If the number of hours worked by existing employees was reduced, then more people would find jobs. It was a rather simple approach to a quite complex problem, and, as will be noted later, there are many crucial assumptions regarding the level of wages, the demand and supply of labor, and productivity that underlie such a policy. But the complexity of the problem did not deter the Mitterrand government from pushing forward with a specific set of policies intended to share work.

The first of these policies was immediately to reduce the length of the normal workweek from 40 hours to 39 hours and then to 35 hours by 1985. Furthermore, the maximum number of hours that could be worked per week was reduced from 48 to 46 in an attempt to curtail overtime work. Second, paid vacation time was extended from four weeks to five weeks. This was not viewed as significant a change as the reduction of the workweek, for over one-half of French firms already were providing their employees with the fifth week of vacation.

These changes in the amount of time an employee worked were to be negotiated between an appropriate government agency and an individual firm. A government representative would sign a "solidarity contract" with the management of the firm, and in return for reducing hours worked and increasing the number of employed, the firm would receive a partial exemption from its social-security contributions for the extra jobs that were created. The legislation approving the reduction in work was rather imprecise on issues of pay and work flexibility, however, and acrimonious debate broke out between management and labor unions.

Initially, government officials had stated that employers only had to maintain the income level of those workers near the minimum-wage level, which meant that the pay of other workers would be reduced by an average of 2.5 percent (a 1-hour reduction in a 40-hour workweek). Also, management would be able to arrange the reduced hours and fifth week of vacation in order to minimize the impact on productivity. Unions, on the other hand, wanted the pay of all workers maintained at the level of 40 hours worked and argued for the fifth week vacation to be continuous with the normal four weeks off in August. The conflict between management and unions was extremely bitter, with strikes and sit-ins occurring at many plants. President Mitterrand resolved the initial disputes by ruling that no decline in earnings should occur for any worker; however, the overall question of how such a reduction in work could be implemented without greatly increasing labor costs was conveniently ignored.

The third policy change aimed at greater sharing of the work was to lower the retirement age of all workers in France from sixty-five to sixty, and to provide incentives for some workers to retire at age fifty-five. The intent of this change clearly was to open up more job opportunities for younger people, but at a tremendous cost in additional social-security payments. At a time when other Western governments were beginning to extend the normal retirement age in order to reduce the social-security burden, the French were moving in the opposite direction.

Fourth, special incentives were given to business firms to encourage the hiring of young people, single women, and unemployed persons over the age of forty-five. If management would recruit and hire from these target groups of high-unemployment individuals, then the firm would receive a temporary remission of required employers' social-security contributions.

And finally, programs were set up to provide training. These programs cover the gamut from professional education to normal on-the-job training for industrial workers. For instance, those participating in professional training programs, lasting six months, receive substantial theoretical instruction as well as more applied knowledge. New entrants to the labor force receive training designed to prepare them for working life, and part of their five- to eight-month program is spent in a specialized training center. Other workers receive on-the-job training provided by a firm that receives a subsidy equal to four times the statutory minimum wage for each trainee.

All of these policy changes appear to be based on an assumption that there is some given amount of employment in the French economy that can be divided up among different numbers of individuals. A smaller number of these individuals could be employed to do the necessary work, but they would be working longer hours, earning more overtime, and working until age sixty-five. Or, alternatively, a larger number of individuals could be employed, each one working fewer hours and retiring earlier.

On the surface, there is no major fallacy inherent in the latter alternative, *assuming* that the workers are willing to absorb a reduction in their total earnings. If the productivity of the new employee is equal to that of the current employee who is now working fewer hours, then the real wage per hour worked will not change. Consequently, a reduction in hours worked by a given individual would mean lower total earnings. The given amount of work could be shared to a greater extent among more employees, without diminishing the total output of the French economy or leading to higher unemployment.

Unfortunately, this is not the case in the French experiment. The workers will not absorb a reduction in total earnings, since the government has decreed that their earnings must not be diminished as a result of work-sharing efforts. This means that wages per hour worked will increase. When this occurs, the labor market responds in a well-known manner: At higher real wages, less labor is demanded by firms and more people are willing to go to work. A decline in the demand for labor, along with an increase in the supply of labor, leads to higher unemployment. The French attempt to share work and maintain income levels confronts a pervasive economic reality that suggests the result will be a reduction in total employment rather than an increase.

The French are attempting to ameliorate the impact of higher hourly wages on total employment in several ways. Since total wages are a combination of payment for actual production work along with such non-work-related benefits as health care, life insurance, and contribution to social security, a firm can offset wage increases through a reduction in non-work-related benefits. Clearly, the partial exemption of social-security contributions offered by the French government as an inducement to firms to participate in work-sharing agreements is an attempt to do just this.

In addition, the higher labor costs can be offset through increases in productivity. And again, the French are attempting to improve the overall productivity in their economy. All of the training programs discussed above attempt to ensure that the new employees will be at least as productive as those who are retiring or working less. If the educational programs are effective, the new workers might even be more productive, for they would be bringing newer skills into the labor force.

The French have set out not only to retrain their labor force, but to strengthen their entire industrial base: modernizing industries, investing in new technologies, encouraging greater entrepreneurship, and nationalizing certain key industries that will form the bulwark of their goal to provide full employment in the future.

Mitterrand and Nationalization

No sooner had the last ballot been counted, and François Mitterrand been declared the new president of France, than the news headlines began to speak to the impending nationalization of much of French industry. It was a foregone conclusion that the new Socialist government would launch a massive drive to bring a great deal of what remained of private enterprise in France under the government umbrella. Nor was there much doubt about which firms were on what the press called "Mitterrand's hit list."[20] The key industries that the Socialists wanted to nationalize had been identified many years earlier in the Common Program of the Left that was developed in 1972.

The list contained some of the greatest names in French industry. Compagnie Generale d'Electricité was the largest electrical and electronics group in France, and the third-largest in all of Western Europe. With 1980 sales totaling Fr 45.8 billion ($4.7 billion), and a third of the sales being exports, this giant conglomerate was a world leader in high-voltage electrical equipment, underwater cables, and telecommunications. Saint-Gobain-Pont-a-Mousson, one of the oldest companies in France, was a highly diversified empire with far-reaching holdings in computers, semiconductors, and office equipment, as well as its mainline activities of flat glass, steel pipe, and insulation material. Thomson-Brandt, an electrical, electronics, and arms group of over a hundred separate companies, was the second-largest television producer in Europe and the leading industry in France in electronics, consumer electrical appliances, and radiology.

It was no simple matter to take over these giant industrial conglomerates. Complex issues had to be resolved, ranging from appropriate compensation for stockholders to whether the foreign subsidiaries of these industries would be nationalized. Nor was the transition period from private to public management going to be easy, for many of the companies were run by strong-willed French capitalists who took a dim view of being replaced by government technocrats.

Mitterrand set up a committee to study these issues, and government officials were dispatched to the headquarters of the companies slated for nationalization to assess their finances and work out the details for the transfer of ownership. Many businessmen accepted these changes with "a Gallic shrug of resignation."[21] A few were supportive, such as the legendary Marcel Dassault, head of a military-aircraft manufacturing empire that he had built into "one of the two or three most brilliantly successful firms in France."[22] Others were quite outspoken in their opposition, denouncing the takeover in newspaper advertisements and stating to the press that "the government has no idea of where it is headed. . . . The entire program is being undertaken regardless of the economic consequences."[23]

Most businessmen seemed to follow the lead of an official at Saint-Gobain: "We knew what was coming and it has come. Everyone is very calm around here this morning."[24] They seemed reluctant to challenge openly the new government for fear of jeopardizing what they were beginning to see as a moderate approach toward nationalization. The government was carefully assessing the situation, and reaching the conclusion that nationalization would be limited. It would not involve foreign firms. The transition would be quietly accomplished through the traditional French approach of "informal mutual persuasion."[25] And even the stockholders were to be royally compensated.

Immediately after the election, stock prices of the firms designated for nationalization plunged, setting the stage for massive speculation. As the time for final decisions on nationalization approached, and rumors began to circulate that the government would be forced to pay a high price for the assets of the companies, prices began to soar. Speculative buying became so prevalent that the Finance Ministry called for the suspension of trading in the stocks of the designated firms.

When the details of the payment plan were finalized, the stockholders had every reason to feel more than adequately compensated — and the speculators were proven correct in their gamble. Stockholders were to be paid in long-term bonds (fifteen-year maturity) that would pay a competitive interest rate. Beginning in 1983, the government would start redeeming the bonds by lottery, so that shareholders could receive cash for the value of their nationalized assets. Even more fortunate for the stockholders was the formula for pricing the assets. Rather than valuing the nationalized companies at the current market value of the stocks — then stalled at a depressed $1.25 billion overall — the government elected to consider current net profits and the capitalized value of expected profits along with asset value. The result was that stockholders received a whopping $8 billion, far in excess of the market value of their stocks.

On February 11, 1982, Prime Minister Mauroy signed into law the historic nationalization bill, representing the largest nationalization of industry by any government in the Western world. A total of thirty-nine banks, two financial holding companies, and nine major industrial groups and large corporations were changed from private to public ownership. (See table 12.)

The Socialist government now had control of the country's two leading electrical-goods manufacturers, the two leading steel producers, nearly all of the military-hardware industry, and most of the electronics, computer, and telecommunications industry. Furthermore, the government added such well-known financial empires as the Banque Rothschild (the French branch of the Rothschild banking dynasty), and Compagnie Financière de Paris et des Pays-Bas and Compagnie Financière de Suez et de Indochine, two strong and aggressive investment banks better known as Paribas and Suez. When added to the previous holdings, nearly one-third of the entire industrial output of the French economy was under government con-

trol, including 70 percent of its advanced electronic capability. And
the government controlled over 90 percent of the nation's financial
deposits, and all of the major banking and investment houses.

In spite of their actions, the Socialists were never clear in their
statements about what they hoped to achieve through nationalization. The official government spokesman announced at the end of
the cabinet meeting during which the decision was made to nationalize that the state takeover of industry would "free the economy
from the financial powers that are suffocating it and restore all its
dynamism."[26] This rather sweeping statement seemed to exemplify
the attitude of the Mitterrand government toward nationalization.
The absorption of nearly one million workers under the government
umbrella, and the assumption of control over several hundred firms
with annual sales exceeding $50 billion, never had a clearly annun-
ciated economic rationale put forth by the Socialists.

The primary impetus for nationalization was not so much an economic one as it was an effort to satisfy political expectations. The
Mitterrand government simply was honoring the nationalization
chapter of the 1972 Common Program of the Left, made nearly a

TABLE 12. COMPANIES NATIONALIZED BY THE SOCIALISTS IN FRANCE

	Major Products	Number of Employees
Compagnie Generale d'Electricité	Electrical equipment, telecommunications, electronics	192,000
Dassault	Military aircraft	16,000
Matra	Military hardware, primarily missiles	6,000
Pechiney Ugine Kuhlmann	Metals and chemicals	80,000
Rhône-Poulenc	Chemical products	84,000
Sacilor	Steel	56,000
Saint-Gobain-Pont-a-Mousson	Building materials, electronics	139,000
Thomson-Brandt	Electronics, consumer electrical appliances	130,000
Usinor	Steel	50,000

SOURCE: Observatoire François des Conjonctures Economiques, Paris.

decade earlier when the Socialists forged the political coalition out of which they launched their successful drive to wrest control of the government from the Right.

Even after winning the presidency, the Socialists did not rush headlong into a nationalization program. Mitterrand established a committee to analyze the issue, setting off speculation that the actual extent of the nationalization might be far less than generally expected. It was only after the Socialists had won a surprisingly strong victory in the National Assembly elections in June 1981 that the government moved ahead with its nationalization efforts. And still the wheels moved slowly. The cabinet did not approve the program until September. It was debated extensively in Parliament through the fall and signed into law in February 1982. Also, there were no surprises in the nationalization legislation. The list of the industries to be taken over by government was nearly identical to those enumerated in 1972, and Mitterrand was quite emphatic that this was the total extent of his nationalization plans. "There is no risk of nationalization in the future," he told the international press. "When I was elected President, I announced the list of firms to be nationalized, and that's been done. And I said that was the end of it. During my term, which lasts seven years, there will be no further nationalizations."[27]

This does not mean that the nationalization was a pure political act without any economic rationale. As the French economic experiment developed, and the industrial policies were more fully enunciated, four major economic goals were attached to the nationalization program. Nationalized industries would (1) lead the development of smaller industries, (2) orient the French industrial structure more rapidly into high technology, (3) make French industry more dynamic and innovative, and (4) ensure sufficient jobs for a growing French labor force.

The Socialist policymakers view the nationalized industries as giant engines that will power a whole network of suppliers and subcontractors. The state-owned companies are expected to help their satellite smaller companies through prompt payment, assistance with research and development, more stable domestic markets for their products, and support in expanding into overseas markets. In addition, the nationalized industries are expected to cooperate with government in stimulating a new breed of entrepreneurs. Employees with new product ideas who want to form their own company are to be encouraged. A potential entrepreneur-capitalist is to be given a three-year leave of absence from the parent company, with a return job assured. The new company will be eligible for government guidance in seeking finance (easy to accomplish with the banks nationalized) and for reduced taxes during the first five years of operation.

Nationalization will enable the French to orient their industrial structure much more rapidly into high technology. The French have long shown a strong proclivity toward the development of new and advanced technologies. From the research laboratories of Grenoble to the corporate headquarters in Paris, the French have established a reputation for advanced engineering and development. Already acknowledged leaders in nuclear power, military hardware, aircraft, and telecommunications, they are planning to move into biotechnology, microelectronics, robotics, advanced energy systems, and other high-technology industries.

To accomplish this leap forward into the industrial future, the Socialist planners are convinced, the state must take the lead. They point to their audacious success in telecommunications. Less than a decade ago, the French telephone system was the brunt of many a joke. It was archaic and ineffective. Telephone communication between Paris and the other capitals of the world was almost impossible, and the same was true between Paris and other regions of France.

By 1980, the French had expanded the number of telephone lines from 6 million to 17 million. Service was fast and efficient. New developments were being made in linking massive data banks to telephone-television communications devices, thus creating an electronic telephone directory, and in using optical fibers to increase efficiency. All of this was accomplished through a massive, centrally backed research program, a strong government purchasing plan, a large concentration of engineering and managerial skills, and a commitment to targeting this major industry. The same approach is to be applied to the newly nationalized French firms, which are heavily represented in high-technology industries.

Through nationalization French industry will become more dynamic and innovative. There will be a new influx of managers oriented toward development, investment, and greater risk-taking. For an American business leader, such an outcome might seem incongruous with nationalization, but in France the opposite is thought to be true. "Do not judge France by American criteria," warned the minister of planning and regional development. "In the U.S., if American management is not efficient, it will not last long because it will be thrown out or the company will be taken over. But in France, management power is not disputed whether it is efficient or not."[28] Consequently, nationalization is necessary to inject new blood into France's managerial elite.

And finally, nationalization will ensure that France can provide sufficient jobs for its growing labor force. This all-important goal will not only be achieved through creating dynamic and growing new industries in the high-technology areas, but also through preserving more basic industries, such as steel and textiles. These industries provide thousands of jobs to French workers, and rather than benignly assume that they are to become the victims of global competition, the French are attempting to rebuild their competitive power. This is far more than just shoring up a dying low-skilled or smokestack industry. "There is no such thing as a condemned sector," the Socialists stated in their interim two-year plan adopted when they took office, "only out-of-date technologies."[29] They intend to encourage the shift by France's more basic and traditional industries to new processes of production, the adoption of more advanced technologies, and the manufacture of higher-value-added products.

Yet none of these goals, including nationalization itself, is unique to the Socialists. Although given a great deal of emphasis in the Western press, and viewed with some alarm by political and business leaders in the United States, the nationalization plans of the Mitterrand government do not represent a major break with the past. Renault, a favorite example among the Socialist leaders of a well-run and highly competitive firm that was nationalized, had been taken over by the government in 1944. The rapid modernization of the telecommunications industry occurred under the rightist leadership of President Giscard. Leading French industrialists have long come from public service. Rather than representing a dramatic change from the past, the Mitterrand government is continuing a long tradition of industrial and financial nationalization and centralized direction.

The French Tradition of Nationalization

During the period of nationalization, the Socialist government was fond of pointing out that it was doing nothing more than continuing a French tradition that dates back to the time of Louis XIV and his brilliant controller-general Jean-Baptiste Colbert. The Sun King had grand visions of building a magnificent new palace on the outskirts of Paris in order to escape from the constant political bickering in the capital. And he turned to his controller to obtain the massive funds that would be required for this edifice.

Colbert developed an industrial strategy that would turn France into an economic power — a strategy based on creating strong government-controlled trading companies, subsidizing export industries, building a large merchant fleet, and constructing a system of roads and canals throughout France. As a result of this energetic intervention of government into the economy, France became the strongest and richest power in the world.

Yet the tradition that is far more relevant to understanding the nationalization policies of Mitterrand is not that of the seventeenth century, but the more recent post–World War II era. Out of the rubble of the war, the unique form of French nationalization was born — a form that entailed three major changes in the French economy: (1) the development of centralized industrial planning, (2) nationalization of carefully selected target industries, and (3) the education of a managerial elite that dominated both government and industry, and moved readily between the two.

A small group of young men emerged from the war bent on reforming France. They had given much thought to the future of their country, and how its economy might be revitalized. And since many of the older generation stood discredited by their part in the Vichy regime or the Occupation, these young thinkers rapidly were able to move into positions of power and influence. The most influential of these men was Jean Monet, a "warm idealist and international visionary"[30] who sold General de Gaulle on the idea of a five-year plan for rebuilding France from a prewar agricultural and static economy into a postwar industrial dynamo.

Moving into an elegant little private house on the Left Bank of Paris, Monet collected around himself a small group of dedicated visionaries. They worked around the clock with missionary zeal. Discussions were held with government officials and French industrialists. Economic growth targets were set. "Modernization Commissions" were established in which the heads of companies, union leaders, and government planners would sit around a conference table for weeks at a time and hammer out an industrial-development strategy that would achieve given growth objectives.

These commissions were the great innovation of Monet's efforts, for they allowed what the French call *une economie concertée* to evolve. The plan was not dictated by government and imposed on the industrialists; such a strategy would never have worked. Under the plan, each of twenty-five different commissions representing a major industry reached a concerted agreement on how to attain specific production, investment, employment, and growth goals for the particular industry. These commissions, later combined into a single overall industrial commission with twenty-three sectoral sub-committees, would collect information, exchange points of view, and attempt to define the foreseeable evolution of their particular industrial sector during the period of the plan. They would review the forecasts of the government planners and modify them, if necessary, to make them more compatible with the perspectives and forecasts that the industries themselves provided.

The success of the plan was in establishing a psychological environment in which cooperation occurred. The process "tore some of the barriers of secrecy from private firms, helped to create a new climate of productivity and competition, and induced different categories of people to think and work together as in France they had rarely done before."[31] Out of the planning process there evolved a climate for economic expansion, and a framework in which that expansion could occur. But most important, all major economic actors were involved in the process, and they willingly agreed to work to make the plan succeed.

The first plan appeared in 1946 and Jean Monet continued as Commissariat General du Plan until 1952. While Monet was busy developing his plans, a second major change was occurring in the French economy: the direct nationalization of much of French industry itself. When the truce was concluded and the war came to an end, many French firms were tainted with Nazi collaboration, which gave a great impetus to nationalization. The most publicized case was that of Renault, whose owners had cooperated with the Germans. Consequently, Renault was quickly taken over by government.

Other firms soon found themselves under government control. The coal mines, the electricity and gas industry, Air France, and the larger insurance companies, along with the four major banking houses, were nationalized. They joined a group of industries that had been taken over by government before the start of the war, including most armament factories and the railways. By the end of 1946, 18 percent of the entire industrial output of the French economy was produced by nationalized firms, a level of government control that remained fairly constant until the Mitterrand nationalizations of 1982.

Obviously, these nationalized industries gave French government officials the involvement in directing and managing industrial activity that was needed to implement the objectives of Monet's plans. A strong precedence was established for government to put its own managers in charge of these firms, so that when President Mitterrand ousted the heads of three major industrial groups and twenty banks in early 1982 and replaced them with his own managers, there was no public outcry. (It is interesting to note that Mitterrand appointed proven administrators and businessmen, who appeared likely to carry out the government's plan efficiently, rather than prominent Socialists. This also continued a tradition of the past, as will be discussed later.)

The postwar nationalizations established other precedents as well. The French did not necessarily nationalize industries that were in trouble and in need of government assistance to remain in business, as was the custom in Great Britain. French firms were carefully selected to achieve well-thought-out government objectives. The prewar nationalizations were an effort to mobilize resources to prepare for conflict. The immediate postwar takeovers represented a desire not only to replace management whose loyalties to the new government were suspect, but also, more important, to achieve rapid modernization along the lines of Monet's first five-year plan. Steel, coal, and electricity were the basic industries that were to be rebuilt, and these were the industries that were either nationalized or given large government subsidies. The banks were nationalized to ensure that these industries would receive "appropriate consideration" when requesting financing.

Thus it was no surprise when the Socialists targeted steel, chemicals, and other basic industries for strengthening, along with military industries (to reinforce the increasing emphasis on a stronger defense establishment) and high-technology industries (to provide growth potential for the future). The remaining banks were taken over to complete the task that had been initiated in 1946. Mitterrand was following in the tradition of Monet and de Gaulle.

Another well-established precedent is the French predilection for large-scale enterprise. All of the postwar nationalizations, including those of the Socialists, were of the largest firms in the target industries. The two largest steel companies, the entire railway industry, the leading producer of electronic equipment, and the four biggest banks were brought under the government umbrella. And when the existing firms were not thought to be large enough, a policy of mergers and consolidations very similar to that undertaken by the Japanese was adopted.

The French policymaker takes a view toward industrial concentration that is quite different from that found in the United States, where the usual assumption is that high concentration reduces competition and permits unfair monopoly profits. The French economist generally looks at industrial structures to see whether concentration "is high enough to allow for big, efficient firms."[32]

During the postwar period, the French government greatly encouraged the concentration of industrial power. Industrial concentration was given top priority in the government's Fifth Plan, for 1966 through 1970, and was continued in the Sixth Plan, for 1971 through 1975. Special tax inducements were given to firms that acquired the assets of other firms. The Industrial Development Institute, an official government agency, provided capital to rapidly growing medium-sized firms to stimulate even more growth, and aggressively approached groupings of firms to encourage them to consolidate. Between 1950 and 1967, a total of 2,068 mergers were effected by French firms responding to these government inducements.[33] Yet most of the consolidation was carefully concentrated in a few select industries — primarily, steel, chemicals, and electronics.

The French desire for large-scale enterprise has a lot to do with national pride. As part of their foreign-policy goal of maintaining a cooperative but independent role for France within the Western alliance, French leaders have felt it essential to develop large industries. As one prominent student of French industrial policy has noted: "To pull some weight and figure prominently in the diplomatic arena, de Gaulle judged it necessary to have a nuclear striking force, however small and insignificant such a force might be. Similarly, to figure prominently in the economic field it has also been judged essential to promote enterprises with an international character."[34]

Enterprises with an international character were thought to be essential also in order to compete with foreign firms. When France became part of the European Economic Community in the mid-1950s, there was great fear among France's policymakers that French firms would not be able to compete against the giants of Germany. Yet the French steel industry soon proved that it indeed was able to compete against the Germans, and government planners admitted that "what we like best about the Common Market is that it helped shock our industry into modernizing."[35] And thus President Mitterrand was on firm and traditional ground when he told the press: "As long as we do not restructure our industry, France will have a difficult foreign trade situation. So it is one of our main goals."[36]

Another major characteristic of the French form of nationalization is the education of a managerial elite that dominates both government and industry. This elite occupies the senior positions in government, and readily moves from high-paying and secure public jobs into even higher-paying and more powerful positions in private industry. Many of them move directly into industry and maintain their close connections with their counterparts in the various ministries. They have been referred to as "a dedicated clergé, the secular priests of progress,"[37] as well as called the "polytechnical Mafia,"[38] but officially they are known as graduates of one of two all-powerful schools in France and members of les Grands Corps de l'Etat.

The newest of these schools, the Ecole Nationale d'Administration (ENA), was founded in 1946 to provide a postgraduate education to a select group of students who would enter public service. Students are selected through tough entrance examinations, but only those who have attended the more prestigious Paris lycées stand much of a chance of gaining admission. Once enrolled, they are given twenty-nine months of education, "acquiring the techniques and correct attitudes of the upper civil service."[39] Before graduation, they take a final exam that classifies them in order of merit — a classification that is all-important to their future career and financial success, for the top 30 or so graduates, out of a class that generally numbers 130 to 150, are offered positions in the Grands Corps.

The Grands Corps are a unique institution. They are official government bodies that operate parallel to the ministries, and each corps has a specific function to perform. The members of the most prestigious corps, the Inspection des Finances, spend their time touring France to ensure that public funds are not being misspent. The Conseil d'Etat advises on legal disputes between citizens and the state. The Cour des Comptes has the job of verifying public accounts. The Corps Préfectoral works in the *préfets,* or local governments, while the Corps Diplomatique operates in foreign service.

Once a member of one of these five corps, an official is a member for life. Members maintain strong loyalties among themselves, and if a member is temporarily out of a high-level position, or simply wants time off to regroup his political fortunes or rethink his career, he can retreat into the corps. There are no financial worries, no need to seek immediate employment. The corps offer their members a sanctuary that enables them to avoid the straitjacket of normal bureaucratic service in government or industry. The system "enables a brilliant and energetic man to make a full and diverse use of his talents."[40] It also provides government with a reservoir of talent, which both the Gaullists and the Socialists have drawn upon to staff their top political and administrative positions.

The second of the two all-powerful schools in France is the Ecole Polytechnique. Founded by Napoleon to train engineers for the armed forces, the school now educates civil servants for careers in the more technical ministries, or in the large state bodies that oversee electricity, railways, postal services, and telecommunications. Students at X, as the school has been nicknamed because of its badge of two crossed cannons, refer to each other as *camarade* and join their own corps upon graduation. Many complete a brilliant career in public service and then move to a high position — generally, head of a major company. Others go directly into industry, bringing with them their precious contacts in government.

These elite members of the Grands Corps have significantly transformed the relationship between government and industry in France. Once a battleground of conflicting priorities, an arena in which government interests clashed with private goals much as in the United States, the French system now makes it difficult to distinguish between the two. The views of the senior government officials and those of the business leaders on the proper functions of state and industry are almost identical.

There is nearly total agreement on the art of management — hardly surprising, since most of the heads of big industry were educated in *grandes écoles* and spent their early years in public service. There is agreement on the desirability of large-scale enterprise, for a concentration of political and administrative power is how the elite maintain control. And there is agreement on the advantages of maintaining a close working relationship between state and industry, for such cooperation has brought great prosperity both to the economy of France and to the privileged members of the Grands Corps. In essence, the success of French industrial planning "is that the same type of men are sitting in the management and civil service posts in this cartel: men of the grandes écoles, present and former civil servants who consider themselves technocrats."[41]

Socialism in Moderation

When President Mitterrand was sworn in to office, there was great expectation of change. After all, this was the first socialist to be elected leader of a major Western power, and the world had been prepared by an eager and aggressive press to expect change. The new president fueled this expectation in his inaugural address with his promise of a new alliance between socialism and liberty to be offered "to tomorrow's world." And in the dawning days of his administration, change seemed to be imminent.

In retrospect, Mitterrand's new economic policies do not seem to have been very radical. He attempted to stimulate the economy, but later was forced to restrain greatly his plans for increasing government spending. He adopted policies to reduce unemployment: lowering the workweek by a modest one hour, encouraging earlier retirement, and developing programs to train the young and retrain the displaced. But these policies are not very different from those that have been tried in other Western economies. He nationalized a sizable portion of French industry, but, as he himself was quick to point out, this did not represent either a break with past French industrial tradition or the beginning of more nationalizations to come. And so one may ask: What was unique about the French economic experiment? Were the French really doing things differently, or was the heralded new order nothing more than a figment of the imagination of the Western press? Most important, where was the socialism?

To answer these questions and get at the heart of the French economic experiment, one must review the socialist heritage of President Mitterrand and his new administration. Out of what background of socialist thought was Mitterrand operating in developing his economic policies?

First of all, there was the legacy of nationalization of major industry. From the very beginning, socialism has been associated with government control of capital, or the means of production.

In 1850, in an address to the Communist League, Karl Marx stated:

We have seen that the democrats will come to power in the next phase of the movement and that they will be obliged to propose measures of a more or less socialist nature. It will be asked what contrary measures should be proposed by the workers. Of course they cannot in the beginning propose actual communist measures, but they can . . . concentrate in the hands of the state as much as possible of the productive forces, means of transport, factories, railways, etc.[42]

Government ownership of industry came to be identified as the major, if not sole, characteristic of socialism. This is particularly true in the United States, where our understanding of alternative political systems has always been somewhat parochial. Yet to equate socialism with nationalization is a rather limited view. We need to move beyond what might be called "the innocence of traditional socialism" to a deeper understanding of the essence of socialism — to a more sophisticated comprehension of "the relationship between social structure and human values."[43]

The issue is not nationalization per se, but the use to which government control of major industries is put. And in this regard the socialist economists have definite views. Arguing that capitalism in its pure form does not exist, they conclude that the innovative drive assumed in capitalist ideology is no longer valid. Therefore, capitalism does not necessarily ensure economic progress. Indeed, they go so far as to state that "the further maintenance of the capitalist system is [not] compatible with economic progress."[44]

Their logic in reaching this rather startling conclusion is quite straightforward: Capitalism assumes that competition forces the management of individual firms to adopt the latest technology, create new products, and reduce costs. The failure to do so means bankruptcy. But this is true only when pure competition exists. The reality is that while purely competitive markets may exist for farmers and small shopkeepers, they certainly do not for large industrial firms.

The management of steel plants, automobile firms, computer companies, and other basic industries "will introduce innovations only when the old capital invested is amortized, or if the reduction of cost is so pronounced as to offset the devaluation of the capital already invested."[45] In other words, they will delay innovation that might cause obsolescence of existing plant and equipment, displace an existing profitable product, or threaten short-run profit goals. The management becomes conservative and protective. It is therefore the responsibility of government to take the lead to introduce new technology into such industries, to assume the risk of large-scale research-and-development efforts, and to prod management into making the necessary long-range investments in new plant and equipment. Only if government assumes these roles will economic progress be achieved.

Yet the highest aim of socialism is not the nationalization of industry, or the expansion of the powers of government, but "the enlargement of freedom" of the individual.[46] This aim was most eloquently expressed by a most unlikely man — poet and playwright Oscar Wilde. Hardly a name associated with socialist theoretical development, Wilde wrote that

Socialism, Communism, or whatever one chooses to call it, by converting private property into public wealth, and substituting cooperation for competition, will restore society to its proper condition of a thoroughly healthy organism, and insure the material well-being of each member of the community. It will, in fact, give Life its proper basis and its proper environment. But for the full development of Life to its highest mode of perfection, something more is needed. What is needed is Individualism.[47]

What Oscar Wilde called individualism, other socialist writers referred to as egalitarianism, fraternity, libertarianism, or simply freedom. Whatever the term, the value and meaning are the same. It is a condition where human beings can live freed from economic tyranny, whether that tyranny be imposed by a capitalistic system in which individuals are driven by profit goals and the fear of job loss, or a communistic system in which coercive power has been centralized under a small group of elite managers. How to achieve this individual freedom is the essence of socialism, and it represents the other two legacies influencing President Mitterrand: to achieve such freedom requires an equitable distribution of wealth and income, and the creation of greater democracy in the workplace.

Traditional nonsocialist economists argue that the existing distribution of wealth and income is primarily the result of individuals receiving their just rewards for the value of their work. The individual worker is paid according to his or her contribution to the market economy. To be more specific, each of us receives a wage that is equal to the market-determined price of the product we make or the service we provide times the marginal product of what we contribute to the production of that service. For those whose marginal product is high, such as a surgeon or a corporate executive, incomes will be high. Alternatively, those with a lower marginal product will receive lower wages. And if we choose to save and invest wisely, rather than consuming all of what we earn, we may accumulate personal wealth. Since this wealth reflects our own individual efforts at work and in investing, we are entitled to keep that wealth for our own economic gratification, and to pass it on to our heirs as we wish.

Not so, say the socialists. Beginning with wealth as the starting point of their analysis, they suggest that the accumulation of personal wealth has more to do with the accident of history than with the talents of the individual. The man or woman who inherits massive quantities of stocks in a company founded by a distant relation or a sizable trust fund, or on whose land oil is discovered, enjoys an economic advantage that has nothing to do with the value of services rendered. Also, the high salaries and fees paid to professional and managerial workers are in part a reflection of the social inequality inherent in a system in which educational opportunities tend to be distributed unequally.

In a society that accepts unearned income based on property as legitimate, say the socialists, such fortunate individuals tend to be treated with greater prestige and deference than those who must work for their living. Furthermore, such a system does not achieve the maximum social welfare. Rather than having income distributed according to the laws of economic efficiency, it is distributed by the inefficiency of fate. "Only a socialist economy can distribute incomes so as to attain the maximum social welfare," observed Professor Oskar Lange of the University of Chicago. "In any system with private ownership of the means of production, the distribution of income is determined by the distribution of ownership of the ultimate productive resources. This distribution is a historical datum which originates independently of the requirements of the maximization of social welfare."[48]

When the issue arises of how wealth and income should be distributed, the socialists quickly split into two camps. The more radical camp argues that income must be divorced from property, and "even from the exertion of labor."[49] All property is to be owned by the state. The tie between wages and value added is to be broken, and income would be distributed to each according to his or her needs. If all individuals have identical needs, and the utility they derive from income is the same, then the distribution of income would be absolutely equal.

But absolute equality need not be the answer, even under this more radical of the socialist systems. Not everyone has identical needs, and some may value money more highly than others. But such individual differences require that the state determine who is to receive what, and this opens the door to political coercion and greater inequities imposed by the bureaucracy than existed originally. And, as George Orwell so aptly pointed out, this perspective assumes "that the world is immensely rich and is suffering chiefly from maldistribution. . . . Actually the problem for the world as a whole is not how to distribute such wealth as exists but how to increase production, without which economic equality merely means common misery."[50]

The second camp takes a position along the lines suggested by Orwell. The goal is to achieve a more equitable distribution of wealth but to maintain the tie between income and value added. It is fully consistent with socialist principles to allow differentials in earned income in order to procure an adequate supply of skilled labor, and to offer incentives if necessary to achieve high output. The problem for public officials then becomes one of determining the appropriate distribution of wealth and income. This is a question of relative degree, rather than absolute fact, and is a problem that is hardly unique to socialism. Capitalism, at least in its welfare-state form, confronts the same dilemma.

In addressing this issue, the socialists seem to come to several conclusions that indicate a willingness to redistribute income more equitably than would occur under welfare-state capitalism. Arguing that great inequalities of inherited wealth should not be allowed to be perpetuated, they would impose higher taxes on larger estates or would only allow fortunes to be passed along untaxed for one generation. Moderate sums that have been accumulated during the lifetime of the worker would be allowed to be transferred to the wife or children, but massive fortunes that have passed through several generations would be heavily taxed.

Similarly, high incomes would be subjected to greater taxes, for these incomes tend to reflect inequalities in the distribution of educational opportunities and the existence of inordinately high salaries for those who occupy favored management positions. Is the value contributed to the economy by the president of a large corporation who earns $500,000 a year ten times greater than that of the senior manager who earns $50,000 a year? The socialists would say no.

And finally, the moderate socialists would only abolish private ownership of large-scale enterprises in which the greatest concentrations of wealth occur, and in which the opportunities for generating inequities in unearned income are greatest. Socialism does not need to abolish the private ownership of the means of production in small-scale industry, farming, and family-operated shops, for the tie between income and value added remains valid in such enter-prises. It is only "in large-scale industry that the great inequalities of wealth occur."[51]

There is probably no tenet of socialism that has created more controversy, been analyzed and discussed more thoroughly, and still remains such an enigma as the second requirement for achieving freedom: the creation of greater democracy in the workplace, or what the socialists call "workers' control." Throughout all of the writings of Marx, there are numerous references to workers: a "working-class party" must be established and each community must become "the center and nucleus of working-class societies." . . . "The workers must demand progressive taxation." . . . "The work-ers must demand that such railways and factories . . . shall simply be confiscated by the state without compensation."[52] This is the language of class conflict and revolution. It is not the language of government administration and industrial management. And herein lies the problem in understanding what is meant by workers' control.

Workers' control is viewed in socialist writings almost entirely in political terms, to be used as the means of shifting the economic power from the property-owning capitalist class to the propertyless worker class. The workers are a political force, and it is assumed that workers' control will automatically lead to the ideals expressed in socialism. But there is almost no discussion of the appropriate role of worker power in achieving greater democratization or in the management of industry in a socialist society. So the question, Work-ers' control over what? can be answered on several different levels.

On the broadest level, the answer can be that the workers should control the entire economy. This seems to be what the early socialist writers had in mind. But as Professor Daniel Bell has pointed out: "This is unfeasible. A syndicalist society is too much a single-interest affair, which, if extended with its own bureaucracy, would simply substitute one form of interest domination for another."[53]

Alternatively, the answer can be that the workers should have greater control over the direction and management of the industry in which they work: they should be represented on the boards of directors; they should sit on the managing committees; they should participate in setting the goals of the company and share in the rewards for attaining those goals. Hardly a radical concept, this has been attempted in many Western countries, including West Germany and the United States. It has not proven to be highly successful, for it tends to obscure the traditional role of labor unions. Historically, unions have been protective organizations, acting to defend the interests of the workers. Where the union has become a participant in the control of workers — as it must when union leaders assume positions on boards of directors and management committees — workers have tended to form substitute bodies. They have felt that their representatives have sold out to management and are no longer protecting worker interests.

And finally, the answer can be that greater freedom can best be achieved in the workplace when the workers have more control over the conditions that most directly affect them: control in the shop or office over "the rhythms, pace, and demands of work; a voice in setting of equitable standards of pay; a check on the demands of the hierarchy over [the individual worker]."[54] Such control includes the opportunity to discuss work methods and procedures, and to plan how work might be accomplished more effectively, as is done in the famous "quality circles" in Japanese industry.

Having inherited three major legacies from socialist thought — nationalization of basic industry to enhance economic progress, greater equality in the distribution of income and wealth, and increased democracy in the workplace — how did President Mitterrand respond? Did he attempt to incorporate these socialist principles in his economic experiment, and, if so, to what degree?

The answer to the first part of the question is an unequivocal yes: the French experiment is definitely a socialistic experiment. But it is an experiment in moderation. In the first place, the French were quite circumspect in their nationalization of basic industries. The particular industries that were taken over by government were known long in advance, and so there was little, if any, feeling of class struggle. The nationalizations did not represent the triumph of the workers over the property owners. There was no confiscation of private property; the stockholders of the affected companies were quite adequately compensated. It was not a victory of socialism over capitalism.

The French government is intent on putting its control to use to stimulate economic progress — a rather moderate goal of the socialist agenda. There is no doubt that the new French leaders have far more confidence in the ability of government to initiate innovation, undertake investment, and stimulate economic growth than they do in the private sector's ability. "The intended nationalizations will make it possible for decisions by the dominant groups in our economy to be subject to the interests of the community as a whole," stated a ranking French official.[55] And those interests are for "the French economy to develop . . . in the spirit of initiative and the virtues of competition," concluded President Mitterrand.[56]

The second area in which the French experiment reflects its socialist heritage is in the redistribution of income and wealth. And in this arena the socialists have ample cause for instituting change, for the French economy is the most inequitable among the Western industrialized countries. In a study of income distribution published by the OECD, France has the greatest inequality of all the countries analyzed. As indicated in table 13, where the countries are ranked according to their overall inequality, the bottom 20 percent of French households receive only 4.3 percent of the total income in France; households among the top 20 percent received 47.0 percent of the total income.[57] Only the Italians, the Americans, and the Canadians live in an economy that comes close to distributing income as inequitably as do the French. At the other end of the spectrum are

TABLE 13. DISTRIBUTION OF POST-TAX INCOME IN
INDUSTRIALIZED ECONOMIES

	Bottom 20% *of Households*	*Top 20%* *of Households*
France	4.3%	47.0%
Italy	5.1	46.5
United States	4.5	42.9
Canada	5.0	41.0
West Germany	6.5	46.1
Netherlands	6.5	43.0
Great Britain	6.3	38.7
Norway	6.3	37.3
Japan	8.0	41.0
Sweden	6.6	37.0

SOURCE: OECD, Sawyer, 14.

NOTES: Data shown are proportions of the total post-tax income for each country. The study covers the years 1969 through 1973.

the British, the Norwegians, the Japanese, and the Swedes, who share income far more equitably.

Even these measures fail to capture the total extent of inequality in France, for "they gloss over one notorious injustice: Not only are the rates of income tax relatively low, but the self-employed can indulge happily in that ancient French pastime, tax evasion. It is this, as much as anything, that leads to the gross inequalities of wealth."[58] And, as other OECD data suggest, the French have mastered the techniques of tax evasion. It has been estimated that only 89 percent of all wages and salaries are reported for tax purposes in France, compared to 98 percent in the United States and 100 percent in West Germany. Only 34 percent of French entrepreneurial income is reported, which is far below the 91-percent level in the United States. And the French report just 34 percent of their property income, the lowest proportion among the major Western countries.[59] Such widespread tax-evasion means that wage earners in France, who have the least opportunity to avoid reporting income, carry an inordinate burden. They pay 84 percent of the total income-tax bill, but receive just 55 percent of all earned income.[60]

President Mitterrand moved aggressively to redress this inequality. In his first budget, announced in September 1981, the government introduced a wealth tax ranging from 0.5 percent to 1.5 percent on fortunes valued at more than Fr 3 million (about $310,000). In order to curtail evasion of this tax, regulations were put into place to require the recording of all gold transactions in the Paris markets. (Previously, both the buyers and sellers of gold remained anonymous — an obvious advantage to those who chose to keep their wealth in gold and did not wish to pay taxes.) Furthermore, a super-tax of 15 percent was imposed on the top category of taxpayers. And finally, taxes were increased on such luxury items as expense accounts, yachts, and fancy hotels. These tax changes, along with increases in family allowances, old-age pensions, and the minimum wage (all of which were introduced shortly after Mitterrand assumed office in May 1981), will go a long way in altering the inequalities of wealth and income. As a knowledgeable observer of French affairs has written: "The rich in France are now being hit quite hard, for the first time since the war, and are having to cut back on smart clothes, expensive holidays and lavish entertaining. The worst extremes of the wealth gap are being closed."[61]

Yet President Mitterrand is still a great distance from the more radical camp of socialists, who advocate severing the tie between income and work, and achieving something close to equality in the distribution of wealth. For while France is moving closer to the average for the industrialized countries, there will still be plenty of inequality.

As with income redistribution, there is plenty of room for action in the third area in which socialistic ideals are being implemented in France — that is, in the area of promoting greater democracy in the workplace. The typical French laborer works in an environment that is far more centralized and rigidly hierarchical than does the American worker. There is a strong tradition of employer aloofness and secretiveness, fear of delegating authority, and rigid and bureaucratic chains of command in the management of French firms. This is particularly true for strong and closely held family firms such as Michelin.

Also, the French worker does not have the advantage of a strong union struggling to alter these conditions, for only about 20 percent of the French work force is unionized, compared to a European average of 43 percent. The unions they have are weak and fractionalized. For instance, unions have never been able to mount effective strikes, and so the French have developed a rather unusual form of labor protest: the one-day walkout. These spontaneous outbursts of labor grievance, which give the impression that France is a highly unionized country, are more effective in venting frustration than in achieving lasting changes in labor-management relationships.

In recent years, French workers have mastered the technique of the sit-in, which was used quite effectively in the May 1968 labor crisis, when nine million workers took part in a nationwide strike that was the largest in Europe since the war. Especially in smaller firms, the sit-ins have proven somewhat effective in persuading management to rethink decisions. In general, though, French workers enjoy few of the perquisites that are available to their counterparts in other industrialized countries.

The socialists are attempting to alter this tradition. The role of the *comités d'entreprise* are being strengthened. These *comités* are work councils that hold monthly meetings with management to consider such issues as welfare and social activities, offer advice, and serve as a line of communication between labor and management. Interestingly, they are not a new creation of the socialists, but were introduced by President de Gaulle as part of his grand design for participation and were strongly supported by conservative President Giscard in his quest for an "advanced liberal society." Yet the *comi-*

tés never enjoyed much success, shunned by the unions as irrelevant to their main objectives and ignored by management, who protectively guarded their prerogatives in setting overall labor policies. "All the comites do is arrange the Christmas parties" is the common view.[62] The Socialists hope to change this, fulfilling the vision first held by de Gaulle.

The Socialists also are attempting to introduce other changes that go well beyond past efforts: flexibility in work hours, more involvement of workers in decisions that affect daily working conditions, and job-enrichment programs. Management will be required to keep workers more informed of company policy and consult them in advance about major new plans.

In summary, there is no doubt that President Mitterrand has created an economic experiment that is unique among those of the Western industrialized world. He came to power at a time when other countries were electing more conservative leadership and launched France on an economic course that is directly contrary to the policies being pursued elsewhere. That elements of his experiment ran afoul of intractable problems is quite clear. But it is also clear that Mitterrand proved himself to be a very pragmatic socialist, not wedded to ideologies that prevented compromise. The initial stimulation plans were scaled back. Efforts to restructure the labor market, particularly the goal of reducing the workweek from 40 hours to 35 hours, were delayed. Nationalizations were constrained and quietly accomplished. Yet Mitterrand retained much of the core of what is the essence of his socialistic experiment. The redistribution of income and wealth is under way. The French worker undoubtedly will enjoy far greater freedom in the future. And the nationalized industries are being used to pull the French economy into a new era of economic progress.

The Economic Experiments Fail to Deliver

No SOONER had the five economic experiments in the United States, Japan, West Germany, Great Britain, and France been launched than they began to clash and to falter. Each was unique. Each was independent of the others. And each failed to live up to expectations — unable to provide the stable growth and new jobs that had been promised.

None of the experiments received as much criticism or stirred up as much wrath as did that of the Americans. The press reported that "alarm is mounting on both sides of the Atlantic that planned high U.S. Budget deficits are keeping world interest rates high and impeding economic recovery."[1] Karl Otto Pöhl, president of the West German Bundesbank, in an unusually blunt and critical speech for a central banker, stated: "I cannot believe that they do not understand that they have responsibility not only for their own economy, but also for the world economy." In the House of Commons, Sir Geoffrey Howe, the chancellor of the exchequer, called for a concerted European effort "to impress upon the Americans Europe's mounting concern over the U.S. deficits." And Willy De Clercq, the Belgian finance minister, warned that "high U.S. interest rates were increasing the temptation for Europe to adopt protectionist policies."

Although the Americans excelled at stirring up criticism for their new economic policies, they were not alone. The Japanese were singled out for their success in expanding export markets abroad while maintaining rigid and cumbersome restrictions against foreign imports into their home markets. The British economy immediately plunged into a recession, generating headlines around the world decrying the failure of monetarism. The Germans stumbled along, replacing their moderate and brilliant leader Helmut Schmidt with a more conservative chancellor who did little to alter the course of the German economy, which was slowly ebbing into stagnation.

The French knew well that their experiment in socialism would clash with the policies of their Western allies, as was indicated by a member of the French cabinet commenting on his country's economic course: "We must recognize that such a path may bring us into conflict that in the case of the Reagan administration might be quite sharp. It is our conviction that we will, in the long run, best protect the interests of all peoples, including the Americans, by acting in this way."[2] But what the French leaders did not recognize was that their experiment would drive the French economy to the brink of disaster and threaten the stability of the European Common Market.

Rather than ushering in a new era of economic growth and strength, the major industrialized countries plunged into a recession in 1981 and 1982. The economic recovery that began in 1983 was weak by past standards. Only the American economy was showing much strength, and this was expected to be short-lived, with another recession being projected for late 1985 or early 1986. And the Europeans were convinced that the American strength was coming at their expense. By 1984, over 30 million workers were unemployed in the industrialized countries, more than double the level only a decade earlier. Thousands of private companies had gone bankrupt, farmers were losing their land in unprecedented numbers, and major international banks were having serious difficulties. Communications between the political leaders over economic matters had degenerated to mere banalities and meaningless press releases. Above all else, the global economy that had worked so well for nearly half a century was being threatened with a return to protectionism and autarky. To many, it seemed only a matter of time until the global economy disintegrated and collapsed.

What went wrong? Why did the economic experiments, so loudly hailed in Washington, London, and Paris only a few years earlier, now lie in disarray? And what is likely to be the outcome?

The Failure of Reaganomics

The American experiment in Reaganomics was launched in February 1981 amid great fanfare and optimistic promises of performance. "If enacted in full, this program can help America create 13 million new jobs, nearly three million more than we could without these measures," announced President Reagan in setting forth his new economic experiment.[3] It will cause inflation to "come down rapidly," unemployment to "decline steadily in the years that follow," real economic growth to "be in the five percent range during 1982 and 1983 and then settle at a sustainable rate of about 4.25 percent." All of this would be accomplished with a budget deficit of only $41.5 billion in 1982, and a completely balanced budget by 1984.[4]

Such economic performance seemed too good to be true, for it was to be achieved with a massive three-year tax cut and with no pain imposed on the American people. The economic growth that the program would stimulate would be so powerful and strong that the budget could be balanced while slashing taxes and significantly increasing spending on defense. Of course, none of this occurred as planned. Rather than enjoying a strongly growing economy, Americans were immediately plunged into a deep and serious recession. Rather than balancing the budget, the program generated the largest budget deficits in peacetime history.

Yet by early 1984, the economy was recovering strongly. Unemployment was rapidly declining and inflation had been brought down to a remarkably low 4-percent rate. On the surface, it appeared that President Reagan was correct in his early promises. He may be faulted on the timing — the low inflation and strong economic growth promised for 1982 appeared a year later — and for being wrong in not foreseeing a recession. But these failings can be forgiven if indeed Reaganomics has succeeded. That it had succeeded was certainly the impression that President Reagan gave during his triumphant campaign for a second term in late 1984, claiming victory for his economic program as one news headline after another announced the latest buoyant economic numbers.

Given the recent strength of the American economy, and the fact that economic growth did occur along with low inflation (thus appearing to have broken the trend of stagflation that had been plaguing the economy for nearly ten years), has Reaganomics succeeded?

Is an economic program built around large tax reductions over an extended period the economic model for the future for all industrialized countries? Would the French and the Germans be well advised to drop their current economic experiments and follow the lead of the Americans?

To many, this might seem to be the case: Reaganomics appears to have succeeded and it is only a matter of time until other political leaders recognize this fact. Unfortunately, a closer reading of the situation indicates that this is not the case: Reaganomics has not succeeded; it has failed. The reasons for the failure are threefold.

First, the current strength of the American economy stands for nothing more than what normally occurs after a deep recession. The nature of the recession and the economic recovery is almost identical to those of the past forty years and does not represent anything new.

Second, current economic policies in the United States bear almost no resemblance to the original design of Reaganomics. The initial experiment has been dramatically altered during the past four years, and is in the process of being altered even more. What is occurring in the U.S. economy today may serve as a model for other countries, but it definitely is not a model of Reaganomics.

Third, the American experiment has saddled our economy with a long-term structural deficit of historic proportions. This deficit is mortgaging our economic future, and will lead to higher inflation, lower levels of productive investment, and lower growth rates. This is not a legacy that Americans or those living in other countries can afford.

The American economy began its recovery from the recession of 1981 and 1982 after the Federal Reserve Bank had greatly expanded the money supply and forced interest rates down. During the summer of 1982, the Fed became quite concerned about the depth and duration of the recession. There were few signs of an economic recovery on the horizon, and the situation was reaching a critical stage. Congress and the Reagan administration seemed in a deadlock about any positive action: the White House refused to budge on its economic policies for fear of having to admit that the president's economic program had collapsed, and Congress did not know what to do about the situation. Only Chairman Paul Volcker of the central bank appeared to have a grasp on both the seriousness of the situation and on a course of action: he began to expand the money supply at a very rapid rate, forcing interest rates down and stimulating the recovery.

The recovery was led by interest-sensitive sectors such as housing and automobiles and other consumer durable purchases. Once the recovery was under way, the consumer began to spend, encouraged in large part because of the large tax reductions adopted by the Reagan administration. (Recall that the tax reductions were supposed to increase consumer savings, not spending.) In early 1984, consumer spending was joined by business investment and the recovery was complete.

It was a classical economic recovery. Inflation had been brought down by the recession, which is what has occurred in every previous economic recession. The recovery was led by sectors responding to lower interest rates, just as in the past. Then consumer spending began to expand, particularly because of large personal tax reductions. And finally, business investment in new plant and equipment rounded out the recovery. There was nothing new this time, with the possible exception that the Reagan administration had given the economy an inordinately large boost through its tax-reduction program. Previous tax reductions designed to stimulate the economy out of a recession had been more modest.

Of course, the Reagan tax cut was not designed for this purpose, for there was no recession planned in Reaganomics. It was designed to stimulate higher savings and greater productive investment, not to expand consumer spending. Tax cuts for stimulating consumer spending was old-fashioned Keynesian economics, and this was complete anathema to the Reagan economists. The president had run on a platform denouncing Keynesian economics as dangerous to the future of our economy: it did no more than turn politicians into big spenders, encouraging them to spend far beyond the nation's means and creating large budget deficits.

It is ironic that the Reagan tax-reduction program, sold to the American public as the basis of a new supply-side economic experiment, should turn out to be nothing more than good old Keynesian economics on a grand scale. The current strength of the American economy owes a lot to the Reagan tax-reduction program, but it does not represent a victory for Reaganomics. Rather than proving the success of a new approach to our country's economic problems, it is no more than another example of what John Maynard Keynes noted nearly a half-century ago: when the economy is in a recession, the quickest way to return to strong growth and full employment is to reduce taxes and increase government spending. This the Reagan administration did with a vengeance, although quite inadvertently.

The second reason that the Reagan experiment has failed is that it had to be altered significantly owing to the recession, the fear of large budget deficits, and a return to high interest rates. The result is that economic policies in the United States today bear little resemblance to the original intent of the Reagan experiment.

It was not long before serious cracks started to appear in Reaganomics. The first crack came from a high-ranking member of the Reagan team. In "The Education of David Stockman," an amazing article published in the *Atlantic Monthly* in December 1981, the brilliant and powerful director of the Office of Management and Budget (OMB) was quoted as admitting that "none of us really understands what's going on with all these numbers."[5] The article went on to describe how in early January of 1981 the staff of the OMB were responsible for preparing the official economic forecasts for Reaganomics. In preparing these forecasts, they estimated the impact of the Republican economic policies on the federal budget. And the forecasts predicted that if President Reagan "went ahead with his promised three-year tax reduction and his increase in defense spending, the Reagan Administration would be faced with a series of federal deficits without precedent in peacetime — ranging from $82 billion in 1982 to $116 billion in 1984."

Such projections caused the OMB officials to gasp. Stockman well knew that if such forecasts were released in Reagan's first budget, the financial markets would panic. Already-high interest rates would go even higher, and the expectation of long-term inflation would be confirmed. And so Stockman "changed the OMB computer." Assisted by like-minded supply-side economists, "the new team discarded orthodox premises of how the economy would behave" and substituted numbers that the White House wanted to see.

Unfortunately, the old OMB model of the economy proved to be far more accurate than did the new one. During 1982, the economy did not grow at a 5.2-percent rate, as assumed, but actually went into a deep recession, with economic growth falling by 1.9 percent. And during 1983, a year of economic recovery, the economy only managed a rather anemic 3.4-percent growth rate, far below the official projections of 4.6 percent. Yet the greatest gap between promise and reality existed in the official budget-deficit forecasts. The deficits were $148 billion in 1982 and ballooned to $173 billion in 1984, many times greater than the official projections.

The actual performance of the economy forced a sense of reality on Reaganomics — a reality that was well recognized by David Stockman, who had engineered the initial set of optimistic projections. "Some of the naive supply-siders just missed this whole dimension. You don't stop the growth of money supply in a three-trillion-dollar economy without some kind of dislocation," Stockman admitted. And then he added the coup de grace: "Whenever there are great strains or changes in the economic system, it tends to generate crackpot theories, which then find their way into the legislative channels."

As the economy failed to respond to the Reagan economic experiment during 1981, pressures began to build up for a significant change in policy direction. By August 1982, almost a year to the day after President Reagan had triumphantly signed into law his historic tax-reduction program, *Business Week* was calling the situation "the most miserable and baffling economic environment that business has seen since the Depression." The budget deficit was seen as the problem — "a built-in deficit that will remain astronomically high" long after the economy has recovered.[6]

A debate had been going on in Congress for some months over raising taxes to reduce this deficit, and on August 19 a bill was passed to raise taxes by $98 billion over a three-year period, thus erasing about one-fourth of the tax reduction of a year earlier. Against the advice of his supply-side economic advisors, President Reagan supported the tax increase as an important part of what he called the "crusade to get the country's economy moving again."[7]

But it was not with a great deal of enthusiasm that this major change in economic policy was signed into law. White House press aides refused to allow reporters to witness the signing at Rancho del Cielo, the presidential ranch in the mountains of southern California. Nor were photographs allowed to be taken — a sharp contrast to the hoopla of a year earlier, when scores of reporters were driven up the mountain road by bus to witness and photograph the signing.

Critics were not long in pointing out that the tax hike represented a major reversal of the supply-side experiment. Congressman Henry S. Reuss of Wisconsin wrote that "Reaganomics is no more."[8] The *New York Times* observed that the "switch in economic policy" was brought about because "the promises of his original program did not materialize."[9] *Euromoney,* an influential European magazine, commented that "it happens to all governments sooner or later. The surprise with Ronald Reagan is that it is sooner. After only 18 months the fire of his crusade to regenerate America with a new spirit of enterprise has been snuffed out by the grim realities of Washington. His economic policy is in a shambles, his economic team rent by dissension and resignation."[10] And one of those who resigned spoke for the supply-side economists, who were witnessing the gradual dismantling of their experiment. Norman B. Ture, formerly the undersecretary of the treasury for tax and economic affairs, stated that the tax increase, "although it does not completely cancel last year's incentive-enhancing tax provisions, . . . very substantially reduces their effectiveness."[11]

Significant as was this change in course, it was not enough. The budget-deficit problem did not dissipate, even with the largest tax increase in history. As Senator Daniel Patrick Moynihan of New York succinctly summed up the events of the year: "Congress passed the largest tax cut in history, which led to the largest budget deficit, which led to the largest tax increase. These latter two were just not supposed to happen."[12]

The deficit problem continued to fester, growing in size with each new projection from congressional and private-sector financial economists. Interest rates rose. The countries of Latin America threatened to default on their debt unless something was done. European political leaders railed against the huge American deficits, fearful that their own precarious economic recoveries would be aborted because of the intransigence of Washington. At home, Continental Illinois National Bank of Chicago tottered on the brink of bankruptcy, demonstrating the increasing vulnerability of all American banks. And economic and financial experts began to forecast another recession.

The White House knew that something had to be done. In his state-of-the-union message on January 25, 1984, President Reagan called for a down payment to deal with the budget-deficit problem. Such a down payment was worked out between the administration and key Republican leaders in Congress, who in March recommended another major reversal of Reaganomics in the form of a tax increase of $48 billion and expenditure reductions and defense-spending stretch-outs of $83 billion. This program would reduce the deficit to $143 billion by 1987, the president announced to the American public. The Congressional Budget Office later corrected this overly optimistic projection, however, and stated that the Reagan down payment would only reduce the deficit to $204 billion.

The Democrats in Congress developed their own program, calling for a similar $50 billion in tax increases but $110 billion in expenditure reductions, mainly concentrated on defense. Unable to reach a compromise on the major expenditure reductions, Congress passed the tax increase and it was signed into law in July 1984 — a remarkable feat in an election year. But it was well known that far greater tax increases and expenditure reductions would have to be approved in 1985 if the budget-deficit problem was to be resolved. Slowly, but surely, the excesses of Reagan's experiment in supply-side economics have been eroded until today most of the original tax incentives either have been or soon will be removed.

The third, and final, reason why Reaganomics has failed — and why it does not offer a viable model for either the United States or other industrialized countries — is the impact of the budget deficit: the deficit is so large and permanent that we are in effect mortgaging our economic future. The situation becomes clear when one examines the proportion of our nation's resources that are being absorbed by the federal budget deficit.

As shown in table 14, the average budget deficit during the years 1965 through 1981 was $24.7 billion, which represented 1.4 percent of our gross national product. In 1982, the deficit was $148.2 billion,

TABLE 14. BUDGET DEFICITS IN THE UNITED STATES

Year	Amount in Billions of $[a]	Amount as Proportion of GNP	Amount as Proportion of Net Savings[b]
1965–1981 (avg.)	24.7	1.4%	12.5%
1982	148.2	4.8	52.7
1983	178.6	5.4	53.6
1984	173.0	4.5	33.1
1985[c]	208.0	5.3	41.4
1986[c]	190.0	4.5	34.2
1987[c]	204.0	4.4	33.5

[a]Calculated on a national-income account (NIA) basis for each calendar year.

[b]Net savings = total domestic savings minus capital depreciation plus net foreign capital inflows.

[c]Estimated by Economics-Policy Research Dept., Bank of America, San Francisco.

or 4.8 percent of our GNP. And in 1985, assuming that there is reasonable economic growth and no recession, the deficit will have grown to $208.0 billion. Never before in our peacetime history has the federal government absorbed so much of the national product.

Yet the most critical aspect of the deficit is what it is doing to the savings in the economy, out of which the deficit is financed. During more normal times, the budget deficit absorbed an average of 12.5 percent of our total net savings (that is, the amount of savings in the economy after replacing the depreciated capital). Net savings includes the capital that is available for consumer purchases of housing, automobiles, and other durable goods, and for financing productive business investments in new plant and equipment. And net savings are what the Reagan economic program hoped to increase significantly, providing the capital for productive new investments in our future. Unfortunately, financing the budget deficit during 1983 required nearly 54 percent of all net savings that were available; and the financial requirements will remain around 33 percent for the foreseeable future.

This tripling of the financial burden of the federal budget deficit will have a devastating impact on the future growth and performance of the American economy. With far less capital available for new investments, we will not be able to incorporate the latest technology into our industry at a time when other countries, and particularly the Japanese, are planning aggressively to modernize their industries. We will find our automobile and steel plants, along with our high-technology computer industry, facing increasing competition in the future. We will not be able to maintain our lead in creating new technologies, let alone rationalize our existing smokestack industries to be more efficient. Housing will be far more scarce and expensive. Mortgage rates will be high as the federal government competes for funds in the capital market — and in such a clash, the federal government always wins. Fewer automobiles will be sold. The appliance industry will decline.

All of these conditions not only mean a lower quality of life today, but greatly diminished quality in the future. For without adequate investments, our growth rate will be slowed. We cannot generate the same number of jobs, the same high employment levels, the same growing incomes that we could with more modest budget deficits. And on top of all of this, inflation will be higher. Diminished investment in new productive capacity means that future wage increases cannot be as readily offset through productivity increases, and this translates directly into higher prices.

This is not a pleasant picture of our future, but it is inevitable when the federal government takes one-third of all net savings in the economy. Reaganomics has failed to achieve the most important goal that it set out to attain: strengthening our economic future. Rather, it greatly weakens our future, and for this reason alone it does not provide an answer in the search for an economy that works.

Japan Confronts a Global Backlash

When one looks at results, the Japanese economic experiment appears to be the most successful. The Japanese have been able to ride out the economic storms of recent years in remarkably good condition. Their economy seems to be immune from recession, at least as recession is defined in other industrialized countries. The only year during the turbulent 1970s in which Japan's real economic growth rate was negative — the traditional definition of a recession — was 1974, when the Japanese economy reeled under the impact of the first OPEC oil price increase. And then the growth rate was only down 0.6 percent. The Japanese avoided the 1981–82 recession that felled the economies of the United States, West Germany, France, and Great Britain. And during the past several years, the Japanese economy has been among the strongest and best balanced of the major industrialized countries.

These results were not achieved without wrenching adjustments on the part of the Japanese. In the first place, they had to adapt to a much lower long-term economic growth rate. From 1960 through 1973, for instance, the economy had expanded at an average annual real rate of 10.5 percent. And since 1973, the average growth has been less than one-half of that rate. Many observers thought that the highly structured and somewhat rigid Japanese society would begin to crack under the pressures of adjusting to the lower growth. But rather than succumbing to the pressures, the Japanese people exhibited remarkable resiliency in adapting their life-styles and industrial base to a new age of higher-cost energy and lower economic growth.

In the second place, the Japanese had to adjust to a major deterioration in their terms of trade. The terms of trade, or export prices divided by import prices, suffered an unprecedented decline as the price of imports, primarily oil prices, soared while export prices rose far less. Between 1973 and 1982, the terms of trade of Japan deteriorated by 43.3 percent, compared to only a 7.4-percent decline for West Germany and a 24.5-percent reduction in the United States. This change had a massive impact on the Japanese economy, resulting in a 10-percent loss of real income.

To compensate for this tremendous loss of wealth, the Japanese turned to what they do best: they greatly expanded their exports and cut back on nonessential consumer expenditures. These adjustments enabled the resourceful Japanese to maintain their relatively strong economy, but as a result, Japan soon encountered a global backlash against its growing trade surpluses. Much of this backlash was based in the United States.

The problem with the Japanese economic experiment lies not in internal inconsistencies, as in Reaganomics, or in over-reliance upon a single policy approach, as is true with monetarism in Great Britain. Rather, the Japanese experiment is in an unfortunate position for three reasons:

1. Japan's economy is directly clashing with the largest and strongest economy in the world — that of the United States — which greatly heightens tensions and focuses public attention.
2. The Japanese economic experiment continues to be successful at a time of much slower growth in global trade markets and a time of increased competition for those markets among the major industrialized economies.
3. The experiment comes at a time when both Japan and the United States are undergoing basic structural changes in their internal economies that make it difficult to accommodate each other.

"The most immediate and politically sensitive issue in U.S.-Japanese relations is unquestionably trade," stated former U.S. ambassador to Japan Mike Mansfield in 1983. "A situation now exists in which, in many different fields — manufactured goods, services, standard codes, investments — Japan enjoys easier access to the American market than America has to the Japanese market."[13]

There is no question that trade between the two countries has reached huge proportions. During 1984, the value of trade between Japan and the United States was $84 billion. And there is no doubt that the Japanese seem to be getting the better end of this trade flow, for their trade surplus with the United States was a massive $37 billion. But to suggest that Japan should operate a trade balance with the United States such that they purchase American products equal in value to their exports to this country is to ignore economic reality.

The structure of both the Japanese and the American economies ensures that there will continue to be a large trade surplus in favor of Japan. As an island economy with few natural resources, the Japanese must import huge quantities of raw materials and food, products that the United States has in abundance. Japan always will be a large market for American coal, timber, wheat, corn, soybeans, and other food commodities.

Likewise, as the largest and richest market for automobiles, television sets, electronic appliances, and computers, the United States will always be a major importer of Japanese-made products. It is an economic reality that the "value added" of manufactured products from Japan is far greater than that from raw materials and goods produced in the United States, which means that the trade balance will continue to favor the Japanese.

To pay for their imports of raw materials, the Japanese must continue to export what they are most efficient at producing, and those products happen to be manufactured goods. And the United States, as the largest market for manufactured goods in the world, will continue to buy from Japan as long as Japanese products maintain their quality and protectionist measures are not imposed. Yet economic reality does not prevent the trade imbalance from being politicized as a "competitive imbalance."

There is a growing attitude among Americans that the Japanese are so successful in their trade with the United States because of an unfair competitive imbalance between the two countries. Americans charge that the Japanese have a distribution system, laws, antitrust policies, and regulations that make it very difficult for American firms to penetrate Japanese markets, while the American system is far more simple and open to competitors from abroad. To correct for this perceived competitive imbalance, many American politicians are recommending reciprocity legislation.

Such legislation ranges from establishing a government agency to systematically catalog the barriers that exist to U.S. exports to Japan, to limiting Japanese penetration in American markets proportional to American penetration of Japanese markets. As Senator John C. Danforth of Missouri, a leading proponent of reciprocity, has said: "It is very difficult to explain why competitive American exports such as cigarettes, telecommunications equipment, oranges, or medical equipment have market shares in Japan ranging from only one to seven percent whereas Japanese autos, steel, television sets, machine tools, and recording equipment have anywhere from 15 percent to 50 percent of the U.S. market."[14]

The Japanese counter that Americans have not invested sufficient time to master the Japanese language and marketing styles, or to design products for Japanese consumer tastes, as they have done in the United States. They point out that American corporations are too driven by the desire for short-term profits, and don't invest on a longer-term basis, as is required for any firm, be it American or Japanese, in order to penetrate foreign markets. While admitting that their language is difficult and that Japanese regulations and distribution systems are quite different from those in the United States, the Japanese maintain that there are no overt barriers to prevent American firms from competing in Japanese markets.

Such discord appears to be generated by a difference in viewpoint over trade reciprocity. The concept of reciprocity dates back to the 1860s, when the standards of the British-French trade treaty were extended to Germany, and German firms were to be treated the same as British or French firms operating in their own home markets. Applied to the U.S.-Japanese situation, reciprocity would thus mean that American firms would be treated the same as Japanese firms when operating in Japanese markets, and Japanese firms would be treated the same as American firms in our markets. American firms would have to conform to Japanese standards and marketing practices when operating abroad, and our methods would apply to Japanese firms marketing in the United States. Such a traditional view of reciprocity seems to be what the Japanese have in mind.

Americans, however, seem to define reciprocity somewhat differently. Many politicians and labor representatives and business leaders suggest that American firms should be treated the same in Japan as Japanese firms are treated in the United States. This means that American firms should be allowed to operate with the same degree of openness and freedom in Japan as they do in the United States. What this implies, of course, is that Japan needs to alter its basic social and economic structure to resemble the United States, or vice versa. Only then will there be true equity and fairness between the two largest markets in the world.

This same attitude, and resulting clash of interests, carries over into such economic matters as the value of the yen and other economic policies. During the past several years, the yen has been greatly undervalued relative to the dollar. Japanese exports to the United States are cheaper than they would be if the yen-dollar relationship were normal, and American exports to Japan are more expensive. Such undervaluation is viewed by leaders in both countries as a major reason for the trade imbalance between Japan and the United States.

American leaders charge the Japanese with directly intervening in financial markets to depress the yen in order to make Japanese exports more competitive. The Japanese leaders counter that the yen is not undervalued, but that the dollar is overvalued. And the reason the dollar is overvalued is the high-interest-rate policies that emanate from Reaganomics. The solution, they say, is for the Reagan officials to correct the serious inconsistencies of the American economic experiment and allow interest rates to decline.

Yet the American officials are not about to alter their economic policies, and instead suggest that the Japanese take appropriate steps to raise their interest rates more in line with those in the United States, which would cause the yen to appreciate. The Japanese argue that they should not raise interest rates and thus choke investment and their economy to accommodate the inappropriate policies of the Americans. And so the clash over economic policy continues, exacerbated by the overall success of the Japanese in maintaining their trade balance and growing economy.

Much of this clash over economic issues — trade imbalances, different viewpoints on reciprocity, the value of the yen, and high interest rates — has occurred at a time of much slower growth in global trade markets and during a period of increased competition for those markets among the major industrialized countries. If the global markets had continued to expand as they did during the 1970s, then it is likely that the Japanese and the American economic experiments would not be at odds to nearly the extent that they are. Japan would have been able to export manufactured products without running headlong into American, German, British, or French opposition. Growing markets at home and abroad would have provided ample room for all of these countries to sell their manufactured products.

Global markets have not continued to grow at the rate of 5.6 percent each year, which had been the experience throughout the 1970s. (See table 15.) Rather, the growth of world trade slowed to a miniscule 0.8 percent from 1981 through 1983. And the slowing of world trade was quite pronounced for manufactured goods, whose growth declined from a 7.1-percent annual increase to just 1.7 percent. Since 1981, global trade has been relatively stagnant and the result has been intense competition for market share.

Underlying the tensions between the Americans and the Japanese is a far more basic problem: fundamental structural changes are occurring in the two economies that make it difficult for one country to accommodate the economic differences of the other. In the United States, these fundamental changes involve learning to live with the fact that exports have assumed a much greater role in our economy, and dealing with smokestack industries that are going through a critical period of rationalization. The Japanese face the problems of structural changes associated with maturing as an international financial center, developing a welfare society, and opening up domestic markets.

The United States can no longer treat its export industries with benign neglect, as was true in the past. Exports have more than tripled in the past decade, accounting for 10.6 percent of our gross national product in 1984, compared to 6.6 percent in 1970, and providing an estimated five million jobs for American workers.[15] We still think of ourselves as a closed economy, however, immune from both the advantages and problems of participating in a global trading economy. And this is particularly true for politicians, who respond to trade competition with the rhetoric of the past.

"International trade is a political issue in our country [and] by far the most important political concern of our constituents is jobs," stated Senator Danforth at a conference on the future course of U.S.-Japanese economic relations held at the Brookings Institution in 1983.

TABLE 15. CHANGE IN VOLUME OF WORLD EXPORTS
(AS ANNUAL AVERAGE, IN CONSTANT VALUE)

Period	Manufactured Goods	Agriculture and Raw Materials, Excluding Fuels	Fuels	Overall
1971–1980	+7.1%	+5.0%	+2.6%	+5.6%
1981–1983	+1.7	+3.6	−8.2	+0.8

SOURCE: Economics-Policy Research Dept., Bank of America, San Francisco.

There is no doubt at all that in the minds of the people of this country their ability to find jobs and hold jobs is very closely related to international trade. Missouri has been a major producer of automobiles . . . yet under even the most optimistic outlook employment in the industry is going to be well below the levels of, say, five years ago. A good part of this problem is that imports have taken over a very substantial share of our auto market — and people know that.[16]

Obviously, Senator Danforth was responding to the difficulties faced by a large industry going through a period of rationalization. He was quite correct in pointing out that the automobile industry will never employ the numbers of workers that it did in the past. The assembly plants in Detroit, as well as those in Saint Louis, will be far more efficient in the future, using the latest technology and robotics. Their costs will be far more competitive with those of Japanese automobile manufacturers. And the American consumer will benefit. The same will occur in other smokestack industries — steel, rubber, and machine tools. American manufacturers will be forced by foreign competition to become more efficient and productive.

It will be a difficult transition for American workers and politicians. As a politician, Senator Danforth could not assert "that protectionism would be bad for the country. Nor, unfortunately, could he point to equal treatment in Japan for American exports or argue that as many jobs were created in the export industries as were lost through import competition."[17] Rather, he was compelled to deal with a constituency who wanted to regain or keep their jobs in the automobile industry, not to be trained for other work elsewhere in the country.

The Japanese face structural changes of their own that make it difficult to accommodate U.S. economic interests. First of all, Japan is maturing into a major international financial center, matching its role as a world economic power. Although the Japanese have taken a number of steps in recent years to liberalize the free flow of capital — for instance, Japanese businessmen no longer have to obtain permission from the government to invest abroad — there are still constraints. Most of these constraints are in the domestic financial markets, where the banks and savings institutions are highly regulated, the home mortgage market is quite undeveloped, and extensive agricultural subsidies exist. These regulations have the impact of keeping the Japanese savings rate artificially high, and raising the price of land and housing.

Furthermore, the regulations create an imbalance between increased financial liberalization on the international side and continued restrictions in domestic financial markets. As the president of the New York Federal Reserve Bank noted not long ago: "No country can have external balance without internal balance. . . . In my opinion, that imbalance is disruptive and damaging to the Japanese economy, and it certainly does not help the world adjustment problem."[18]

Yet to create a truly open and liberalized financial system will be a long and drawn-out endeavor in Japan. As we have learned in the United States, the deregulation of financial markets is very difficult and threatening. And the Japanese have much further to go along these lines than was the case in this country. The Bank of Japan must relinquish some of its traditional control over the money supply and its power to reinforce restrictions on international capital flow. The yen would need to become a true international currency, much freer to fluctuate in value. The rigid structure of Japanese banks, the postal savings system, and other financial institutions would have to be deregulated. The Japanese consumer would have to be given greater opportunities to borrow for housing and durable goods. Such changes are not easy, nor can they be made rapidly.

The second area of ongoing structural change in Japan involves the attempt by the Japanese to develop what they call "A New Welfare Society." This new society will attempt to balance the traditional overemphasis of the Japanese economy on industrial development with more investments in housing, highways, sewage systems, urban parks, and facilities for the elderly. National priorities are being shifted from economic development to improving the overall quality of life of the Japanese people. And this change in priorities will require the investment of millions of yen. Therefore, when the United States suggests that Japan alter its economic policies to raise interest rates more in line with those in this country, we are confronting a Japan whose own interests are for low interest rates in order to finance the development of its new welfare society.

Finally, the Japanese are going through a structural change in opening up their markets, and society, to increased competition from abroad. Japan has long been a somewhat closed society, insulated from the rest of the world by geographic distance, a difficult language for foreigners to learn, social customs that are much more stylized than in the West, and an oriental rather than an occidental cultural history. In the past, such insulation was heightened through outright economic protectionism: customs tariffs were imposed on products from abroad and tight restrictions were placed on the flow of Japanese capital abroad. Most of these restrictions have now been removed, and Japanese tariffs are among the lowest in the world.

Some nontariff barriers do remain, however — primarily customs clearance procedures related to health, safety, and other standards or regulations, as well as a traditional multilayer distribution system that makes it exceedingly difficult for foreign producers to market their products. Many of these nontariff barriers are being reduced — admittedly, under intense pressure from Americans and Western Europeans, although it appears that leading Japanese officials desire such a change. They face a difficult task, for there are numerous government bureaucrats at lower levels who can impede a liberalization of nontariff barriers, as well as a powerful lobby of Japanese farmers who want domestic markets protected from foreign competition. And there is a conservative and somewhat insular Japanese public that must accept the advantages of increased liberalization — a public that is rather skeptical of outside influences upon their traditions.

The German Economy Stagnates

For the first couple of years it appeared that West Germany's economic experiment in moderation was going to succeed. The 1978 and 1979 economic growth rates were strong, and the economy seemed to be well balanced. Productivity was expanding, consumer confidence was rising, and German exports continued to be in great demand in foreign markets.

Beginning in early 1980, however, the economy began to deteriorate seriously, and it was soon mired in a recession. The most apparent reason for the weakening of the German economy was the large increase in energy prices precipitated by the second round of OPEC oil price hikes in 1978. The German officials tightened up economic policy to contain this new inflation threat and, as a result, the economy slowed down.

Other signs indicated that all was not going well for the German economic experiment — signs of basic structural and longer-term problems that went far beyond oil-price shocks and restrictive monetary and fiscal policies. The value of the mark fell owing to a large gap between interest rates in the United States and those in West Germany. This development put the German officials in a bind, for to raise German interest rates to match those of the United States would dampen business investment and consumer spending within Germany even more. But to ignore the high interest rates in the United States would be to invite disaster in external markets.

The German current-account balance already had plunged from a surplus of DM 18.4 billion during 1978 to a deficit of DM 29.1 billion in 1980, and this rapid deterioration in the balance of payments was threatening the entire German experiment. Above all, it drove home to German officials the fact that no single country, even one as large and powerful as Germany, could long withstand the policy imbalances pursued by the United States.

Even though the Germans were the first major country to recognize the emerging interdependence among the industrialized countries of the world, and though they are following an economic course that they view as a policy of reliable partnership, the same is not true of their peers in Washington. And so the first major weakness of the German experiment is not one of their own making. Yet it is forcing the Germans, as well as other world powers, to confront the reality of a global economy that has grown far more interdependent. And such interdependence greatly limits the economic policy choices that any single country can pursue in its respective experiment.

Other basic weaknesses in the German experiment are of the nation's own making, however, and these concern the pride of the German economy: the industrial base. The Germans are counting very heavily upon the strength of their underlying industrial base to provide economic growth and jobs for the future. Their attempt to maintain a free-enterprise economy while pursuing moderate budgetary and monetary policies is strongly predicated upon the continued strength of their industries. Unfortunately, many of their most important industries are beginning to show signs of obsolescence and ponderousness.

West Germany's industrial base is no longer the lean and dynamic machine that catapulted the country to economic power during the postwar era — making Germany a leader in new technologies and lifting it to the forefront of expanding global markets. Rather, the Germans are saddled with an industrial base that presents four problems: (1) it is called upon to play an inordinately large role in the German economy compared to the role of the industrial base in other industrialized countries; (2) it suffers from an industrial policy that places primary emphasis on preserving the older and more mature industries in the economy while giving little support to the development of new industries; (3) it suffers further from a policy that makes it difficult to restructure even these older industries into more efficient and competitive organizations; and (4) it lags in the development of high-growth export markets.

The Germans depend upon their industrial base to provide a greater proportion of jobs and exports than do most other major Western industrialized economies. (See table 16.) In 1981, over 36 percent of all jobs in West Germany were in manufacturing industries, as compared to just over 22 percent in the United States and slightly more than 28 percent in France, Japan, and Great Britain. And in 1983, manufactured exports accounted for nearly three-quarters of all German exports, a proportion exceeded only in Japan. Such a large role for the industrial base of West Germany means that the success of the German economic experiment is highly vulnerable to any weakness in the country's primary and basic industries. Unfortunately, such weakness has begun to appear, beginning with an industrial policy bent on propping up industries whose time has come and gone.

As discussed in chapter 4, German officials intervene and direct the development of their nation's industries to a much greater extent than is commonly perceived. Large conglomerates of economic power are encouraged. When the public interest is thought to be at stake, there is little hesitation about supporting important segments of the industrial base. And rather sizable amounts of public funds are targeted to specific industries, to assist them in a broad range of

TABLE 16. THE ROLE OF MANUFACTURING IN MAJOR INDUSTRIALIZED ECONOMIES

	Manufacturing's Share of Total Employment (1981)	*Manufacturing's Share of Total Exports (1983)*
United States	22.1%	58.3%
Japan	28.5	92.2
West Germany	36.7	73.4
Great Britain	28.5	57.7
France	28.8	62.3

SOURCES: OECD, *OECD Labour Force Statistics, 1970–1981* (Paris, 1983); Economics-Policy Research Dept., Bank of America, San Francisco.

activities; from help with research and development to direct operating subsidies, the government plays a significant role.

Nearly all of this industrial support is allocated to basic and mature industries. Railroads and the coal, steel, shipping, and aircraft industries received about three-fourths of all federal government support during 1983. While these industries were important in the postwar recovery of the German economy, and provided a strong industrial base during the growth era of the 1950s and 1960s, they are not the rapidly growing industries of the future.

German coal is costly to produce and noncompetitive on the world markets. The global steel and shipping industries are overbuilt, and newly industrialized countries have emerged as strong competitors. The German aircraft manufacturers face severe competition from the Americans, as well as the French and the British. But German industrial policy seems to be mired in supporting these older industries, as if in hope that they can be rationalized into leaner and more efficient organizations in spite of evidence to the contrary.

By 1982, the future of the German steel industry was so bleak that the government devised a rescue plan in which the five largest steel producers would be merged into two new groups: a Rhine group, comprising Krupp and Thyssen, and a Ruhr Valley group, made up of Hoesch, Salzgitter, and Kloechner. These two groups account for 75 percent of total German steel production, and are slated to receive some DM 3 billion in government subsidies. The remaining smaller steel producers are apparently being cast aside to sink or swim on their own.

Minimal production floors are to be established for the two consolidated steel groups, and if total demand falls below these floors, the German steel companies will be protected from foreign competition. Even such sizable public financial support and the acceptance of outright protectionism may not work. Many problems regarding the protectionist measures have to be worked out within the European Economic Community, and difficult negotiations are anticipated with German unions on job security and with the individual companies on the apportionment of assets and liabilities.

Even the newer industries in Germany are encountering great difficulties in adjusting to the future. The chemical industry, long a major flagship in the German industrial fleet, has encountered intense price competition and excess global production capacity. The biggest three producers — Hoechst, Bayer, and BASF — have seen their profits decline. Existing capacity is being reduced, particularly in plastics production. And less investment in new plant and equipment is being made. While there is some hope that the bottom has been reached, there is no expectation of a strong rebound in the demand for German chemical products.

The proud electronics industry also is floundering. AEG Telefunken, the country's second-largest electrical and electronics group, nearly collapsed in mid-1982 and has appealed to the government to write down its debts by 60 percent. Massive government loans are being provided to keep Telefunken from going bankrupt. The company's twenty-five banks have agreed to write off 60 percent of its loans, and plans were made to merge the consumer electronics section of Telefunken with Grundig, the leader in consumer-electronics production in Germany. At least that was the plan until Grundig agreed to merge with Thomson-Brandt, the nationalized French electronics giant — a merger that was blocked by the German cartel office. The turmoil is so immense that there is some "doubt on the ability of West Germany to compete effectively in the markets and products of the late 1980s and 1990s."[19]

This turmoil is carrying over into the export markets, where the German economic experiment has failed to keep abreast of competitors in developing high-growth markets for the future. In such areas as scientific instruments, telecommunications, office machines and computers, and medical and pharmaceutical products, where global markets are expected to be expanding in the future, German exports accounted for only 6.6 percent of the country's total exports in 1983. (See table 17.) This was far below the 12.2 percent for Japan, and well below the 8.6 percent share in the United States.

Rather than exporting into high-growth markets, the Germans continue to rely upon their traditional exports, from such mature industries as motor vehicles, machinery and appliances, and iron and steel products. A total of 41.1 percent of their exports are in these slower-growing markets, far above the proportion of the French, the British, or the Americans. Only the Japanese, with their dominant position in automobile exports, depend to a greater extent than do the Germans on mature product-markets. The Japanese, however, have balanced their slower-growing export markets with a very sizable role in high-growth markets.

The Germans are heavily concentrated in the moderate-growth industries, which include organic chemicals, plastic materials, chemical materials, and petroleum products. Such markets account for 9.4 percent of German exports, which is among the highest of the major countries. But, as noted earlier, these industries are having a great deal of difficulty in adjusting to the increased global competition.

German policymakers increasingly have become aware of these problems with their country's industrial base, particularly in the past couple of years, and they are attempting to develop growth industries through stimulation of small and medium-sized firms. New programs have been established to provide research and technical support for these firms. A more innovative economic environment is being encouraged. And it is hoped that out of this environment, with minimal support from the federal government, a large group of new entrepreneurs will emerge. If all goes well, some of these entrepreneurs will then develop into the Grundigs and Hoeshsts of the future.

Such a "Silicon Valley approach" to developing new growth industries has a lot of merit. It is extremely difficult to preselect growth industries, and particularly to predict which individual firms within those industries will be successful. Government officials are notoriously inept in making the tough investment decisions that are necessary in a dynamic and rapidly expanding new market. And entrepreneurs and politicians generally do not mix well. The German approach to an industrial policy for the future is very similar to that

TABLE 17. EXPORT MARKET CONCENTRATION IN MAJOR INDUSTRIALIZED ECONOMIES, 1983

	High-Growth Markets[a]	Mature and Slow-Growth Markets[b]	Moderate-Growth Markets[c]
United States	8.6%	37.1%	8.2%
Japan	12.2	60.1	3.2
West Germany	6.6	41.1	9.4
Great Britain	7.5	34.8	15.1
France	5.5	33.9	9.3

SOURCE: Economics-Policy Research Dept., Bank of America, San Francisco.

NOTE: Data shown are proportions of total exports for each nation, excluding oil and fuel.

[a]Scientific instruments, telecommunications, office machines and computers, and medical and pharmaceutical products.

[b]Motor vehicles, machinery and appliances, and iron and steel products.

[c]Organic chemicals, plastic materials, chemical materials, and petroleum products.

which is emerging in the United States. But there are major differences between the two countries that may prove critical to the success of the Germans.

In the United States, there is a strong tradition and acceptance of entrepreneurship and there exists a well-developed venture-capital market to support new high-risk firms, neither of which is true in West Germany. While the Germans may be successful in stimulating the creation of many small and innovative firms, the founders of those firms will have difficulty obtaining the capital and personnel essential for development. In the first place, there is a generally conservative attitude toward investment risk. The problem is not a lack of opportunities for investment, writes Gregor Mettinger of the Associated European Capital Corporation, but rather "the uncertainty of the realization of the ultimate goals of the [venture] capitalist substantially augmenting his capital."[20] German investors apparently want guarantees and assurances that a high-risk firm simply does not offer. In other words, the Germans seem to lack the "high financial rollers" that dot the landscape of California.

Second, venture capitalists are not held in high esteem in Germany, as they are in the United States. They are often referred to in the press as speculators or as greedy, and their critical role is not well understood by the public. In the United States, in contrast, the new breed of venture capitalists and high-tech entrepreneurs are prominently displayed on the cover of *Time* magazine and have developed a following that is reminiscent of the old Yankee inventor-capitalist of an earlier era.

Third, large German companies and banks have not established venture-capital subsidiaries, since the executives know that free-wheeling entrepreneurs typically find normal business bureaucracy stifling. Very few German firms have taken the venture-capital route, preferring to keep their investments in more stable and mature industries.

Finally, German scientists and engineers appear to lack the entrepreneurial spirit and independence that is prevalent among Americans. "Most German engineers prefer security in a large, comfortable company to running their own business," notes Klaus Luft, a managing board member of Nixdorf Computer, a small German firm. Furthermore, "the engineers you meet in the United States usually know something about financing. That's less so here."[21]

The Germans' attempt to maintain the golden middle road in

their economic experiment has not suffered from the internal problems of the supply-side experiment in the United States or the monetary experiment in Great Britain. The Germans have avoided the policy extremes and the wrenching adjustments of the Americans and the British, and thus will face fewer problems in the course of correcting their experiment as time goes on. Nor will they have to go through a soul-searching exercise upon asking what comes next in the way of economic policy. Their balanced approach toward monetary and fiscal policies offers a good model for those countries who have gone the route of extremes and whose economies are suffering accordingly. Nonetheless, the Germans' experiment suffers from a weakness in the industrial base, and it remains to be seen whether their attempt to develop new small and medium-sized firms can overcome the inherent conservative German attitude toward entrepreneurism and the lack of adequate financial markets to provide necessary risk capital.

British Monetarism Leads to Recession

"WHAT HATH THATCHER WROUGHT?" read headlines after four years of British monetarism.[22] The answer: an economy that began deteriorating immediately after the monetarist policies were imposed and continued to sink into a deep and serious recession.

During 1980, the first full year of the Thatcher experiment, the growth rate of the British economy plunged to -2.0 percent and continued to fall through 1981. Unemployment jumped to 12.3 percent in 1982, the highest among the major industrialized countries. Manufacturing output dropped by over 14 percent and remained at a very low level. British products were being priced out of international markets as wages exploded during 1980, leading to relative labor costs that were approximately 35 percent higher than those of other industrialized countries. The British brought the inflation rate down from 18 percent in 1980 to a remarkably low 5-percent rate during 1983, the one area in which the experiment in monetarism succeeded — but many British experts thought that the cost in terms of lost output and unemployment was far too great.

So devastating was the impact of the policies of Margaret Thatcher on the British economy that 364 university economists, over one-quarter of England's academic specialists in the field, and nearly all of the retired senior economic advisors to British governments of the past thirty years, issued a public statement condemning the monetarist experiment. This unprecedented statement declared that

First, there is no basis in economic theory or supporting evidence for the Government's belief that by deflating demand they will bring inflation permanently under control and thereby induce an automatic recovery in output and employment;

Secondly, present policies will deepen the depression, erode the industrial base of our economy and threaten its social and political stability;

Third, the time has come to reject monetarist policies and consider urgently which alternative offers the best hope of sustained economic recovery.[23]

In many respects, the British experiment suffered from the same mistake as Reaganomics: naive and overly optimistic promises of economic performance were made that far exceeded what could actually be achieved. British leaders, however, did not make the same mistake as the Reagan economists, who set specific targets for economic performance. The British promises were generalized commitments for change, but even these were unattained. Large reductions in government spending were not made, and there was a considerable rise in the public-sector share in the economy. Organized labor was not brought under control, for the government backed down under pressure from the National Union of Mineworkers over the issue of closing redundant coal pits. British industry was not cut loose: massive loans and advances were made to British Steel, British Leyland, Rolls-Royce, British Shipbuilders, and British Airways.

Yet it is not these mistakes nor the inability to effect change that most mar the British experiment: it is that an economic experiment based primarily upon monetary policy cannot succeed. While monetary policy is highly successful in the theoretical world of academics, it fails to perform when applied in the real world. And it fails to perform for three basic reasons: (1) monetary policy, by itself, is insufficient to deal with all of the problems of a complex and rapidly changing industrialized economy; (2) the economic costs in terms of unemployment and lost output in the initial stages of monetary tightening are too great to be sustained by the political and social system; and (3) monetary policy is very difficult to implement and to sustain.

The British experiment in monetarism placed major emphasis on reducing the growth rate of the money supply and holding it at a low level for an extended period. Such a lowering of the growth of the money supply was expected to reduce inflation and bring interest rates down. This is indeed what occurred, for by 1983 inflation had been lowered to 3 percent from the 18-percent rate of 1980. And short-term interest rates were reduced from roughly 16 percent to 10 percent. But the economy was expected to respond automatically once these reductions in inflation and interest rates occurred. New investments in productive plant and equipment were anticipated to occur spontaneously, while British workers would work harder, entrepreneurs would emerge, and new technological breakthroughs would appear.

Such a dynamic response to passive monetary policies placed a lot of faith in the mysterious black box of monetarism. The great weakness of monetarism is that it does a poor job of explaining exactly *how* the economy moves from lower growth in the money supply to higher real output and greater employment. And, indeed, Milton Friedman and most other monetary experts argue that the real output of the economy is determined by such nonmonetary factors as technology, the growth of the labor force, and the availability of natural resources. Monetary policy can provide a stable background for the economy to operate in, but it does not stimulate the economy to faster growth. This is the task of other economic policies.

This critical point was recognized by leading British officials. Sir Keith Joseph, who served as minister of industry in the early days of the Thatcher government, declared that "monetarism is not enough. . . . It is not enough unless there is also the essential reduction of the state sector and the essential encouragement of enterprise."[24]

Unfortunately, the British did not aggressively encourage greater enterprise and directly stimulate the growth potential of the economy. Supply-side incentives, while emphasized in policy statements, were never very central to the British experiment. Overall, tax reductions were too small. Private incentives were blunted by massive pay increases given to public employees. The policy of denationalization of British industry was quite bland: simply sell selected companies to private owners and curtail public subsidies. Yet it is not at all clear why the management of British industry would become any more efficient under private as opposed to public ownership. Nor is it obvious that private owners would be willing to make more long-term investments in new research and development than would the public owners.

To revitalize the British economy — or the American or French economy — to meet the challenges of the future will require much more active policies. Aggressive efforts will have to be made to stimulate the development of new technology. Displaced workers in obsolete and declining industries will have to be retrained and relocated. The quality of education must be improved. And none of these changes are a natural outgrowth of monetarism.

The second area in which the British experiment in monetarism has run aground is the tremendous costs in terms of unemployment and lost output inflicted upon the economy. The experience in Britain, along with a similar experience in the United States, raises the specter that monetarism imposes too great a cost to be a viable economic policy. And this cost can be critical when it is totally ignored, as was the case in both Britain and the United States. Neither the Thatcher government nor the Reagan administration included in their official forecasts any indication of a recession induced by tight monetary policies.

This oversight did not occur because the politicians lacked sufficient evidence from the experts. Monetary economists have long known that the short-run impact of deflating the economy — that is, of moving the economy from high to low inflation rates — would create unemployment. They generally view this wrenching adjustment as a necessary cost in order to return the economy to a more stable growth path, with lower inflation. Unfortunately, the Thatcher and Reagan economists seemed to have been lulled into complacency on this matter by a new school of thought that suggests that the adjustment to lower inflation can be instantaneous, with no accompanying economic costs.

A group of very bright and articulate American economists, known as the "rational-expectations school," argue that people will rapidly adjust their expectations to future levels of inflation on the basis of recent policy actions and expectations about future policies. (The monetarists, on the other hand, maintain that inflationary expectations are formed exclusively on the basis of past inflation experience.) Therefore, they contend, if a new leader such as Margaret Thatcher can convince the public that she is serious about controlling inflation through tight and stable monetary policies, and she states her intent openly and unequivocally, the response will be quite dramatic. Built-up expectations of continued inflation will rapidly evaporate, and actual inflation will decline, with no loss of economic output and no increase in unemployment.

Needless to say, such a painless solution to our inflation problem was too enticing to the political leaders not to be readily built into their economic experiments. But the actual experience of the British and the American economies in adjusting to tighter monetary policies has proven the rational-expectations school wrong. There are quite substantial economic costs associated with disinflation. But how large and long those costs are is another matter on which the monetarists and their primary critics, the neo-Keynesians, strongly disagree.

Empirical evidence by monetary economists suggests that it requires around five to seven years for a gradual and sustained reduction in the money supply to reduce inflation to 3 percent. Measured in constant 1972 dollars, the cost in terms of lost output in the U.S. economy is approximately $330 billion. The neo-Keynesian economists, however, obtain results that are more pessimistic. To reduce inflation to 3 percent would take about fifteen years of sustained reduction in the money supply, and would reduce output by $1 trillion.[25]

While such results only give a crude estimate of the costs of monetarism, it is clear that the disinflation adjustment period is long, drawn out, and costly. To rely upon monetarism as the dominant policy in an economic experiment, as are the British, is to invite political and social backlash. Five to fifteen years is a long time for any society to sustain the economic costs associated with the gradual wringing out of inflation in the economy.

The third and final area where the British experiment is floundering is in the difficulty in implementing monetary policies. The difficulty arises from three causes: (1) monetary policy is esoteric and difficult for the public and politicians to understand; (2) there is no agreement among central bankers regarding the appropriate targets for guiding the effectiveness of monetary policy; and (3) there seem to be too many external factors that intervene to cause monetary policy to go astray.

Monetary policy is far more mysterious than fiscal policy, for the latter involves rather straightforward concerns such as raising or lowering taxes and changing government expenditures. Politicians and the public can easily relate to these policy changes. Monetary policy, on the other hand, deals with such unfamiliar matters as the monetary base, money supply, nonborrowed reserves, M1, and sterling M3.

The public tends to view monetary policy as an enigmatic machine that allows the central bankers to pull mysterious levers that somehow affect such recognizable conditions as interest rates and inflation. There is an underlying sense that all is not aboveboard, that the central bankers work in concert with the commercial bankers to keep interest rates artificially high and impose on the economy undue hardship in order to keep inflation down.

The inability of the public to comprehend monetary policy easily means that the central bankers can operate far more independently from the political scrutiny that surrounds taxes and government expenditures. But it also means that the central bankers are always suspect and that monetary policy is viewed with a certain amount of skepticism. Periodically, attempts will be made to bring the central bank under more control — if not by incorporating it under the direct supervision of Congress or Parliament, at least by imposing specific conditions for measuring its performance. The central bankers resist such attempts, for they know that monetary policy is not a science and requires a great deal of flexibility in implementation. Furthermore, they tend to feel that their independence is essentially a "check and balance" on fiscal policy. And all of this jockeying for independence versus control only adds to the uneasiness of the public regarding the role of monetary policy in the economy.

Much of this uneasiness arises because the central bankers cannot agree upon an appropriate measure of the effectiveness of monetary policy. If the Fed or the Bank of England, for instance, would announce to the public that during the coming year monetary policy will be implemented to achieve an inflation rate of 5 percent or a real economic growth rate of 3 percent, then much of the concern would dissipate. The public and the politicians would know what to expect from the central bank. They could assess performance against some measure of economic activity that is readily understandable. But, unfortunately, the central bankers cannot do this, for the tie between monetary policy and economic performance is very loose at best. And so the central bankers must rely upon some proxy or close substitute for the ideal measure. And here the central bankers violently disagree.

There are at least three monetary targets that are currently in vogue among the central bankers of the industrialized economies: (1) monetary base, (2) money supply, and (3) interest rates. Officially, the central bank of the United States manipulates the monetary base, which is the sum of the currency in the economy plus the reserves held by commercial banks in the federal reserve system.

Yet the official monetary targets are "M1" and "M2"; the Fed is required by Congress to announce a year in advance the range within which these measures of money supply will expand or contract. And while dutifully reporting its target ranges, the Fed still adheres to its official position that it is the monetary base, and not money supply, that it is controlling.

The Bank of England officially targets money supply, but it aims at money supply M3, a far broader measure of the amount of money in the economy than the M1 and M2 used by the Fed in the United States. Moreover, the British central bank appears to be actually targeting interest rates, manipulating the money supply in order to keep these rates within a specific range that is never revealed to the public.

The public searches among these various measures of monetary performance for clues as to what the central bank is doing, and the press attempts to interpret what this means for the economy. "Fed watching," as the process has been named in the United States, has become a fine art. But it is an art that does not engender much confidence in the effectiveness of monetary policy in stabilizing the economy.

Even if the central bankers could agree upon specific monetary targets, they would have great difficulty in implementing monetary policy to achieve these goals, for far too many external factors intervene and cause monetary policy to go astray. Part of the problem arises from the dynamics of the financial markets themselves. "Money supply" is a broad generic concept that includes many different forms of money. Traditionally, it has meant currency — that is, money held in checking accounts and cash held by the public to pay for economic transactions. But in recent years, the innovative commercial bankers have invented a number of very close substitutes for money. NOW (negotiable order of withdrawal) accounts, money-market funds, and automatic transfer from savings to checking accounts all represent recent innovations that play havoc with the traditional measures of money supply. So dynamic have been these changes that some observers argue that the central bank cannot control the money supply, for it is unable even to count the amount of money circulating in the economy.

Further complicating the implementation problem is the fact that the amount of money in the economy is a function of two major factors: (1) the monetary base, which the central bank can control, and (2) money velocity, which is determined by the behavior of the public. Money velocity is the ratio of the gross national product to the amount of money in the economy. During 1984, for example, the money supply (M1) in the American economy was $550 billion and the gross national product was $3,661 billion. Thus the velocity of money was 6.7, which means that, statistically, each dollar in circulation turned over 6.7 times during the year.

Changes in money velocity are determined by public behavior — such as economizing on the use of cash when interest rates are high in order to maintain more in interest-earning savings accounts — and by the efficiency of banks in circulating money more rapidly. Money velocity normally increases over time, but there is a great deal of variability in the rate at which it grows. This variability makes life exceedingly difficult for the central bankers, for their attempts to change money supply can be totally negated by an unexpected shift in velocity. And this is exactly what has happened in the United States and Great Britain in recent years: money velocity has plunged far below the historical trend. So destabilizing has been the behavior of velocity that a British monetary expert curtly noted: "If velocity is that unpredictable then monetarism is worthless."[26]

The French Go to the Economic Brink

It did not take long for the French economic experiment in socialism to run into difficulty. Almost from the day that François Mitterrand was elected president in 1981, pressures began to appear that would eventually force the country to the economic brink. The value of the French franc began to decline. French investors attempted to move their capital out of the country, and foreign investors took a wait-and-see attitude toward the new leadership before investing in France.

The first economic actions of President Mitterrand did nothing to ease the growing difficulties, for those actions were immediately to stimulate the French economy through increased government spending. The problem was not that the stimulation policies were unsuccessful; indeed, they were too successful. The French economy grew at a real rate of 1.7 percent during 1982, a time when nearly all of the other countries of the world were suffering from economic stagnation or recession. Of the major industrialized countries, only Japan grew more rapidly than France. The rate of economic growth in the United States declined by 1.9 percent, and that of West Germany by 1.1 percent. The economies of the European Community and the developing countries — major markets for French products — were stagnant.

What the French very rapidly learned was that a strong economy at home sucked in imports while weak economies abroad greatly reduced the demand for French exports. The result was a trade deficit that nearly doubled, from Fr 50 billion during 1981 to Fr 92 billion in 1982. There was no way the French economy could sustain such a decline in its trade fortunes, for the growing deficits meant a loss of jobs for French workers, depressed profits and low levels of investment for French manufacturing firms, and a French franc that was continually under pressure in the financial markets.

The ill-fated attempt to stimulate the French economy to faster growth lasted for only a year, from June 1981 to June 1982. Mitterrand was then forced to change course, adopting rather stringent measures to control inflation and ease the pressure on the franc. A wage and price freeze was imposed, followed by an incomes policy designed to limit wage and price increases in the future. Government spending plans were scaled back and taxes increased, but even these tightening actions were not enough.

In March 1983, further policies were put into place, representing the "most deflationary postwar austerity package."[27] New spending cuts and increased taxes were adopted in order to reduce the 1983 budget deficit. Taxpayers were required to lend the government 10 percent of their 1982 taxes for three years. French travelers were limited to $275 per year for foreign travel expenditures, and the foreign use of credit cards was banned. An 8-percent increase in gas, electric, telephone, and rail rates was imposed. And the money supply was further tightened, along with a drastic reduction in the allowable expansion of consumer credit.

The French people were becoming increasingly worried about the future of their economy under the socialist experiment, and these new austerity measures only intensified their concerns. Fears of higher unemployment and anger over the new taxes and travel regulations were rampant. "Today we have had a cold shower, and I assure you that our militants and members will not accept it," warned André Bergeron, head of the moderate Force Ouvrière labor union when the changes were first announced.[28] In a slightly more humorous vein, but still to the point, was the reaction of a typical Frenchman to the controls on foreign travel: "We are condemned to vacations with our grandmothers in the countryside."[29]

The austerity programs began to have their intended effects. During 1983, growth of the French economy was slowed to zero, and inflation was lowered from an annual rate of 12 percent to 9 percent. The trade deficit was reduced by over one-half, falling from Fr 92 billion in 1982 to Fr 44 billion in 1983. The French franc finally stabilized against the German mark and the U.S. dollar (although at a quite low rate). It appeared that the bottom had been reached in the French economic experiment.

The lesson that the French were learning — a costly one, for it came close to scuttling the entire French economic experiment — is that no single major industrialized country, no matter how large and powerful, can sustain an economic experiment that runs counter to those being tried in the other major industrialized countries. The global economy is now too interdependent for any country to go off on a tangent. All of the major Western countries are inextricably tied to one another through foreign trade, international capital markets, and dependency upon global sources of oil, food, and other basic commodities.

When the French attempted to stimulate their economy to faster growth at a time when far more conservative and austere economic policies were being implemented in West Germany, Great Britain, and the United States, the result was a weakening of the French franc and of trade balances. France had no choice but to alter course: to adopt economic policies that were more compatible with those of her trading partners. And even though French leaders took corrective action rather quickly, the damage to their economic experiment may have been irreparable.

In the first place, the reversal of economic course in regard to France's short-run stimulation policies has raised doubts regarding the efficacy of the entire French economic experiment. French leaders are now operating from a defensive posture, both with regard to international opinion and the attitudes of the French people themselves. They are being questioned about their intentions, their plans for the future, and their ability to implement the remaining — and far more important — elements of their economic experiment. President Mitterrand and his economic advisors have lost a lot of their initial momentum in their effort to achieve a new alliance between Socialism and liberty.

In the second place, the French have created great uncertainty about their commitment and future role in the European Monetary System. As a member of the EMS, France is obligated to maintain the value of her currency in a stable relationship to that of the other major currencies, and primarily the German mark. If the value of the franc declines and is no longer stable, then the French are responsible for taking corrective action in their economy. But when the franc ran into difficulty in early 1983, the French blamed their problems on the Germans and threatened to leave the EMS.

"It was up to our German partners to make the biggest step," announced Jacques Delors, the French finance minister, at a press conference. And "they made it."[30] What the Germans agreed to do was to revalue their currency upward by 5.5 percent, thus making German exports more expensive within the European Common Market. The French franc was devalued downward by only 2.5 percent — a remarkably small adjustment for a country whose weak currency was creating havoc in Europe.

The French victory, however, left a bitter legacy among her trading partners and a deep suspicion that the French could not be relied upon as a committed member of the EMS. "The threat to leave the monetary system and perhaps pull the whole Common Market down was in the great tradition of Gaullist diplomacy, when France never shied from the most bruising confrontations with its partners in pursuit of national objectives," reported the *New York Times*. "France's skill in turning what should have been a mechanical exchange rate adjustment into a major political crisis left scars on many of its Common Market partners."[31]

The third area in which the French economic experiment is threatened is in the rise of political opposition to President Mitterrand within France and his loss of political support among the French public. Although Mitterrand enjoys the longest incumbency of any major Western leader — the term of office is seven years — there are national municipal elections during his tenure that are widely viewed as an indication of the political strength of the French president. These elections also provide an opportunity for political opposition to rise. In the municipal election held in early 1983, the Socialists lost control in thirty cities — a loss that was described by Socialist leaders as a warning. The party's general secretary, Lionel Jospin, interpreted the results as requiring government policy to become "simpler, more concrete and more coherent."[32]

It did not take long for Mitterrand's major political opponent — Jacques Chirac, the outspoken and aggressive mayor of Paris — to offer a simple solution: himself as the next leader of France. The Gaullist leader began to criticize openly the economic policies of Mitterrand, claiming that the government has lost its moral mandate and calling for a referendum on economic policy. These criticisms fell upon sympathetic ears. Mitterrand's rating in the public-opinion polls plunged to a low of 30-to-35 percent by late 1983. Opposition parties won a string of victories in local elections and for the French senate. Mr. Mitterrand's own left-wingers, it was reported, "abhor his government's forced economic austerity."[33] This loss of political support is making it increasingly difficult for Mitterrand to sustain the leadership that is required for his economic experiment to survive.

The early change in course, the difficult lessons of learning to live in an interdependent global economy, and the loss of political support at home and abroad have certainly taken their toll. But the most important aspects of the French experiment are still intact. The use of the nationalized industries to build a stronger French economy in the long run, and the commitment to achieving a more equitable and open French society have not been abandoned. Indeed, Mitterrand has put into place several major changes to strengthen these, his most important economic objectives. First, there has been a shift in the overall goals of his economic program; second, the French are attempting to buy time for their experiment while the global economy gains more strength; and third, French industrial policy has been moderated.

During the crisis week of March 21, 1983, when France won its currency battle with the Germans, President Mitterrand made a television speech that formally altered the entire course of the French experiment. After defending his policies of the past twenty-two months, Mitterrand voiced the need to beat "the infernal machine" of inflation and "the unacceptable trade deficit and the indebtedness it brings."[34] He announced that France was setting two new economic goals: (1) reducing inflation to levels comparable with France's competitors, and (2) totally eliminating the trade deficit within two years.

These were not simply statements made to satisfy promises made to the Germans in the heat of the negotiations over currency levels; it was reported that French officials were subjected "to a severe inquisition" on the details of the proposed French austerity measures at the meetings of the EMS before the Germans would agree to revalue their currency to help the French save face.[35] President Mitterrand had made a very critical decision during this fateful week: he rejected the nationalistic and protectionist positions being advocated by his more leftist advisors and committed France to an economic direction that would allow her to remain within the Western alliance.

In many respects, however, the French were taking another calculated risk with their new austerity policies. They were again electing to move against the economic trend in the global economy, but rather than stimulating their economy while other countries adopted more constrictive policies, as they did from mid-1981 through mid-1982, they planned to hold down French growth while other major countries expanded. "France will be the rare — if not the only — Western country not to benefit from the international economic recovery," commented former president Valéry Giscard d'Estaing.[36]

Indeed, the French projections for growth in 1984 looked rather pale when compared to those of the other industrialized countries. The official forecasts were for the French economy to expand by 1.0 percent in real terms, while the United States was expected to grow by nearly 7.0 percent, Germany by 2.5 percent, and Japan by over 5.0 percent. As for 1985, the French economy was expected to expand only 1.5 percent — well below that of most other industrialized economies.

The French seemed to be betting that their slower growth would reduce imports from abroad and that the higher growth in other countries would mean expanded markets for French exports. The result would be a rapid shrinkage in the French trade deficit, with a resulting strengthening in the value of the franc and French confidence and prestige. Once the problems of the trade deficit and weak currency had been resolved, the French economy would be in a position to resume faster economic growth. The risk was whether the French people would tolerate continued austerity at a time when the people of other countries were enjoying a return of economic prosperity.

In altering their economic goals and constraining economic recovery to solve France's inflation and trade problems, the Socialists seem to be buying time for their industrial policy to work. The French are betting a lot of their economic future on a revitalization of the nation's industry, and President Mitterrand took steps to strengthen and moderate his industrial policy in March 1983. In a dramatic move, he swept clean his cabinet, reducing the number of ministers from thirty-four to fifteen and eliminating the most leftist among them. Prominent among this ousted group was Jean-Pierre Chevenement, who was France's minister of research and industry.

Chevenement, well known for his outspoken views on the need for more state intervention in industry, was replaced by the former budget minister Laurent Fabius.

"The private sector is predominant in France and it's going to stay that way," announced Mr. Fabius in his first major statement after being appointed to office. "The state can't do everything. It can't stand in for businesses; it can only provide incentives and arbitration."[37] The young minister immediately set out to moderate the industrial policies of France. There was to be less legislation and far more negotiation on such critical issues as working hours, adapting industrial policy to local needs, and recognizing the reality of the market for the companies involved. New investment and professional research and training were to receive increased emphasis. A five-year, $25-billion plan for developing the electronics and computer-science industry was launched. The growth of medium- and smaller-sized firms, which are expected to provide the bulk of the new jobs in the future, would be encouraged. Mr. Fabius was given the task of ensuring that French industrial policy succeeds, for that policy will be a major issue in the 1986 parliamentary elections.

And in July 1984, Laurent Fabius, at the age of thirty-seven, was appointed the youngest-ever prime minister in modern French history. In the second-most-powerful position in the French government, he was expected to broaden his mandate from modernizing French industry to updating Mitterrand's version of socialism and thus regain lost political support. On the shoulders of the brilliant, tough-minded, and pragmatic Fabius fell the task of turning the ebbing political tide of the Socialists and preserving the French experiment in socialism.

Conclusion

"President Mitterrand deserves more cheers than jeers for the choices he has made," editorialized the *Economist* in March 1983, "because in the process he has saved France and Europe from much worse ones that were on offer."[38] The editorial writers were commenting upon the crucial events of the week of March 21, when France and Germany squared off against each other over their currencies and President Mitterrand announced the new directions of his economic experiment, simultaneously cleaning the leftist opposition out of his cabinet. But what the editorialists were really commending was Mitterrand's strong stance against the rising tides of protectionism within his own Socialist party and his administration.

At a time when the French economic experiment was failing, many of the politicians were turning to protectionism. President Mitterrand was being pressed to go on television and announce that the franc was not going to be devalued by the "speculation of anti-socialist bankers." Rather, the government would impose new controls on foreign imports and protect French workers from unfair foreign competition. To his credit, Mitterrand did not follow this advice. Instead, he said in his television appearance that France should not "isolate itself from the European Community or distance itself from the Atlantic alliance."[39]

The situation the French president encountered is far from unique. As the economic experiments in the United States, Great Britain, West Germany, Japan, and France struggle to succeed, they will encounter difficulties and will fail to deliver on all their promises. As a consequence, pressure for a protectionist alternative will continue to mount.

Politicians in the United States already are introducing numerous bills that would protect American workers from foreign competition. "If you look at the record of the Ninety-seventh Congress on trade, you will find over 250 substantive trade bills were introduced," stated Senator John Danforth at a 1983 conference on trade problems. "I might add," he continued, "that of these almost 20 percent were focused directly or indirectly on Japan."[40]

The continued pressure on the Japanese appears to be wearing thin in that country. The Japanese claim that their markets are already some of the most open in the world, and when harangued to do more, they respond that there is little more that can be done. In proposing a new package of economic measures to ease trade problems with the United States in late 1983, Prime Minister Yasuhiro Nakasone said the measures "represent a maximum that can be taken under the severe fiscal constraints we face at the present."[41]

Political leaders throughout the industrialized world are being courted to embrace protectionism, and while the current leaders of the five major industrialized countries have all publicly taken a stand against such a move, the pressures are building. Many of them are relying upon industrial policies that encourage the development of such high-technology industries as electronics, communications, and robotics. The appeal of protecting these "infant industries" is great. At the same time, unemployment continues to mount in the old smokestack industries, and rather than face a future without a basic steel, rubber, coal, or shipbuilding industry, the present Western leaders may turn to outright protectionism. For many of the aspiring politicians waiting in the wings for the five economic experiments to fail (providing them the opportunity to move into power), protectionism appears to be the only alternative in a search for an economy that works.

The Threat of Protectionism

*G*ENTLEMEN, at this time of widespread economic stress, it is with a feeling of deep responsibility that I welcome you to this country," announced King George V to 168 delegates who had gathered at the Geological Museum in Kensington, England.[1] It was June 12, 1933, and the occasion was the opening of the World Economic Conference.

In the audience were powerful political leaders such as Secretary of State Cordell Hull, leading the American delegation, and Prime Minister Ramsay MacDonald of Great Britain, who was serving as chairman of the conference. The delegates, representing sixty-six nations, had come to what the *New York Times* called the "greatest economic clinic of all time."[2] They came knowing that the fate of thirty million unemployed people hung in the balance, and, indeed, that the future of not only international economic stability but world peace was at stake.

A general feeling of pessimism hung over the conference as the delegates debated whether it was possible to solve the complex problems facing the world economy. Unprecedented levels of unemployment, lack of adequate productive investment by businesses, a stagnant economy in every industrialized country, and mounting trade and financial barriers were hastening nations down the road of protectionism. The major countries were attempting to deal with these issues quite independently of one another, implementing economic policies that only exacerbated the global problems. "Never before in a world conference have the interests seemed so irreconcilable, the obstacles so difficult and common ground so hard to attain," reported the press from London.[3]

There was a growing belief that the Great Depression of 1929 was finally coming to an end, yet most of the delegates knew that the global economy was faced with serious structural and long-term problems.[4] Former British prime minister David Lloyd George warned that "mankind is getting nearer the brink year by year, revolution by revolution, conference by conference."[5] Sir Arthur Salter, a leading British economist and member of the British Economic Advisory Council, cautioned that "the world now stands hesitant between alternative systems, one designed to develop world trade, the other to develop national or regional self-sufficiency."[6]

Although these events occurred over fifty years ago, they bear remarkable similarity to conditions of today. The same problems of unemployment and stagnant growth confront the global economy today as in 1933. Now, as then, the economy is recovering from a serious decline, but there is an underlying sense that all is not right. We face the same choice of whether to accept protectionism or take steps to maintain free trade. Most important, the economic policies being tried by individual countries fifty years ago were unsuccessful, much as the fate of the five economic experiments of the present.

It was to solve these critical economic problems that the 168 delegates gathered in Kensington a half-century ago. Unfortunately, they failed. Many laid the blame on the Americans, who rejected a proposal to preserve the gold standard in order to stabilize international currency markets. Rebuking the gold bloc composed of such strong allies as Great Britain, France, Switzerland, Holland, and Belgium, President Franklin Roosevelt stunned the conference with the forceful statement that he "would regard it as a catastrophe amounting to a world tragedy if the great conference of nations, called to bring about a more real and permanent financial stability and a greater prosperity to the masses of all nations, should . . . be diverted by the proposal of a purely artificial and temporary experiment affecting the monetary exchange of a few nations only."[7]

Others blamed the conference itself for failure, observing that it was impossible to expect much agreement from so many different countries, while a Russian delegate "openly scoffed" at the collapse of the proceedings, proclaiming "the great superiority of his own brand of economic rationalization over this impotence of capitalism."[8]

Whatever the reason for failure, on July 27, 1933, the World

Economic Conference came to an end "amid mingled reproaches, regrets and expressions of pious hope."[9] The last opportunity for a peaceful resolution of the problems vanished. The global economy plunged back into depression. The international currency system broke down. World trade totally disintegrated, and the forces of extreme nationalism dominated nearly all aspects of international relations. The world rapidly embarked upon a course of autarky that was eventually followed by the Second World War.

Nowhere was the growth of economic nationalism more virulent than in Japan. The Japanese government had adopted an aggressive strategy of promoting economic growth, and with the passage of the Major Industries Control Law of 1931, the government began to "rationalize industry, sponsoring mergers, eliminating wasteful competition, and streamlining industry for foreign competition."[10] So successful were the Japanese efforts that by early 1933 Japan's exports had increased a remarkable 50 percent above their level a year earlier. Despite strong trade competition from the United States, Britain, and Germany, Japan became the first major power to recover from the depression, in large part as the result of her exports.

Japan's success in her export drive led to increasing resentment in the United States and western Europe. Japan was accused of unfair business practices and artificially depreciating the yen in order to price her products more competitively in world markets. The United States imposed high tariffs on Japanese imports and the British Parliament voted to take action to check Japanese competition, which further convinced the Japanese that they were being excluded from the global economy because of their accomplishments.

It was Japanese "enterprise, industry and natural advantages rather than so-called exchange dumping" that were responsible for the success of Japanese goods in American markets, Kensuke Horinouchi, consul general of Japan, told the Foreign Commerce Club of New York in November 1933.[11]

Feeling isolated and on the defensive, the Japanese became even more nationalistic. Determined to consolidate their economic fortunes in Manchuria by extending control in northern China, they blundered into a long, drawn-out war with the Chinese. Driven by military extremists who were rapidly gaining power over the government in Tokyo, the traditional Japanese concern for economic security soon was turned into economic imperialism. They moved southward toward the French, Dutch, and English colonies, which held vital supplies of oil, rubber, and other raw materials. Finally, in the summer of 1941, when Japanese troops moved into southern Indochina, the United States, Britain, and Holland imposed a total embargo on all exports to Japan, thus cutting off Japan's oil and rubber supplies. And in September 1941, Japanese leaders determined to go to war against the United States if agreement on lifting the oil embargo was not reached by October. Agreement, of course, was not reached and Pearl Harbor was bombed on December 7.

The economic concerns and trade competition between Japan and her major trading partners today is frighteningly similar to developments of the 1930s. Now, as then, the Japanese are seeking economic security. In recent years they have been remarkably successful in developing export markets, relying upon their enterprise and prodigious abilities, just as they did earlier. And the reaction from other industrialized countries, struggling with problems of unemployment and declining industries while confronting Japanese competition, is to charge the Japanese with unfair practices.

"Pondering Japan's behavior in the current trade disputes," wrote Professor Yoshihiko Seki of Tokyo's Waseda University in 1983, "I am struck by how little the Japanese people seem to be heeding the lessons of the past. This observation is prompted not by fears that my country is about to revive militarism, as some critics claim. Rather the real danger lies, once again, in Japan's growing isolation from the rest of the world."[12]

Growing isolation is not unique to Japan. Nor are the Japanese alone in failing to heed the lessons of history. Isolation and increasing economic nationalism are strongly present in the United States and Western Europe as well, and just as in the past, the threat of economic disintegration of the world economy, if not military conflict, is a clear danger.

Addressing this danger and suggesting ways in which the world economy can pull back from the brink of disaster will be the focus of the remainder of this book. We have examined in some detail the major economic experiments that are being attempted in the United States, Japan, West Germany, Great Britain, and France; we have analyzed why they are failing to solve current economic problems; and we have considered the probability that to continue along our present course will only lead to economic disaster, if not war. It is therefore imperative that we seek an alternative course. Such a course is the Power Economy — and the first step in attaining the Power Economy is to stop the growing threat of protectionism.

What Is Protectionism?

Protectionism, which has a long tradition in economic history, has usually taken the form of duties or tariffs imposed on certain imported products. Generally levied to provide protection to newly developing industries — to "infant industries," as they are frequently called — high tariffs on the products of foreign competitors gave domestic firms time to develop the economic strength to compete successfully. Although ideally the protective duties were to be imposed only for short periods, they frequently remained long after the domestic firms had matured.

Protective tariffs reached their height during the early 1930s, after the United States adopted the Smoot-Hawley tariff of 1930. At the time, agriculture prices were depressed on world markets, and Congress believed that by raising tariffs on food products American farmers would be made prosperous once again. The thinking seemed to be that since industry had done well in the 1920s, and since American industry was protected by high tariffs, the same would be true of the farmers. The fallacy in such thinking was that manufacturers were prosperous not because of the tariffs but because of the strength of the American economy: high growth rates, rising incomes, and increased consumer spending. All the tariffs did for farmers was raise the price of their products to consumers and depress the markets even more — a lesson learned much later.

In any event, Congress began to logroll the original agriculture tariff bill, extending proposed tariffs to numerous manufactured products in addition to farm goods. And in June 1930, the Smoot-Hawley bill was enacted, which broadened tariff coverage to 25,000 products and provided for substantial increases in over 800 tariff rates, raising American rates to an average of 50 percent on all imports. The reaction of the rest of the world to this stunning increase was immediate. Widespread protests erupted. Tariffs were raised in a dozen major countries, and they were targeted against American products. The League of Nations, which was working hard to halt the upward trend in tariffs, was powerless. The seeds of economic isolation had been deeply planted.

While efforts were made by the Roosevelt administration to lower the high tariffs in the United States, it was not until after the end of the Second World War that tariff reduction was really achieved. Beginning with the Geneva round of tariff negotiations in 1947 and extending through the Tokyo round, which were concluded in 1979, tariffs have been greatly reduced. Once the results of the Tokyo round are completely implemented, as is scheduled for 1988, the average tariff on raw materials of the major industrial countries will be a mere 0.3 percent, that on semimanufactured goods will be only 4.0 percent, and that on manufactured goods will be just 6.5 percent.

For all intents, tariffs are no longer an issue in international trade. They have been almost totally eliminated among the industrialized countries, and there are only isolated cases where high duties are now imposed. (A recent case is that of the Reagan administration raising the duties on large Japanese motorcycles from 4.4 percent to 49.4 percent to save the Harley-Davidson Motor Company, the sole remaining survivor of 143 companies that once made motorcycles in the United States.)

The end of the high-tariff era does not mean that the protectionist issue is dead — far from it. For new forms of protectionism have been developed. These include nontariff regulatory barriers to trade, and the formation of trade cartels and orderly trade markets. Such nontariff barriers, which generally take the form of lengthy customs procedures, exhaustive safety and inspection requirements, mandatory licenses, complicated procurement regulations, and similar government restrictions and red tape, have become a critical sore point between the Americans and the Japanese.

Frequently, an exporter will find a product tied up for months on some foreign dock while local inspectors ponderously check to make sure that the appropriate paperwork has been done. The product will be sent to government laboratories for extensive testing to ensure that it meets safety and environmental requirements. Many times, these requirements appear to be far more stringent for foreign products than for those manufactured domestically. And in Japan and Western Europe, foreign producers are sometimes excluded from bidding on contracts.

It was the French who most highlighted the use of nontariff barriers to trade. In November 1982, the French government suddenly declared that all imported videotape recorders must be cleared through a tiny customs station at Poitiers, in southwestern France, hundreds of miles from the northern ports where the recorders initially landed. This action received a great deal of international publicity, in part because of the history of Poitiers itself. Reporters delighted in pointing out that it was at Poitiers that "Charles (The Hammer) Martel saved Christendom by crushing an advancing Moorish Army in A.D. 732" and in suggesting that the latest Battle of Poitiers was "to save the French video recorder market from being overrun by Japanese imports."[13]

The following month, the French filed an antidumping suit with the European Economic Community against three Japanese producers, further tying them up with lengthy hearings. The "Battle of Poitiers" was not settled until the Japanese had entered into negotiations for voluntarily restraining shipments to France and had announced plans to place manufacturing plants in Europe.

Under strong pressure from the Americans, the Japanese have taken steps to streamline their trade procedures. In 1982, they established the Office of Trade Ombudsmen to deal with the complaints of foreign exporters. Outside of agriculture products, there are only a few remaining quotas on imports. Customs procedures have been streamlined. A survey made by the American Chamber of Commerce in 1982 failed to find pervasive patterns of major nontariff barriers to imports into Japan.[14]

Currently, protectionism does not take the form of the old-fashioned tariffs of the 1930s, nor even the form of the more recent nontariff regulatory barriers, such as burdensome procedures for customs evaluation and for meeting safety and environmental standards. Rather, the latest and most virulent type of protectionism involves negotiating orderly marketing agreements and voluntary trade restraints, as well as forming trade cartels.

The Growth of Protectionism

On the surface, protectionism is not being openly embraced by the major industrialized countries, whose leaders ritualistically reaffirm their faith in free trade at their annual economic summit meetings. Once a year they gather and proclaim: "We commit ourselves to halt protectionism, and as recovery proceeds to reverse it by dismantling trade barriers.[15] . . . The growth of world trade in all its facets is both a necessary element for the growth of each country and a consequence of that growth. We reaffirm our commitment to strengthen the open multilateral trading system.[16] . . . We reaffirm our strong commitment to maintaining liberal trade policies and to the effective operation of an open multilateral trading system."[17]

Yet there is very little detail on just how and when trade barriers are going to be reduced, either at the economic summit meetings or in the postsummit discussions. Nor are there many indications that actions are actually being taken to encourage free trade. The fact of the matter is that while the political leaders annually go through the ritual of embracing free trade, they are putting into place policies that threaten to lead to outright protectionism and trade warfare.

The cases of protectionism are increasing each year, and in the United States, long viewed as the bastion against the growth of protectionism, political forces are mounting for even more curtailment of imports. Secretary of Commerce Malcolm Baldrige in late 1982 foresaw protectionist pressures "increasing this year and for a period of years," reversing decades of progress toward a more open world trading system. Meanwhile, William Brock, U.S. trade negotiator, predicted that protectionist legislation would continue to be a threat in Congress and warned that it was "going to be tough to resist those pressures." Former vice-president Walter Mondale, while crisscrossing the nation during his unsuccessful 1984 campaign for the presidency, argued forcefully that "we have got to get tough — and I mean really tough — with nations that use our markets but deny us their markets."[18]

These political leaders were simply responding to a growing attitude among the American public that free trade is not feasible, or even desirable, in today's world. "Unemployment is the big issue," warned Mayor Bud Ayres of New Castle, Indiana, a small midwestern manufacturing and agriculture center. "Trade restraint and the preservation of American jobs is going to be a big factor in local and national politics for the next few years," he predicted. According to Marvin Luellen, who farms thirty-five hundred acres outside New Castle: "We're going to have to have more government intervention. Free trade just won't work in today's world economy." And Jack Hill, manager of an Allegheny Ludlum steel plant, added: "We've got to set acceptable limits on imports. Everybody's getting desperate."[19]

What the American farmer and manufacturer are saying is being repeated by their counterparts in Japan and Western Europe, and the politicians are not ignoring these protectionist sentiments. It is becoming increasingly evident that the high point in free trade was reached in 1974, and that since that time the pendulum has swung toward far more protection.

A 1981 study for the National Institute of Economic and Social Research in London, for instance, found that the proportion of trade of the industrialized countries that was controlled or managed by federal governments had grown from 36.3 percent in 1974 to 43.8

percent during 1980. (See table 18.) The most rapid growth in protected trade had been in manufactured goods, where the proportion had increased from 4.0 percent to 17.4 percent. It is interesting to note that the United States has continually led the major industrialized countries in protection of manufactured goods.

The New Protectionism

When confronted with rising unemployment that is concentrated in specific basic industries, such as automobiles, textiles, and steel, the solution seems easy: simply curtail imports of those products from abroad through agreements with the countries involved. Thus, if a loss of jobs occurs in the American automobile industry, the United States should just force the Japanese and the Europeans to limit voluntarily the number of automobiles they export to this country to a stated number per year. Such action would preserve a certain proportion of the American market for American producers. It does not close the door to foreign imports, nor totally isolate domestic manufacturers from foreign influence in terms of product quality and greater efficiency. It seems to be a fair and rational solution.

It is a solution that is easy to achieve. Quotas can be set on the number of foreign-produced items that are allowed into the country, or they can be set as a certain proportion of the domestic market.

TABLE 18. CONTROLLED TRADE IN MAJOR INDUSTRIALIZED ECONOMIES (AS A PROPORTION OF TOTAL TRADE)

	All Goods		Manufactured Goods	
	1974	*1980*	*1974*	*1980*
All industrialized countries (OECD)	36.3%	43.8%	4.0%	17.4%
United States	36.2	45.8	5.6	21.0
Japan	56.1	59.4	0	4.3
West Germany	37.3	47.3	0	18.3
Great Britain	38.5	47.9	0.2	17.4
France	32.8	42.7	0	16.2

SOURCE: S. A. B. Page, "The Revival of Protectionism and Its Consequences for Europe," *Journal of Common Market Studies* 20 (Sept. 1981): 29.

A country can be pressured to limit exports of a particular product, or agreements can be reached between countries on how much each can export into world markets. Such agreements can be formalized, with the major exporting countries meeting periodically to parcel out the global markets exclusively among themselves.

All of these restrictions on trade are now being used by the major industrialized countries, including the United States. These new protection measures date back to 1973, when the Multifiber Agreement was signed as a means of enlarging textile trade. It was an agreement that did very little to expand the global markets for clothing and textile materials. Rather, it set in place a global trade cartel that tightly controls world markets by setting limits on how much is produced and traded by the fifty countries who are principals to the agreement and by excluding other countries. When the latest agreement was signed, in late 1981, it was estimated that for the American consumer the price of clothing would be increased by 5 to 10 percent — a total cost of $4 billion per year.

Unfortunately, the textile cartel has become a model for dealing with other difficult trade problems. While formal agreements among the major trading countries are so far limited to textiles, many of the elements of trade cartels have been put into place in steel, television sets, footwear, shipbuilding, and automobiles, and many of these have been initiated by the United States.

In 1977, the United States negotiated orderly marketing agreements limiting imports of footwear from Korea and Taiwan, and color television sets from Japan. The controls on television-set imports were extended to Korea and Taiwan in 1979. In 1978, American steel manufacturers were provided with protection of their domestic markets, and the Reagan administration has taken an "orderly marketing" approach to the problem of excess steel capacity among the industrialized countries. In 1981, the United States forced Japan to accept "voluntary" restraints on automobile exports to this country. And in 1982, we adopted sugar quotas and negotiated voluntary quotas with the European Community on steel products.

Such actions by the United States and other countries to negotiate trade agreements sets off reciprocity actions by the other trading countries of the world, who fear that their own markets will be inundated by diverted trade. The result is a widespread adoption of cartel-type trade restrictions, with resulting higher prices to consumers and reduced economic growth. Such actions have now become so commonplace and accepted that anytime a trade problem occurs, politicians quickly turn to orderly marketing agreements, voluntary restraints, or some other form of control.

The formation of trade cartels will do for the 1980s what duties and tariffs did during the 1930s. Global trade will be greatly curtailed, domestic markets will be protected from foreign competition, and the existing world markets will be carefully parceled out among the rich and powerful countries to the exclusion of most of the less-developed countries. We will have created a world market of the haves and the have-nots. Since it is rather unlikely that the have-nots will idly stand by and accept this fate, we are inadvertently generating a highly unstable world order.

Other forms of new protectionism are generating friction between the haves — that is, the major industrialized countries — themselves. The most important type of these protectionist devices are subsidies. Trade subsidies can take the form of reduced interest rates for export finance, credit for taxes earned on export profits, or direct government subsidies for the costs of developing export business. Such export credits cover around 45 percent of all exports of Japan, France, and Great Britain, but only 10 percent of the exports of Germany and the United States.[20]

The greatest point of contention between the United States and Europe is over the treatment of tax subsidies. According to international rules, indirect taxes, such as the value-added tax in Europe, are a legitimate subsidy and such taxes can be rebated. But direct taxes, such as the American corporate income tax, cannot be rebated. In response, the United States established the Domestic International Sales Corporation (DISC), which permits the postponement of federal taxes on income from export profits until it is distributed to shareholders. This practice was ruled inappropriate under the General Agreement on Tariffs and Trade (GATT), the international compact for resolving trade differences.

Some governments establish limitations on government procurement, so that only domestic firms are allowed to bid on contracts for equipment used by companies owned or controlled by the government. Thus, only French firms can bid on electronic and communications equipment to be purchased by the state-owned telephone company. And many manufacturers, particularly Americans, charge that Japanese buyers have an unwritten "buy Japanese" policy. (Although foreign producers are now allowed to bid on Nippon Telegraph and Telephone contracts, it took years of pressure to open up this government monopoly to outsiders.)

Another form of protectionism that is receiving increasing attention in the United States is so-called domestic-content legislation. Yet studies suggest that this is a rather expensive means of preserving jobs — an approach that leads to higher prices and reduced efficiency. Such legislation would require that a designated foreign product must contain a certain proportion of domestically produced parts before it is allowed into our markets. Most of the discussion concerns automobiles, and numerous bills requiring that up to 90 percent of an automobile's components be made in the United States as a precondition to export into this country have been introduced in Congress. Union leaders are pushing the idea as a way of preserving American jobs, and Democratic presidential candidate Walter Mondale endorsed the concept. Content legislation is common in the developing countries, who adopt it to help build up a new industry, as well as in industrialized countries such as Canada, Mexico, Brazil, Spain, and India.

The Agriculture Trade Problem

The most difficult of the trade issues to resolve, and the one that threatens to prevent progress from being made on resolving other trade problems, is agriculture. All countries subsidize their farmers. In the United States, these subsidies totaled $16 billion during 1984 through the Commodity Credit Corporation alone. Established in 1933 to support farmers' income, this massive government program now provides price supports and other direct grants to farmers. Furthermore, American dairy farmers are protected from foreign competition, and the price for butter, cheese, and milk is kept at a level above free-market prices. Tariffs and quotas are imposed on imported beef, sugar, tobacco, and peanuts.

European farmers are among the most protected in the world. In an area where 3.6 million farmers try to make a living on an average of twenty acres or less (just one-twentieth the size of the American farm), and where 35 percent of the entire labor force is working in jobs that are related to agriculture, the economic position of the European farmer is extremely vulnerable. There are few jobs in the cities to absorb displaced farmers. Many are barely able to scrape out an existence on small plots of land. And most lack the capital to compete against their more productive peers in the United States.

To protect its farmers, the European Economic Community, composed of the ten major Western European countries, has established a Common Agricultural Policy that guarantees farmers high and uniform prices for their products regardless of their efficiency or prices in world markets. When the world prices are lower than the costs of production, the farmers receive an export subsidy to bring the price of European products down to the level of American farm exports. These protection and subsidy programs have enabled the Europeans to capture an increasing share of world markets. During the 1970s, Europe's share of the milk market increased from 41 percent to 63 percent, its share of the butter market grew from 27 percent to 61 percent, and its share of the sugar market nearly tripled, rising from about 5 percent to 15 percent.

The Japanese farmer enjoys similar treatment. Operating small farms much like those in Europe, and living in a country where they enjoy an inordinate amount of political power, the Japanese farmers have long been protected. Of the twenty-seven quotas the Japanese maintain on imports, twenty-two are for agriculture products. State trading companies control the purchases of foreign tobacco, salt, and livestock. Burdensome procedures for customs evaluation and for meeting health and environmental standards are applied against food imports. And whenever the Japanese government attempts to eliminate any of these protections, primarily responding to American pressure, the farmers are quick to react. Since 60 percent of the members of the Diet are from rural districts, the Japanese farmer is easily able to influence government policy.

Even though farmers in the United States, Europe, and Japan all receive government support and protection, the clash over these policies is tremendous. Wedded to an ideology of free trade, the Reagan administration is threatening Europe with retaliatory export-subsidy programs unless the Common Market policy is changed. And given the nature of trade with Japan, which primarily buys raw materials from the United States, American officials are quick to note that without greater access to Japanese food markets, there is no way that the trade gap between the two countries can be closed.

The Europeans respond that they are not about to change their agricultural-support policies, but that they would be willing to work out a cooperative agreement with the United States and other major food producers. What they have in mind is an informal cartel that would divide up world food markets, giving the United States primary access to Latin America and Asia while European farmers supply Africa, the Middle East, and Eastern Europe. In addition, food would be stockpiled to avoid wide fluctuations in world prices and to maintain stable markets. All of this, of course, means much higher prices to the consumer. The Japanese politely ignore the pressure to change their agriculture policies, and go about their business of protecting their farmers.

Significant differences in farm-support policies and the nature of farming between the major industrialized countries make it almost impossible to achieve either free trade, as proposed by the United States, or informal cartels, as suggested by Europe. Free-trade suggestions are simply ignored in Europe and Japan as a totally unrealistic posture by Washington right-wing ideologues, while previous attempts at food cartels have failed. This is the one area of trade in which the best that can be done is to isolate the issues from spilling over into other trade matters, and continue to muddle through.

The High Cost of Protectionism

Protectionism is not cheap. The American consumer is paying around $100,000 annually for each job saved by protection of television sets, footwear, and speciality steel. The total cost per year for the protection of the textile industry alone is a staggering $13 billion. European consumers are in a similar situation, for during 1984 they paid about $20 billion for the protection of European farm products.[21]

Yet the impact on the economy of protectionism goes far beyond increased costs to the consumer. Not only are prices higher, but the consumer has fewer choices of consumer products. The manufacturer has less incentive to remain competitive, to develop new technologies, or to invest in more productive plant and equipment. The resurgence of the American automobile industry, for instance, is due in large part to the stimulus from Japanese competition. Detroit has invested billions of dollars to reduce production costs and improve quality in order to compete with Japanese imports.

Furthermore, the economy suffers from a less efficient allocation of resources, for protection tends to maintain the status quo. It is the mature and declining steel and textile industries that are protected — industries that should be allowed to shrink to a more efficient and cost-effective size, given declining world markets. The resources that would be saved from this adjustment could then be shifted to industries that offer the potential for higher growth, such as computers, biotechnology, and health care. The consequence of

THE HIGH COST OF PROTECTIONISM

freezing the economy through protection of slow-growth industries is higher inflation and slower economic growth.

Nor does protection save jobs; it simply redistributes jobs from potential high-growth industries to mature and declining industries. A job in steel is saved at the cost of a new job in high-technology computers. In sum, protectionism imposes tremendous economic costs: the consumer pays more for products and has less choice, inflation rises, and the economy is less efficient and its growth is slowed down.

These economic costs, serious as they are, do not represent the complete story, for there are also tremendous political costs inherent in protectionism. The political costs are twofold: (1) tensions increase between the industrialized countries themselves, and (2) the economies and political systems of the less developed countries break down.

The recent surge of protectionism has done more to weaken the Western alliance than any other single factor since the end of the Second World War. Indeed, the current trend in international discussions brings to mind disputes among warring neighbors rather than disagreements among family members. The increase in antagonism between the Japanese and the Americans over trade issues has been well publicized, for instance — and, unfortunately, the dialogue has taken on quite strident tones: "We've been running up the white flag when we should be running up the American flag. . . . What do we want our kids to do? Sweep up around Japanese computers?" said Walter Mondale on the campaign trail.[22] "If we don't win this battle, you can forget the U.S. as an industrial power," charged Charles Sporck, president of the National Semiconductor Corporation.[23] And on the Japanese side: "DON'T SURRENDER TO UNDUE U.S. DEMANDS" and "DON'T SACRIFICE JAPANESE FARMERS" read banners among those carried by ten thousand protesters when they demonstrated in front of the U.S. embassy in Tokyo in early 1983.[24]

The anti-Japanese rhetoric is just as strong in Western Europe, where the Europeans have taken the unprecedented action of formally charging that under the GATT the entire Japanese economic system is a huge trade barrier. Normally, formal complaints on trade disputes concern specific products and protectionist actions. But frustrated with the Japanese trade success, and unable to pinpoint the specific cause of presumed protectionism, the entire Japanese economic and social system has been charged with being unfair.

The warring rhetoric is nearly as strong between the Europeans and the United States. In response to the attempt by the Reagan administration to curtail trade with the Soviet Union, the European Economic Community responded that such moves were "contrary to international law and comity" and called them "unacceptable in the context of relations with friendly states."[25] Diplomats on both sides of the Atlantic said that they could not recall a time when tougher language had been used in formal Europe-U.S. communications.

The French have accused the United States of "contempt and insensibility" toward its allies over foreign exchange and trade policies.[26] The Germans said that recent American trade policy has "cast a shadow over relations" between Europe and the United States, "damaging confidence as regards future agreements."[27] The European Common Market formally charged the United States with not complying with trade agreements that had been reached at the economic summit meeting at Versailles in 1982, and in a later action threatened to tax imports of American farm products if the United States took action to curb imports of European steel. As the *New York Times* editorialized: "Skirmishes all, but that's how big and bloody wars begin."[28]

Protectionism will not only damage the relationships among the free industrialized countries, but it could well destroy those between these rich developed countries and newly industrialized areas such as Brazil, Mexico, Argentina, South Korea, Singapore, Hong Kong, and Taiwan. During the 1970s, these economies greatly expanded their industrial base, became strong exporters in world markets, and were able to attain high growth rates. These advances were achieved in large part because they were able to borrow extensively, following the normal pattern of a rapidly developing industrialized economy. And herein lies the further threat of protectionism.

The newly industrialized economies, along with the less developed ones, currently are in debt for $730 billion, most of it owed to large international banks in the United States, Japan, and Western Europe. There is no way that this debt can be repaid under protectionism. As suggested by the data in table 19, which lists the countries with the largest external debt, the major source for financing the debt will have to be export earnings.

Brazil, for example, owed a long-term debt of $82.2 billion in 1984. The total reserve holdings of Brazil — which includes the amount of gold and foreign hard currencies (such as dollars, pounds, deutsche marks, Swiss francs, and Japanese yen), along with special drawing rights and reserve positions at the International Monetary Fund — amounted to only $5.3 billion. So if Brazilian authorities took the highly unlikely step of giving up all of the country's financial reserves to pay off part of the national debt, they would still owe $76.9 billion. The only way to pay off more of the debt is to use part of the $8.6 billion Brazil earned during 1984 in net exports (the total value of exports minus the cost of imports). Clearly, Brazil will have to earn a surplus in foreign trade for a number of years to pay off its total debt obligations.

If protectionism occurs and global markets are closed to Brazilian products, the country thus has no choice but to default on its debt. This will not occur suddenly; the decline will be painful and drawn out. The IMF will attempt to impose even tighter conditions for continued loans than are now in place — and the current ones are causing riots in the streets and threatening massive social unrest. The Brazilian economy will slowly deteriorate. Extremist politicians will come to the fore and use the unrest for political gains. Anti-

TABLE 19. DEBT BURDEN OF NEWLY INDUSTRIALIZED AND DEVELOPING ECONOMIES, 1984 (IN THOUSANDS OF DOLLARS)

	Total External Debt[a]	*Total Reserves*[b]	*Net Exports*[c]
Brazil	82,200	5,300	+ 8,600
Mexico	76,000	5,215	+10,800
Argentina	45,000	4,950	+ 3,000
Iraq	40,000	10,000	− 5,000
Indonesia	28,700	5,200	+ 3,000
South Korea	28,000	2,880	− 1,250
India	25,100	8,870	− 3,900
Israel	23,000	4,700	− 5,300

SOURCE: Economics-Policy Research Dept., Bank of America, San Francisco.

[a]Obligations with maturity of one year or more owed to foreign institutions and international agencies.

[b]Includes gold, foreign hard currencies, and IMF drawing rights and reserve positions.

[c]Value of total exports minus value of total imports.

American and anti-European feelings will surface, providing ample opportunity for the communists to attempt to enlarge their foothold in Latin America.

The picture is not pleasant — but there is more. A Brazilian default will generate massive shocks throughout the international financial markets. The Federal Reserve Bank in the United States, in concert with the central banks of Japan and Western European countries, will move quickly to stabilize their nations' commercial banks, which will incur massive losses. But Brazil will not be alone: many other countries will be in the same boat if protectionism takes hold, and will have to default on their debt. The result will be massive bankruptcy of large international banks, and the global economy will be plunged into an economic depression. It will be a repeat of the 1930s all over again. And the stage will have been set for wider military conflict, particularly in the volatile areas of Latin America, Central America, and the Middle East.

Containing the Threat of Protectionism

Obviously, protectionism does not hold out much hope for the future of the global economy and international security, and so the question remains: What can be done to contain this threat? Fortunately, there are six definite actions that can be taken, building upon the general attitude that still exists among world leaders that free trade is far more preferable. But these actions will require that these leaders take a much more aggressive role to implement the conditions that would contain protectionism than they have evidenced so far. They will require a willingness to compromise, to adjust domestic economic policies to support trade, and to challenge proposed legislation aimed at increasing protectionism.

Action one. The Western powers must sign a "Standstill Agreement" to stop any further trade barriers. In taking this action, the leaders of the major industrialized countries would pledge to counter aggressively the proliferation of such trade barriers as domestic-content legislation, export subsidies, and voluntary restrictions. The agreement would freeze the current situation, stopping the growing trend of protectionism, and would allow the normal GATT channels of trade negotiation to deal with the longer-term problems.

To implement the agreement, a monitoring committee would be created under the authority of the GATT. This committee would investigate protests filed by any signatory country that believed that another country had violated the conditions of the trade-barrier freeze. The committee would be given a limited time — say, thirty days — in which to reach a decision, so as to avoid the possibility of months of delaying tactics or bureaucratic haggling. If a country was found in violation, it would be given fifteen days to take corrective action or else would face retaliation from all other countries party to the agreement.[29]

Obviously, such a Standstill Agreement would only be effective if the leaders of the major countries were willing to back it up with decisive actions on their part, for there is no way under the GATT to force countries to comply. But the retaliatory aspects of the proposed agreement go far beyond current GATT rules and introduce a new and powerful element — peer pressure — into trade relationships.

Action two. The major industrialized countries must agree to stimulate the growth of the global economy, for trade is highly responsive to the rate of overall economic growth. Trade does not behave in a nice, normal manner, increasing gradually and in direct proportion when the global economy is expanding and declining in a like manner when the global economy is in recession. Rather, trade grows at a rate about three times faster than that of overall growth when the global economy is expanding at a real rate of 1.5 percent or more, and declines at a rate three times faster than that of world economic growth when the global economy grows at a rate of less than 1.5 percent. This rather peculiar behavior means that when the global economy is stagnant, as it was during the period 1980 through 1983, there is very little growth in trade. And when the economy is expanding, trade growth booms.

It is not surprising that protectionist measures surfaced so dramatically during the stagnant years of global growth. Coming at a time when all of the industrialized countries were faced with rising structural unemployment and declining smokestack industries, the loss of trade markets greatly exacerbated problems. The global recession simply threw more automobile- and steelworkers out of work, and the response in the United States was to blame Japanese automobile imports, place limits on European steel imports, and consider adopting domestic-content legislation.

As former U.S. special trade representative Robert Strauss noted, to "men wearing work shirts and drinking beer in a neighborhood bar in Gary, Indiana, . . . it's lost jobs, misery and suffering caused by imports."[30] The most effective way to counter such misery is to have a strong, growing world economy. This will not necessarily put the men in the Gary bar back to work in the steel mills, but it might open up new jobs in other industries. While the relocation of the displaced steelworker to new work is far from easy and typically is accompanied by tremendous social and personal costs, it is a relocation that is far more readily accomplished in a growing economy than in one that is stagnating.

Action three. The United States must adopt policies that would keep the value of the dollar in line with other major currencies, reflecting its normal worth — a value determined by such basic economic factors as inflation and economic growth of the United States economy vis-à-vis those in Japan and Europe. Our basic unit of currency would not be artificially overvalued through extreme and unbalanced economic policies, pricing American products out of world markets, as has been the case in recent years under Reaganomics.

Action four. World leaders must be willing to curtail their current practice of negotiating bilateral trade agreements that fail to involve all affected countries. The major countries frequently negotiate two-party agreements between themselves, then present them for GATT review as fait accompli. GATT rulings often are ignored. Certain problem areas are ruled to be outside GATT purview, such as agriculture trade and the rapidly growing trade in services. While the GATT still serves a significant role in maintaining order in world trade markets, its power and influence is being eroded by the independent actions of the United States, Japan, Canada, and Europe.

If this piecemeal approach to dealing with trade problems continues, we will gradually extend cartel-like constraints into most major trade markets. Today, the affected markets are textiles, automobiles, steel, shipbuilding, and some electronic appliances. The Europeans are suggesting that food cartels be formed to solve the friction between the United States and the European Common Market over agriculture subsidies. And tomorrow the markets could easily include computers and other high-technology products, along with banking and financial services.

Given the current trend, it is easy to project a global economy in which every major market is subject to cartel-like trade barriers, such that free trade ceases to exist. Unfortunately, the ability of any country to develop new products and expand its export markets will be determined by politically negotiated market shares rather than innovation and economic resourcefulness.

Action five. The growing trade in services must be brought into the framework of the GATT and rules must be established to regulate trade in this burgeoning market. Trade in such services as banking, insurance, accounting, consulting, advertising, transportation, communications, education, motion pictures, and legal and health services is growing far more rapidly than is trade in manufactured and agriculture products. And with recent advances in computers and telecommunications, service trade is likely to grow even more rapidly in the future.

Services are rapidly becoming the dominant growth industry in nearly every advanced country. Seven out of ten jobs in the United States are now in a service industry, and the output of services accounts for two-thirds of our entire gross national product. In Japan and Europe nearly one-half of the jobs are in services, and advanced developing countries such as South Korea, Singapore, Taiwan, and Brazil are quickly approaching this level. Much of this output is being exported, with an estimated 20 percent to 30 percent of total global trade now in services. Yet in spite of the clear importance of service output and trade to the future of the Western nations, the service industries have remained outside the scope of the GATT. As a result, numerous barriers to service trade have been erected — an estimated one thousand have been identified by the Office of the United States Trade Representative. It is imperative that these barriers be rolled back and that appropriate rules be established for service trade, as have been put into place under the GATT for merchandise trade.

Action six. The current practice of negotiating marketing agreements and voluntary trade restraints must be recognized for what it is: industrial policy. These agreements are not being made to limit trade or to saddle world markets with constraints that would lead to economic stagnation. They are being made to preserve jobs.

Most of the politicians who are pushing for these measures would be appalled at being labeled protectionist. They would undoubtedly speak quite openly in support of the general principles of free trade under normal circumstances. But they would argue that we don't have normal circumstances today, and that therefore actions must be taken to ease the adjustment of declining smokestack industries and to protect the development of infant industries in high-technology, upon which future job security and economic growth depend. Yet protectionism is a poor substitute for an effective industrial policy. In international trade, it is very difficult to go back. Once protectionism gains a foothold, it moves ahead with alarming speed. It would be far wiser to address the jobs question in the context of an appropriate industrial policy.

The Issue of Industrial Policy

*I*NDUSTRIAL POLICY has received more attention and has been debated more extensively than any other issue of economic policy
in the United States, yet it remains the least understood. Discussions
were escalated over four years ago when President Jimmy Carter
called for a new partnership "to foster cooperation between government and the private sector in dealing with the complex issues
of industrial policy."[1] Since then, attempts to explain industrial policy and suggestions on how the federal government could better
guide the development of American industry have been profuse.

In spite of the increased attention, confusion still reigns. The
average well-informed American does not know what to believe.
On the one hand, he or she is being told by such eminent business
leaders as Reginald H. Jones, retired chairman of the General Elec-
tric Corporation, Felix Rohatyn, well-known Wall Street investment
banker, and Irving Shapiro, former head of the du Pont Corporation, that in the United States, as Jones put it, "we face now the
need for a new industrial policy."[2]

These business leaders are joined by a few leading academics, as
well as labor leaders in the AFL-CIO. Many of the major Democratic politicians have endorsed some version of an industrial policy.
The Senate Democrats have united in favor of an industrial plan
that calls for a council on economic competitiveness and cooperation, federal funding for state and regional economic-development
banks, and special training and benefits for workers who are displaced because of foreign-trade competition.

On the other hand, most business leaders and professional economists are cool to the idea of an industrial policy for the United States. Characteristic of their concern is the position of Charles L. Schultze of the Brookings Institution in Washington, D.C. The former chairman of President Carter's Council of Economic Advisors and longtime liberal economic advisor to numerous Democratic politicians states that "one does not have to be a cynic to forecast that the surest way to multiply unwarranted subsidies and protectionist measures is to legitimize their existence under the rubric of industrial policy."[3]

All of the leading Republican politicians share this view, beginning with President Ronald Reagan. "Government's legitimate role is not to dictate detailed plans or solutions to problems for particular companies or industries," President Reagan has argued. "No, the government serves us best by protecting and maintaining the marketplace, by insuring that the rules of free and fair trade, both at home and abroad, are properly observed."[4]

There is no similar ambivalence abroad. All of the major developed countries have practiced industrial policy in some form for a number of years. The Japanese have relied for several decades upon consensus management, a strong role by MITI, and support of industrial development. West German industrial policy dates back to the early postwar years of Ludwig Erhard, while modern French industrial policy was first implemented by the brilliant visionary Jean Monet in 1946. The British began nationalizing and subsidizing industry at the end of the Second World War, and even with the recent denationalizations — or privatization, as the Thatcher government prefers to call the sale of national industries to private interests — the government still retains a strong role in influencing the development of British industry.

Indeed, as the advocates of a more aggressive policy for American industry point out, every major country has a significant industrial policy, including the United States. During 1984, for instance, an estimated $93 billion was spent by the U.S. government in supporting nondefense industry through such programs as subsidies, loans and loan guarantees, and special tax breaks.[5]

But nearly all of our government's industrial support goes to agriculture, takes the form of general tax incentives for business investment, or exists as ad hoc bailouts for such well-known companies as the Chrysler Corporation and Continental Illinois National Bank. It does not emulate the coherent and planned efforts of our major trading competitors. Nor does it offer the necessary incentives to develop new high-technology industries and provide for the stable adjustment of our older smokestack industries.

Even our most successful example of industrial policy, that of agriculture, is not faring so well under present conditions of increased global competition and growing economic interdependence. Government support of the agriculture industry goes back some 120 years to the Morrill Act of 1862, under which the federal government donated public lands to the states and territories to establish colleges for the study of agriculture. Since then, there have been numerous government programs designed to advance agricultural technology, to control farm production, and to subsidize farmers' income. Twelve regional farm-loan banks were set up in 1916 to lend money at highly favorable rates to cooperative farm-loan associations. Elaborate demonstration education for farmers (1914), grants for vocational education in agriculture (1917), cash subsidies to farmers who reduced crop production (1933), and payment-in-kind support (1983) are only a few of the many government programs instituted over the years to aid the agriculture industry. During 1985, the federal government will spend $14 billion on various support programs for agriculture and will provide another $13 billion in subsidized loans.

American technology joined the federal government in advancing the agriculture industry, providing the farmer with the most modern machinery for production and with computers for planning and control. Today, no farmer anywhere else in the world can match the productivity of those in the United States. But has this highly successful example of an industrial policy made the life of the farmer more secure and affluent?

No. And why not? Because the farmer suffers from an industrial policy that is uncoordinated and out-of-date with current economic realities of global interdependence. Although our proficient agriculture schools, sophisticated farm equipment, advanced chemical and computer industries, and certain progressive federal government programs have combined to make the American farmer highly productive and extremely efficient, other government agencies are busy trying to limit production in order to keep prices of farm products artificially high. Many farmers are losing their land because of the high interest rates caused by massive budget deficits. And still other farmers are finding their export markets abroad diminished by the overvalued dollar, by the inability of the American government to reach agreement with the Europeans on agriculture subsidies that are undercutting American producers, and by the Japanese government, which protects its domestic market from foreign competition. Never before has the American farmer been so dependent upon foreign markets — in 1984, agriculture products valued at $36 billion were our most important exports — and never before has the American farmer faced such intense competition from foreign producers.

What is true in agriculture is even more so in industries that have received far less federal support in the form of favorable U.S. industrial policies. The mature heavy-manufacturing industries of automobiles and steel confront intense global competition and are being forced to modernize quickly and reduce their labor forces. Yet, despite the emergency ad hoc bailout of the Chrysler Corporation, they are suffering from the lack of a positive industrial policy, for — as the outspoken president of Chrysler, Lee Iacocca, has pointed out on many occasions — the overvalued dollar has made it nearly impossible to sell American automobiles abroad and thus take market share away from foreign imports.

Smokestack-industry executives are not the only ones who complain about our nation's ad hoc industrial policies. The leaders of the aggressive computer industry in California's Silicon Valley argue that they are losing to the Japanese manufacturers, who receive far more favorable access to bank financing and support from their government. And thousands of new entrepreneurs complain that our current tax laws highly favor the larger and established industries while offering precious few incentives to the young and growing firm.

It is one thing to recognize that there is need for a more coordinated industrial policy in the United States and quite another to develop one that makes sense. The issue is far more complex than simply creating a new national development bank, as is being advocated by Felix Rohatyn, or setting up a new Department of International Trade and Industry, as proposed by the Reagan administration and other political leaders.

Establishing a better industrial policy requires answers to three major questions: (1) What are the goals of an industrial policy? (2) What policies should be adopted? and (3) How should an industrial policy be implemented? In answering these questions, we can learn a lot from the Japanese and the Europeans, who have far more experience in industrial policy than does the United States.

The Goals of Industrial Policy

Industrial policy is one side of the economic triangle, and most professional economists are beginning to recognize it as an essential complement to the other two sides — fiscal policy (taxes and government spending) and monetary policy (interest rates, quantity of money in the economy, and credit demand). But in assuming such a major economic role for industrial policy, one must define it very broadly: Industrial policy involves an attempt by government — working with industry, unions, and academic research centers — to (1) coordinate its many programs and policies in order to provide an environment more conducive to economic growth; (2) strengthen industry for the future; and (3) ensure that domestic manufacturers and service industries can compete effectively with those in other countries.

More-specific goals of industrial policy are not easy to define, however, for industrial policy lacks the clear purpose and intent of fiscal policy and monetary policy. Every voter understands what Congress means when taxes are lowered in order to increase aggregate demand in the economy: that our after-tax paycheck is larger and so we can spend and save more. And we have a fairly good comprehension of what the Federal Reserve Bank means when it announces a tightening of the money supply: that interest rates will be higher and so we will pay more for a home mortgage or an automobile loan. But what are the purposes and intent of industrial policy? And what happens when some of the goals seem to be in conflict with one another?

As Hiroya Ueno, one of Japan's leading experts on industrial policy, states: "Unlike traditional fiscal and monetary policies, industrial policy demonstrates no clear relationship between its objectives and the means of attaining them. Its conception, content, and forms differ, reflecting the stage of development of an economy, its natural and historical circumstances, international conditions, and its political and economic situation, resulting in considerable differences from nation to nation and from era to era."[6]

Indeed, another Japanese expert has suggested the following goals for industrial policy — a list that would find few dissenters among American and European experts:

- Promoting the nation's economic development and growth
- Accelerating the structural transformation of domestic industry in a desired direction

- Improving the international competitiveness of designated products
- Encouraging the development of new technologies
- Smoothing the phasing-out of chronically depressed industries
- Assisting the rationalization and reorganization of a weakened industry that is judged to have a chance for recovery
- Protecting domestic employment
- Programming regional development[7]

The problem with these goals is that emphasizing one frequently means sabotaging another. For instance, a common practice in "protecting domestic employment" is to adopt trade restrictions, which results in the type of protectionism discussed in the previous chapter; but protectionism has a decidedly negative impact on the goal of "promoting the nation's economic development and growth," and generally is not conducive to "improving the international competitiveness of designated products." Similarly, many proposals for "programming regional development," including numerous bills introduced in Congress, would make it very difficult and expensive for companies to close down their aging and obsolete facilities; such programs therefore impede attempts at "accelerating the structural transformation of domestic industry in a desired direction" of greater efficiency and competitiveness.

Such conflicts create enormous confusion over industrial policy in the United States. As a result — and rather surprisingly — conservative Republican business leaders as well as liberal labor officials turn up as supporters of a strong industrial policy; and those who oppose emphasizing industrial policy hold equally diverse political views. Unfortunately, such conflicts among different goals are nearly impossible to resolve, which means that the role of industrial policy must be broader and more general than simply stressing one or more of the specific goals listed above. But what is the appropriate role of industrial policy in the economy? What role gives it equal status with fiscal and monetary policies as the third side of the economic triangle?

The answer lies in the arena of international trade economics, which involves the matter of what gives one country a production and trading advantage over another. It has long been known that countries specialize in producing those products in which they have a comparative economic advantage. Such an advantage may be the existence of raw materials — an advantage that the United States enjoyed for many years in iron ore, oil, and timber, for instance.

Or it may be a highly trained labor force — as in Japan and West Germany — or a low-wage labor force, as in Taiwan. A comparative advantage may be the result of geography, such as Singapore's location at the center of trading and financial routes in southeast Asia. Or, frequently, a country can gain a comparative advantage through high levels of technology.

Whatever the source of the comparative advantage, it used to be that a country could maintain that advantage for a number of years. Raw materials did not suddenly disappear. Labor costs did not escalate overnight relative to those of other countries. Technological leads were not quickly overcome. But with the growing interdependence of the global economy, these traditional sources of comparative advantage have lost much of their significance.

Low-cost and rapid transportation, along with sophisticated communications and computer systems, have made it possible for American manufacturers to locate production facilities as far away as Hong Kong and Taiwan and operate them as effectively as if they were next door to the corporate headquarters in Chicago. Producers in a competing country no longer have to invest for years in order to develop their own technology; they can simply buy the latest technological advances from the most sophisticated producer in the world or enter into a joint venture with that producer. The opportunity to maintain a comparative advantage over competitors from abroad thus has diminished greatly in recent years.

This does not mean that the economic principle of comparative advantage is no longer relevant, for the trade statistics tell us otherwise. If the Japanese don't have a comparative advantage in certain products, why are they enjoying a $30-billion trade surplus with the United States? Why do 18 million Taiwanese export about four times as much as 75 million Mexicans, even though Mexico is located next door to the world's largest market and Taiwan is six thousand miles away?

What has happened is that comparative economic advantage has taken on a new meaning. This newer concept replaces the traditional criteria "with such elements as human creative power, foresight, a highly educated work force, organizational talent, the ability to choose, and the ability to adapt. Moreover, these attributes are not conceived of as natural endowments but as qualities achieved through public policies such as education, organized research, and investment in social overhead capital."[8]

Rather than enjoying a comparative advantage because of a plentiful supply of natural resources or a low-cost labor force, individual countries must develop new comparative advantages. These new advantages will be in a growth environment that encourages continuous technological development, entrepreneurship, and flexibility. Priority will be given to investment. Tax and expenditure policies will encourage savings, and result in low interest rates. Business executives will take a long-run view in regard to profits and return on investments, and they will emphasize quality and service. Government policies will be more closely coordinated to build for the future, with adequate public investments in education and in research and development.

Nor will any particular country necessarily enjoy a natural endowment in these conditions, for the new comparative advantages are critically dependent upon policy actions. They do not occur automatically. Rather, they are carefully built in to the economy and nurtured. Planning will be required — a fact obviously being recognized by American business, as evidenced by its growing concern with strategic analysis and planning. Greater cooperation between government, labor, and business is essential, a condition well understood in Japan and West Germany.

All of this sounds very much like supply-side economics, and appropriately so. The characteristic that most distinguishes industrial policy from fiscal and monetary policies is the long-term supply-side orientation of the former, while the latter concentrate on stabilizing the economy in the short run. This third leg of the economic triangle provides the growth emphasis that has long been missing from more traditional economic policies. But it is a supply-side perspective that is quite broad and oriented toward creating what is frequently called "a dynamic comparative advantage," meaning the adoption of policies that provide an overall economic environment more conducive to economic growth and that ensure that the major industries upon which the economic strength of the country is built are strong and compete effectively in the world economy — our original definition of industrial policy.

The danger is that the politicians will take a much more narrow view of industrial policy, attempting to identify one or two specific objectives, such as primarily preserving jobs in declining smokestack industries or simply encouraging the development of high-technology industries. Such a narrow view will do no more than set one interest group against another and quickly take on geographic-political overtones — the "rust belt" versus the "sun belt." This in turn undoubtedly will lead to dire results: protectionism, centralized government control, and the political logrolling that so many critics fear.

The Policy Choices

The choice of an industrial policy, whether in Europe, Japan, or the United States, is not so much a question of ideology — that is, of whether it is appropriate for government to be involved in influencing the future development of industry or not — as it is a question of pragmatic policy implementation: To what degree does a country desire to influence the investment and development behavior of specific industries as opposed to providing general support to all industries? And here the range of policy choices is broad, ranging from those that are the most neutral in their impact on specific industrial behavior to those that are highly targeted.

The numerous policies that are available for assisting industry can be conveniently grouped into the ten areas described below. The first three fall under the larger category of "General Industrial Policies" — those that impact industry in general and come closest to achieving the dynamic comparative advantage discussed above. The next three are grouped in this chapter under the heading "Moderately Selective Industrial Policies" — those that are essential in an effective industrial policy but that require the setting of some broad priorities. And the remaining four are called "Targeted Industrial Policies" — those that are highly selective in terms of the industries that would be supported or ignored, which are also those that can create serious problems in the economy.

General Industrial Policies

1. Macroeconomic policies. The most general of the economic policies that impact industrial development are the standard fiscal and monetary policies that are adopted by all governments. These involve the level and type of taxes that are imposed, the nature of government spending, and the amount of money that is created. For instance, a country can choose to rely upon consumption taxes rather than income taxes, to balance the budget, and to adopt a relatively loose monetary policy. Such a policy choice would be very conducive to industrial development, for the taxes on business would be minimal, higher-income individuals would be taxed less and consequently would save more, and interest rates would be low.

Alternatively, a country could choose to adopt highly progressive income taxes on both individuals and corporations, and to operate with large budget deficits and a tight monetary policy. In this case, the policy would discourage industrial development, for savings would be lower and interest rates higher. The important point is that even the most general economic policies are not neutral in their impact on industrial development.

2. *Tax incentives.* The second-most-general set of industrial policies, which comprises those that are strongly preferred in the United States, uses tax incentives to encourage business investment. While the United States has forty-seven different tax-incentive programs, nearly all of the tax benefits are concentrated in three major areas: (1) the Accelerated Cost Recovery System, (2) the Preferential Treatment of Capital Gains, and (3) the Investment Tax Credit.

ACR
ITC

Under the Accelerated Cost Recovery System, businesses are allowed to depreciate most of their capital investments over a period that ranges from three to fifteen years. These "tax-defined useful lifes" are intentionally designed to be much shorter than the actual useful life of the asset. This encourages firms to reinvest in new plant and equipment in order to maintain their tax deductions, and thus helps to keep plants modernized and productivity high.

The Preferential Treatment of Capital Gains permits the gains earned on an investment to be taxed at one-half or less the normal rate. The Investment Tax Credit allows companies to deduct 10 percent of the purchase price of machines and equipment (but not buildings) from their tax obligations, and is actually a federal government discount on the price of capital investment. Other tax-incentive programs allow firms to deduct the entire cost of certain investments in research and development in the year in which the investment is made rather than spreading the tax write-offs over the actual life of the investment.

While many other smaller tax programs provide benefits to specific industries, the dominant approach in the United States is to provide industrial assistance through general tax incentives that are available to all firms, consequently avoiding the difficult problem of targeting assistance to particular industries.

3. *Public investments.* Government investments in such areas as education, basic research and technological development, and trans-

portation and communications systems are the third of the most general industrial policies. And these policies have been used extensively in all industrialized countries for many years.

The value of such investments as a source of economic growth has been well documented. It is estimated that investments in education and advances of knowledge, for instance, accounted for nearly one-half of the growth of the American economy in recent years, 40 percent of the growth of the European economy, and 26 percent of the growth of the Japanese economy.[9] In spite of this past success, a major issue has surfaced in the current debate over industrial policy: Should governments target public investments, and particularly research-and-development efforts, into specific areas of expected future industrial growth?

In the United States, the response to targeted support has been mixed. The development of a more efficient and productive agriculture industry has long been supported by massive research-and-development subsidies from government, in large part explaining why the American farmer is the most efficient producer in the world. But outside agriculture, government assistance has tended to be a spin-off from military and space development. Yet it is questionable whether such spin-offs are an effective means of supporting industrial research and development, for the highly specialized requirements for modern defense and space programs have limited applications in consumer markets.

Other industrialized countries are targeting their research-and-development efforts to a much greater extent. The French are attempting to do this through the nationalization of key industries that offer the potential for future growth or that require modernization in order to remain competitive. The Germans recently announced a $1.2-billion program (DM 3 billion) to develop their microelectronics, computer, and communications technologies. And the Japanese have launched a joint effort by government and private industry to develop a "Fifth Generation Computer System."

Moderately Selective Industrial Policies

4. Regional development assistance. In recent years, all of the industrialized countries have adopted numerous programs to assist regional areas that have large concentrations of such basic industries as mining, steel production, and automobile manufacturing. These large and mature manufacturing industries face declining world markets, intense competition from abroad, and, in many cases, high labor costs.

The impact of these industries on the local community is immense. The basic industries are so large that they dominate the local economy. When the automobile industry lays off workers, thousands of others also lose their jobs. Small suppliers are forced to cut back, restaurants and bars close, and the local retail stores lose many of their customers. The housing market becomes depressed as unemployed workers attempt to sell their homes and move to other parts of the country. Government loses substantial tax revenue and must reduce critical public services, adding to the general economic and social decline of the community.

This is undoubtedly the most difficult of the industrial problems, for the issues go far beyond those of economics. It is essentially a problem of what to do with workers who have spent many years in the high-paying steel or automobile industry and are suddenly terminated with no prospect of reemployment in that industry. Since they typically have no experience outside of heavy manufacturing, are in most cases strongly committed to remaining in a community where their family has lived for several generations, and are usually accustomed to wages that are significantly higher than those in service jobs, which offer the most likely opportunity for employment, such workers are extremely difficult to relocate.

Industrial policies generally provide income support in the form of unemployment compensation and family grants. Retraining assistance and relocation aid are given to the displaced workers. The impacted industries frequently receive loans and grants to help them scale back to a smaller and more efficient size, although such assistance is far more prevalent in European countries than in the United States or Japan. And subsidies and other government inducements are given to potential employers who agree to locate in the impacted area.

5. *Export promotion.* With the increasing importance of exports to the economic security and growth of the industrialized economies, more countries are incorporating export-promotion programs in their overall industrial policy. Almost daily, any reader of a major American newspaper or magazine can open the pages and find a flashy special section extolling the virtues of the products from a particular country: buy German products because of their superior technology and quality, or buy Italian goods for high-fashion design. Most countries, including the United States, send delegations of business lead-

ers and politicians to foreign countries in order to push local products. A delegation of California bankers, farmers, and industrialists headed by the governor of the state has become a common sight in most foreign capitals in recent years. And large delegations of export-minded Japanese have become so frequent that some pundits call them the kamikaze advance teams for the trading companies.

These are the more visible of the typical export-promotion policies, but most countries have far more substantial programs. They range from loan guarantees for banks that finance exports to tax reductions for corporate earnings from exports. Government agencies will provide direct loans to foreign companies who purchase domestic products, or will insure domestic producers against loss in export trade. Trading companies have long been a major force in the expansion of Japanese markets, and the United States recently passed legislation encouraging American banks to establish similar trading companies to expand the markets for our products.

All of these various promotional efforts and government policies attempt to build an export-oriented attitude among domestic producers — a task that is far easier in Japan and Western Europe than in the United States. But Americans are rapidly learning that exports can no longer be treated with benign neglect, and promotional policies are expanding.

6. Risk sharing. A major reason why politicians are becoming so infatuated with industrial policy is their belief that private business cannot, or will not, undertake the risk investments that are necessary to build a stronger industrial base: private industry supposedly lacks the resources, banks are unwilling to provide the capital, or the investments are simply too risky. Government therefore must take a stronger role in industrial development in the form of risk sharing.

Sharing the risk is the idea behind the numerous proposals to resurrect the old Reconstruction Finance Corporation in the United States. Originally established in 1932 to lend funds to failing banks and railroads, the RFC later broadened its mandate to lending to other businesses before it was liquidated in 1953. A new bank has been advocated by investment banker Felix Rohatyn and several bills for its creation have been introduced in Congress. To be started with something like $5 billion in capital stock provided by the government, and authorized to lend up to $50 billion, the government investment bank would provide low-cost loans to firms that did not have access to financing in the private markets if they met other criteria.

The bank would be aggressive in influencing the course of industrial development, for as Rohatyn has stated, the loans would be used "as a tool or a weapon . . . to leverage concessions from unions, suppliers, banks, management, legislatures."[10] Whether the problem was high wages, old-fashioned management practices, or the unwillingness of legislatures to provide sufficient investments for public infrastructures, "loans would be given and withheld to induce changes in business behavior."[11]

There are, however, other ways to bring about the sharing of risk besides creating a new government investment bank. Subsidized interest rates and government-operated insurance programs are standard and well-proven means of joint risk sharing. The highly successful Federal Housing Administration (FHA) was created in 1934 to insure housing mortgages made by commercial banks and savings-and-loan institutions. A guaranteed-loan program for students was established in 1972 to provide funds for education. And the federal government guaranteed private bank loans to the Chrysler Corporation in late 1979, on the condition that sacrifices would be made by the workers, dealers, and creditors, in order to enable the company to regain its economic strength.

A great advantage of loan-guarantee programs, as compared to a government bank, is their smaller impact on the federal budget. Loan guarantees do not require government funds unless the private loans wind up in default, while the public bank would require substantial amounts of government capital. But more important, a general loan-guarantee program such as that of the FHA wisely leaves the difficult problem of selecting and servicing qualified borrowers to experienced private institutions; a public bank would become involved in selecting the winners and losers among individual companies — a task at which government bureaucrats have proven to be notoriously inept.

Targeted Industrial Policies

The major policies available to government for targeting industrial-development programs are *(7) trade protectionism, (8) government contracts and procurement, (9) industrial restructuring,* and *(10) nationalization.* In all four of these areas, government officials must select the industries and individual companies that are to receive the assistance, and thus these represent the most narrow of the industrial policies that are available.

As noted earlier, *trade protectionism* can take the form of tariffs and duties imposed on individual products; however, this traditional form of protectionism is being reduced under international agreement. The newer type of protectionism involves the formation of trade cartels that impose ceilings on the allowable imports of specific goods — such as Japanese automobiles into the United States — with government officials making the decision as to what specific product or industry is to receive such preferential treatment.

Even greater targeted control is exercised by using *government contracts and procurement* to assist industry. The government contract can specify the price, quality, and quantity of the specific product that is to be purchased. Government purchases can guarantee a market to a new or struggling firm and thus protect the company during a critical period of transition. And the price the government pays can be calculated so as to offset expensive yet crucial research-and-development costs.

The use of government procurement to assist industries has long been practiced by all of the major industrialized countries, including the United States. The American computer industry is deeply indebted to the federal government, which provided a guaranteed market for its early products. During 1954, the government purchased all of the computers made in the United States, and during the crucial development years of the mid-1950s and the 1960s, the government bought over 40 percent of all computers. The Japanese government long restricted its procurement of communications equipment to Japanese firms, while the French government will generally only purchase from domestic producers.

9. Industrial restructuring. A targeted form of industrial policy that is rarely practiced in the United States — but one that has been used to a great extent in Japan and Europe — is the restructuring of a specific industry. Generally, such restructuring involves combining several smaller companies into a larger firm: government officials select companies that they believe could be more competitive in international markets and either force or induce them to merge. The restructuring may link one firm that is strong in research and development with another that has a well-established marketing base. The ultimate in restructuring is when an industry is nationalized — the last and most aggressive of the industrial policies.

10. Nationalization. Nationalization occurs when government takes over the ownership and management of an individual company (or an entire industry). The assets of a privately owned company are appropriated by the government and private managers are replaced with public officials. (Frequently, the private managers simply change hats and join the public service.)

Nationalizations are undertaken for many different reasons, ranging from quite political considerations, as in the case of British Rolls-Royce — its bankruptcy would have done "irreparable harm to British prestige"[12] — to purely economic reasons, as in the case of most of the recent French nationalizations. There is no general consensus on when nationalization is an appropriate tool of industrial policy, and the practice in individual countries is more a matter of historical and political precedence than of proven policy. Nor is there any agreement on whether nationalizations have been beneficial or harmful. This last of the targeted industrial policies remains an enigma, albeit one that often elicits powerful emotional responses that stem from deeply held political views.

Industrial Policy in the United States

It is clear that the range of choices the United States, or any country, has in developing an industrial policy are numerous. And it is obvious that every developed country, including the United States, currently has an industrial policy. The issue is not one of accepting the concept of an industrial policy or not; we already have such a policy. In assessing our nation's current industrial policy, and in searching for a more effective policy for the future, we must accept several facts:

• First, there is no miracle solution that can be imported from abroad. MITI cannot be transplanted into the American social and economic culture. Nor is the United States going to change its economic structure to resemble that of West Germany, with its large concentration of power in the hands of a few banks and industries. We must build our own industrial policy, although there are important lessons to be learned from abroad.

• Second, the American political system is incapable of advance selective targeting in its industrial policy. To propose that individual winners and losers be selected in advance is utopian fantasy. Other than in ad hoc and crisis circumstances, such as with the Chrysler and Lockheed loans, Congress cannot favor one company over another. As Charles Schultz of the Brookings Institution has succinctly noted, "the one thing that most democratic political systems — and especially the American one — cannot do well at all is to make critical choices among particular firms, municipalities, or regions, determining cold-bloodedly which shall prosper and which shall not."[13] To implement an industrial policy that requires targeting is to invite political logrolling.

• Third, it is impossible to forecast future growth industries. The perceived success of the Japanese and Europeans in doing so is a misunderstanding of economic history. These countries simply followed the technological lead of the United States during the postwar growth era. And now that economic, and to a large extent, technological parity has been achieved, all of the industrialized countries face the same question: How do we ensure that our economy appropriately invests for the future strength of its industrial base?

• Fourth, an appropriate industrial policy for any country, and especially for the United States, must initially identify the inherent and traditional strengths in the economy, then select from among the ten areas of industrial policy those that build upon these strengths.

Once these four basic facts have been accepted, we can begin to develop a more rational and effective industrial policy. Our first task is to identify the traditional strengths and weaknesses of our economy, since they will influence our choice of an industrial policy.

The greatest source of strength in the past has been our willingness to invest in education and research and development. Nearly one-half of our past economic growth has come from these two sources. It was some twenty years ago that Edward F. Denison, who was quickly to become the nation's leading expert on sources of growth in the U.S. economy, first pointed out that "the education that the United States labor force has received has increased at a rate that can only be described as phenomenal." And with such enormous advances, Denison stated in his path-breaking study, "it is not surprising to find that improved education has made a major contribution to economic growth. By my calculations, from 1929 to 1957 it raised the average quality of labor by 29.6 percent" and accounted for a phenomenal 23 percent of the growth rate of the economy.[14] In numerous studies made since that time, Denison and other researchers have found that education continues to be a major source of growth.

This is hardly surprising, for education not only upgrades the skills of the American labor force but gives the worker far greater versatility. An educated worker, as opposed to an uneducated one, is far easier to shift from one occupation to another, in large part because he or she has a much greater awareness of job opportunities and can be more easily retrained. Also, a more educated labor force is better able to learn about and use the most efficient production practices. All of these attributes become even more important to our country's economic future when we confront the problems of significant changes in our industrial structure, the shifting of job opportunities from the Middle West to the South and the West, and the rapidly increasing importance of computers and information processing throughout our entire economy.

Advances in knowledge — meaning improvements in technology itself, better understanding of how to organize and manage more effectively, and progress in developing new products and services — is the single most important source of growth in the American economy. According to Denison, it "is the biggest and most basic reason for the persistent long-term growth of output per unit of input."[15] It is technology that has made our agriculture industry the most productive in the world, that enabled us to place a man on the moon, and that has given our computer industry such a dominant position in world markets. These accomplishments have not come easily. They have required massive amounts of research-and-development expenditures, along with substantial investments in education.

Unfortunately, we have witnessed a significant decline in both the quantity and quality of education and of research and development in recent years. The reasons for such a decline are manifold: President Nixon began to slash general government support for these public investments in 1969 and President Reagan continued the trend through his first term in office; there has been a taxpayer backlash against property-tax increases, the major source of funding for education; large budget deficits and high interest rates are not conducive to private research and development; investments in military and space research have limited applications in the private markets, yet these represent our major source of federal funding for basic research activities today.

Our second-greatest strength is our inherent entrepreneurial spirit — a spirit that does not conform to centralized planning but draws its strength from a basically free and dynamic economic system. This spirit has spawned numerous technological breakthroughs in the past, and it underlies the energetic high-tech environment of Silicon Valley, as well as the resurgence of the American automobile industry. But America's entrepreneurial spirit is one that responds to economic incentives, not to government directives.

It is interesting to note the recent deluge of foreign visitors to the United States (and particularly to California) who want to learn more about how we spawn venture capitalism, promote entrepreneurs, and stimulate the development of new technology. These visitors range from President Mitterrand of France to groups of Japanese business executives — and they all ask one major question: How can we duplicate in our own country the entrepreneurial spirit that seems to pervade much of American industry?

Our greatest weakness in the United States is our ineptitude at consensus forming, even though there has been a surge of interest here in various means of forming a better consensus regarding industrial development. Much of this new interest is based upon a vague feeling that if we could only get government, management, and labor to better communicate, if not cooperate, then an effective industrial policy could be implemented. Labor would be willing to accept lower wage settlements for the broader economic good. Management would take a longer-term and more socially concerned position in regard to investments and other activities. Government would be able to provide better information and intelligence about the potential growth areas of the future.

Numerous suggestions have been made on how such consensus forming would be accomplished. At a minimum, a high-level council would be established to provide advice to government officials on industrial-development matters. Or, alternatively, a new government agency or a cabinet-level Department of International Trade and Industry would be created. The model for such proposals is MITI, the famous Ministry of International Trade and Industry of Japan, but advocates of a new agency are also quick to point out the merits of the Ministry for Industrial and Scientific Development in France, along with the National Economic Development Council of Britain.

Yet, in typical American fashion, there is a certain degree of naivety with regard to the role and effectiveness of these various institutions in forming a consensus on industrial policy. It is almost as if the backers believe that the creation of a new council or government department will solve the problem effortlessly: with the transfer of various current programs to the new department, the selection of a senior council of advisors from labor, business, and academia, and the appointment of a highly visible captain of industry as the new head of the department, the issue of an American industrial policy would be miraculously resolved.

Consensus forming clearly is an important and integral part of any effective industrial policy. Without basic agreement between government officials and business and labor leaders on the overall course of such a policy, there is no possibility of success. But, unfortunately, consensus forming is a far more complex task than simply forming a new government agency. What makes consensus forming successful in Japan and some of the European countries is that industrial policy is based upon a recognition of the indigenous factors within the country that enable a consensus to be reached.

The success of MITI in Japan, for instance, is largely due to an underlying relationship of trust between government, labor, and industry. This trust is built upon the mutual understanding that exists between the various groups, the continuous contact maintained by their representatives, and a strong national desire in Japan to maintain harmony.

The French are able to build a consensus on industrial policy because of their strongly centralized political and economic structure, and the existence of a managerial elite that moves readily between high-level positions in government and industry. These graduates of the Ecole Nationale d'Administration and the Ecole Polytechnique provide France with a cadre of top managers, which makes the problems of achieving and implementing a consensus a far easier task than in the United States, where public officials and corporate managers tend to view each other as adversaries.

The Germans achieve consensus through their great concentration of economic power among a small number of banks and major industries. German banks own sizable shares of German industry, and the boards of directors of the banks and large companies are tightly interlocked. Such a combination of economic concentration and interlocking directorships provides a ready framework for consensus formation on broad issues of industrial policy.

The task we face in the United States is how to implement a more effective industrial policy than we now have, building upon our inherent strengths and taking into account our weaknesses. Given our difficulty in forming a consensus along the lines of Japan, and the political reality of being unable to target winners and losers among individual firms and regions of the country, we should avoid an industrial policy that calls upon government to select which firms and industries will receive assistance and which will not. This would certainly rule out the highly selective policies of trade protectionism, government contracts and procurement, industrial restructuring, and nationalization discussed earlier.

Also, it would rule out a government industrial-development bank of the sort that would operate along the lines of a private commercial bank but simply provide loans to firms that were unable to receive private financing. Such a bank would quickly succumb to the same fate as the original Reconstruction Finance Corporation. The RFC was supposed to make loans to companies that were unable to receive private financing and to follow prudent and conservative banking practices in doing so — meaning that loans should be made with the intent that they would be paid back. But the process quickly became politicized. Congressional hearings beginning in 1948, for instance, began to bring to the public's attention attempts to influence the banking decisions of the RFC through political pressure. Many loans of very doubtful financial success were being made. And loans were made "to a host of businesses and individuals whose merits consisted solely of their political significance to the Truman administration and the Democratic National Committee."[16] Finally, the RFC met its demise after bribery and other forms of corruption infected the top echelons of the bank.

An effective industrial policy for the United States should have one major objective: strengthening the dynamic comparative advantage of the United States in the global economy. The comparative economic advantage that the United States had in its early history — massive sources of raw materials and an abundance of easily tillable land — launched our country toward becoming a world power. We built upon these natural assets, making tremendous investments in educating our labor force and constructing the infrastructure of highways, ports, and communications systems that is essential for an industrialized economy. Furthermore, we expanded upon a long tradition of Yankee ingenuity, developing a comparative advantage in technology. And all of this was embedded in an economy in which entrepreneurship and innovation were highly regarded and rewarded.

What worked in the past will work in the future. Our problem is that we have not kept pace with other countries in recognizing that the comparative advantage we enjoyed in the past must be modernized. Such modernization means that our industrial policy must primarily focus on creating an environment that encourages human creative power, flexibility, foresight, and organizational talent. Emphasis must be given to education, research and development, productive investment, and technology. Fortunately, these are attributes that can readily grow out of our inherent strengths. And reducing the budget deficit, lowering interest rates through more expansive money supply, and allowing the value of the dollar to return to more normal levels would go a long way in solving our industrial-development problems.

The Power Economy

*T*HERE CAN BE a world of faster growth, more jobs, less unemployment, and increased economic security and stability. It is
the world of the Power Economy. The Power Economy would reduce unemployment, and not accept thirty million unemployed
workers in the industrialized countries as a fait accompli; it would
achieve a stable real growth rate of 3 percent or more rather than
continued stagnation; it holds out the hope of far greater economic
and political security than is our present fate.

The Power Economy can be built by the five major industrialized
countries that have been the focus of this book. The economies of
the United States, Japan, West Germany, Great Britain, and France
hold the power to change the future course of the world, and our
lives. Collectively, they produce $6.9 trillion in goods and services
each year, one-half of the world total. They employ 230 million
workers, who are the most sophisticated, best educated, and most
productive in the world. From their universities and industrial laboratories are emerging the new technologies that will shape our
future. Within their corporations and banks are concentrations of
economic power unprecedented in world history.

Yet the Power Economy will not be realized from any of the
current economic experiments. While many of these experiments
held out the hope of faster growth and more jobs, none have been
able to deliver on their promises. The supply-side experiment in the
United States blundered into a recession, and has left a legacy of
massive budget deficits that are destined to sap the investment needed

for the Power Economy. The Japanese are struggling to fend off a protectionist backlash, and are turning more insular in their search for economic security. The German experiment in moderation has stagnated. The British attempt at monetarism has brought down inflation, but has failed to rejuvenate the industrial base. The French attempt to introduce socialism into the Western industrialized world is floundering.

The first step in building the Power Economy is to contain the threat of protectionism. We know from a careful reading of history what protectionism means: Trade disappears. Individual economies are quickly isolated. Tensions rise. Routine economic disagreements and differences easily escalate into threatening encounters. And military conflict looms as the ultimate menace.

We also know from a careful reading of our current situation that protectionism is more threatening today than at any time in the past. For one thing, the global economy is much more interdependent. Economic and financial ties bind the industrialized economies into a complex network of economic relationships such that conditions in one country are quickly transmitted into other countries. The high interest rates of the United States strongly impact the financial markets in Europe and Japan. Large differences in growth and inflation rates immediately affect exchange rates, disrupting trade flow and domestic economic policies.

In the second place, the industrialized economies are irreversibly tied to the fate of the less developed countries because of massive loans. A small group of countries, many of whom are on the threshold of emerging as newly industrialized economies, owe a combined $730 billion to private banks and official government agencies in the wealthier countries. Protectionism would curtail the exports from these countries — exports that are essential if the debtor nations are to repay their obligations. And any large default on these loans would produce an international financial crisis.

Finally, no major economy can long survive without trade. No country, including the United States, has sufficient resources to sustain a strong and growing economy without importing products from other countries. Without imports of food and oil, the Japanese economy would quickly collapse. The United States is no longer energy independent, and cannot become so. The European countries depend upon trade for one-quarter of their economic strength. Protectionism would have a devastating impact on the industrialized countries.

The second step in building the Power Economy is to adopt in- ②
dustrial policies that are reasonable and nonprotectionist in nature.
The greatest danger of the current infatuation with industrial policy
is that it could be implemented only to protect domestic markets.
When confronted with the difficulties of displaced coal-, steel-, and
automobile workers, politicians are hard pressed not to respond
with protectionism wrapped in the garb of industrial policy.

The industrial policy must be reasonable, which means that it
must enable mature and declining industries gradually to shrink in
size, must encourage the development of new high-technology industries, and must assist displaced workers in adjusting to new careers. None of this is easy. Nor does any one country hold the magic
solution. Industrial policy is unique to the country in which it is
practiced; it is deeply woven into the basic economic history of the
country, and its success is greatly dependent upon its ability to blend
in with the entire economic and cultural capability specific to the
country. It is not a single thread that can be removed from the
tapestry of one country and woven into that of another.

Consequently, individual countries will select from among several
different options in adapting their industrial policy to their specific
needs. This means that the United States will place far greater emphasis on tax incentives and general encouragement of a growth
environment than, say, the French, who have a much stronger tradition of nationalization of industry. The Japanese will continue
their practice of consensus forming, with MITI providing a "vision
of the future." The German practice will be closer to that of the
Americans, while at the same time attempting to promote the development of small and middle-sized firms. And it is not known if
the recent British attempt to sell nationalized industries to private
investors will continue under a Labour government, or whether
there will be a return to the traditional British practice of subsidizing
a significant portion of the industrial base.

These different approaches must be compatible and must not
degenerate into competitive economic warfare. To a great extent,
this will depend upon achieving a faster-growing global economy
and expanding trade markets — an outcome that is critically dependent upon the third step in building the Power Economy of the
future.

This third, and final, step is the main subject of this chapter. It
is a step that requires the political leaders of the major industrialized
economies to cooperate to a far greater extent than they have in

recent years, by putting into place economic policies that are characterized by four major objectives: (1) accepting the reality of global economic and financial interdependence; (2) working toward greater coordination of economic policies; (3) striving for a better balance between fiscal and monetary policies, and avoiding the extremes of Reaganomics or British monetarism; and (4) adopting policies that are more conducive to growth.

The Reality of Economic Interdependence

During the past decade, the global economy has become far more interdependent than ever before, with the industrialized countries greatly expanding their trade and financial ties and a group of newly industrialized countries emerging as manufacturing and trading powers in international markets. OPEC served as a major catalyst for the rapid increase in this interdependence. With the quadrupling of oil prices beginning in late 1973, all of the oil-importing countries immediately turned to their export markets, hoping to earn the money to pay for high-cost oil. And, alternatively, the suddenly cash-rich OPEC countries began to undertake lavish development programs, purchasing billions of dollars' worth of equipment and capital projects from abroad.

There were other forces operating to increase global interdependence. Relationships with the Soviet Union greatly thawed under the leadership of President Richard Nixon, and as a result trade increased between the West and the Eastern-bloc countries. The communist countries began to purchase grain in large quantities, and their development plans incorporated major acquisitions of Western capital goods and technology.

The less developed countries began to borrow heavily in international capital markets to finance their burgeoning trade- and internal-development programs. Western bankers, eager to grow with this wave of the future and impelled by the necessity to recycle the petrodollars being earned by OPEC, greatly expanded their international loans, further consolidating the ties binding the global economy.

So rapid was the increase in economic interdependence that by 1983 global trade amounted to a total of $4,000 billion, a fourfold increase over the $970 billion in 1973. International lending mushroomed from $345 billion to $1,600 billion during this period, nearly a fivefold increase.

Even the United States, for many years seemingly oblivious to issues surrounding trade and international finance since they played such a small role in our economy, is suddenly confronted with the reality of global interdependence. Since 1970, exports as a proportion of our total gross national product have grown from 5 percent to 10 percent, and there have been a threefold increase in direct investments abroad by American companies and a tenfold increase in the foreign liabilities of U.S. banks. Today, over five million jobs in the United States are directly related to exports, and between 1977 and 1980, an amazing eight out of ten new manufacturing jobs created in the United States were linked in some way to exports.[1]

The extent to which the future of our economy is inextricably tied to that of the world economy is even more evident when we examine the importance of exports to some of our major industries, and our reliance upon imports. It is expected that during 1985 we will export about $415 billion worth of goods and services. As shown in table 20, our largest exports in recent years have been in civilian and military aircraft and other aerospace equipment. During 1983, we exported nearly $17 billion worth of these products, and exports accounted for 25 percent of the total output of companies in this industry.

Many of our most important industries are critically dependent upon export markets. Computer-equipment-manufacturing firms export 27 percent of their total output; makers of semiconductors, 33 percent; and producers of oil-field machinery, 46 percent; fertilizers, 42 percent; and grains such as corn and wheat, 40 percent. The dollar value of these exports each year is in the tens of billions.

All of the high-technology industries — those that are critical to our future growth and strength — are highly dependent upon export markets. Aerospace, computers, semiconductors, and scientific instruments are the growth industries of our future. Without export markets, these industries would be far smaller and would offer far fewer benefits in terms of jobs, profits, and potential growth to the rest of the economy. And most of our farmers would be out of business if it were not for foreign markets — in particular, our large corn and wheat farmers, who depend upon foreign consumers for two-fifths of their entire output.

Without imports, our economy could not operate. It is as simple as that. Nowhere is this more evident than in energy: we import 20 percent of our total energy from abroad and are dependent upon foreign sources for 52 percent of our crude oil. We learned the importance of energy to the economy during the OPEC oil embargo of 1973–74. Furthermore, we learned that we could not become energy-independent, even though a highly publicized government effort to do so was proposed. It went nowhere, since our demand for energy — especially oil and natural gas — far exceeds our domestic sources.

Our dependence upon imports goes far beyond oil and natural gas, as the data in table 21 make clear. During 1983, we imported nearly $18.4 billion worth of foreign-made vehicles, almost $7.5 billion worth of steel-mill products, and more than $6.3 billion worth of radios and television sets. We even imported billions of dollars' worth of electronic components and semiconductors, though the United States is itself a major exporter of these products. The fact that an industry is both an importer and exporter reflects the high degree of specialization and interdependence of the global economy. Many of our automobile parts, for instance, are manufactured across

TABLE 20. MAJOR EXPORTS OF THE UNITED STATES, 1983

	Value (Millions of $)	Proportion Exported (of Total Produced)
Aerospace vehicles and equipment	16,863	25%
Miscellaneous farm products	15,764	—
Grains (corn, wheat)	12,603	40
Computer equipment	10,300	27
Soybeans	5,913	17
Electronic components	5,851	17
Semiconductors	4,184	33
Oil-field machinery	3,488	46
Construction machinery	2,600	29
Industrial chemicals	2,451	28
Farm machinery	2,100	23
Scientific instruments	1,687	28
Paper pulp	1,550	41
Fertilizers	1,133	42

SOURCES: U.S. Dept. of Commerce, *1984 U.S. Industrial Outlook* (Washington, D.C.: GPO, 1984); U.S. Dept. of Agriculture, *U.S. Foreign Agriculture Trade Statistical Reports* (Washington, D.C.: GPO, 1984).

the border in Canada and then shipped in to Detroit for assembly. Computer firms import parts from abroad, and then export the completed computer hardware and software as finished products.

It might be argued that if we did not import so much from abroad, we would have more jobs at home. Why should we buy television sets and automobiles from the Japanese? Why not manufacture these products at home? The answer is that American consumers like the lower prices and higher quality that imports provide. To close the door to foreign products would greatly raise the prices of nearly everything we consume. Furthermore, other countries would no longer be able to buy our exports, and so our aerospace, computer, electronics, and agriculture industries would greatly suffer. We would simply be trading off increased jobs in automobile and television-set manufacturing for fewer jobs in computers and agriculture. And the net result would be an overall reduction in jobs — for as mentioned earlier, we gain far more jobs because of our exports than we lose because of imports.

TABLE 21. MAJOR IMPORTS OF THE UNITED STATES, 1983

	Value (Millions of $)	Proportion Imported (of Total Domestic Consumption)
Energy (total)	—	20%
Crude oil	47,444	52
Motor vehicles	18,381	17
Steel-mill products	7,491	12
Electronic components	6,770	16
Radios and television sets	6,334	53
Semiconductors	5,048	29
Farm machinery	1,360	15
Machine tools	900	32
Copper	860	21
Textile machinery	600	42
Zinc	419	55

SOURCES: U.S. Dept. of Commerce, *1984 U.S. Industrial Outlook* (Washington, D.C.: GPO, 1984).

There is another reason why imports are so important to our economy: the effect of foreign competition on our domestic industry. American manufacturers have lost out to foreign competition in large part because of too little competition rather than too much competition. Why did our automobile and steel industries lose out to the Japanese and South Koreans? "It would appear that complacency bears much of the blame," observed Regis McKenna, an industry marketing expert who was president of the National Commission on Industrial Innovation. "Security provided a sense of safe markets and predictable competition, so that manufacturing strategies revolved around such things as product standardization and incremental cosmetic changes rather than product innovations."[2]

Despite our early complacency, foreign competition has led directly to the recent rejuvenation of the American automobile industry. The continuing investment in new research and technology by our computer industry is, to a significant degree, a reaction to fears of losing out to the Japanese. While the process of adjusting to a more competitive environment is not easy or pleasant, there is no alternative other than protectionism, with its attendant stagnation and inflation.

Economic and financial interdependence also brings problems. The major economies of the world are now so intertwined that problems in one country are quickly transmitted across national boundaries and impact the economic fortunes of other countries. The high interest rates in the United States, the weakness of the French franc, and the burgeoning trade surpluses of Japan are well-known examples. Somewhat less publicized, but clearly a sign of the times, are the political uncertainties in Argentina and the economic problems in Brazil — problems that would have received only passing attention a few years ago, but that now capture front-page headlines because the possibility of a default on these nations' foreign debt has great import for the United States, whose banks are deeply involved in multi-billion-dollar loans to such countries.

Such changes in the world order are generating repercussions. As the *Wall Street Journal* observed, "there are serious questions whether the long-sought-after interdependence hasn't finally reached the point where its costs may be outweighing its benefits. Growing protectionism, both in the U.S. and in other major industrial countries, may be one sign that a backlash is in the making."[3] Yet as Anthony Solomon, former president of the Federal Reserve Bank of New York and an expert in international finance, correctly noted, "in today's context, the interdependence of national economies is a hard reality" that we must accept. There is "little that anyone can do to reduce interdependence among countries, and the best thing for policy makers to do is to recognize this and search for new ways to cope with it."[4]

The alternative to learning how to cope with the reality of economic and financial interdependence is political isolation and protectionism — with all of the attendant threats of global economic disintegration. Such an alternative has little to offer. Nor is simply searching for stopgap ways to cope with the problem a very appealing course of action: it suggests passivity and resignation. Rather, we should recognize the tremendous benefits offered by a strong and growing world economy with dynamic trade and financial markets. Achieving such an economic order must be our goal — and such a goal can be attained through greater coordination of economic policies by the major industrialized countries.

The Need for Policy Coordination

The single most important lesson that has been learned from the five economic experiments discussed in this book is that no single country can implement economic policies without affecting the other nations. There must be closer coordination between the major industrialized countries, for the economic and financial ties that now bind these countries are simply too strong. Any country that acts on its own and adopts extreme policies will disrupt foreign economies and create tension.

Nowhere is this lesson more evident than in the relationship between the United States and Japan, and between France and her European trading partners. In its infatuation with Reaganomics, the United States has been generating massive budget deficits, which have been countered with extremely tight monetary policies by the Federal Reserve Bank. The results have been high interest rates, an overvalued dollar, and trade warfare with the Japanese. The overvalued dollar has priced many American products, including automobiles, out of international markets, which has contributed greatly to domestic unemployment and has generated a surge of protectionist sentiment in the United States.

The economic policies of the Japanese have run totally counter to those of the Americans. The Japanese have been imposing tight fiscal policies, scaling back on government spending and balancing their budget, while easing their monetary policy in order to keep interest rates low. Such a course quickly led to a direct conflict with policymakers in Washington, who suggested that the solution to the trade gap between Japan and the United States was for the Japanese to ease their fiscal policy and tighten their monetary policy — in other words, to adopt policies similar to those of Reaganomics. The Japanese response was polite but firm: No — why should we jeopardize our plans to increase productive investment and strengthen our economy in order to conform to the ill-fated American experiment?

The French initially attempted to stimulate their economy to faster growth in order to generate jobs. They moved in quite the opposite direction from the Germans and the British, and the outcome was inevitable: The French franc rapidly deteriorated, creating massive uncertainty among French businessmen and the general public. French leaders clashed with their counterparts in West Germany as the two countries struggled to stabilize the relationship between their currencies. The Germans accused the French of being irresponsible members of the international community, and the French threatened to withdraw from the European Economic Community. After several devaluations of the franc, the French leaders were forced to reverse course, raising taxes and reducing government spending, but it was too late. Irreparable damage had been done to their economic experiment in socialism.

In the past, such major international clashes over economic policies did not occur. There was far more general agreement on how to operate in the global economy than there is at the present time. Yet such compatibility did not occur because of any strong effort on the part of political leaders to carefully coordinate their policies, but rather as a natural outcome of several powerful economic conditions. The most important of these was the dominance of the United States economy. During the 1960s, the American economy accounted for nearly 50 percent of the total gross output of the entire global economy, as compared to 25 percent today. Given such a dominant U.S. position, other countries had no choice but to follow in the footsteps of the American policymakers. Yet this choice was quite acceptable to them, for they were rapidly adapting American technology and management styles into their economies. They derived great benefits from following the American lead.

Furthermore, the rapid growth of the global economy during the period from the end of the Second World War to the early 1970s made policy choices an easy matter: simply adopt those that promoted the most rapid growth. These policies, which were all quite similar for the industrialized countries, emphasized investments in new plant and equipment, implementation of new technology, and large government expenditures on research, education, highways, and other infrastructure. And with a rapidly growing economy generating high corporate profits and tax revenues, there were few of the tough trade-off issues that torment politicians and business executives today.

These conditions came to an abrupt end during the turbulent 1970s. Policy coordination no longer will occur automatically; it must be aggressively sought and nurtured. Three important questions immediately surface in this regard: (1) What does policy coordination mean? (2) What does policy coordination involve? and (3) Why will policy coordination work?

What Does Policy Coordination Mean?

In its most straightforward definition, *coordination* means "to bring into proper order or relation, to organize, to systemize, to regulate, or to fix." It also has a less rigid and broader meaning: "to achieve harmonious adjustment or functioning." This latter definition is the one most applicable to policymaking in the international arena, for attaining harmony in economic policies is far more feasible than is trying to organize a systematic and fixed relationship between the economic policies of various countries.

The intent behind extending these meanings to economic policy is obvious. *Harmony* means "a combination of parts into an orderly whole, an achieving of congruity, a fitting well together." The leaders of the major industrialized countries must adopt economic policies that are congruous with each other. "Fitting well together" is a most apt concept. But more important for achieving the Power Economy: the combination of the individual economic policies of each country will add to an orderly whole. To use an overworked concept, but one that is quite relevant to our discussion: The total is greater than the sum of the individual parts.

By achieving greater harmony in economic policy among the major industrialized economies, the total effect on the global economy in terms of economic growth, employment, and trade will be far greater than if we simply add up the results of each country adopting its own independent policies. As explained at length in earlier chapters, the sum of such individualistic actions is likely to be worldwide economic stagnation.

What Does Policy Coordination Involve?

Policy coordination requires that the major industrialized countries agree upon economic policies that are generally consistent, that are moderate, and that avoid unrealistic and politically motivated goals.

Consistency means, for example, that if the European countries adopt a broad policy of monetary constraint, the United States and Japan should agree to do likewise, and vice versa. When a serious recession occurs, or several countries are mired in economic stagnation with high unemployment, there should be agreement to follow more stimulative policies.

This does not mean that the leaders of the major countries should sit around a conference table and agree upon specific rates of growth of the money supply for each country, or detail government expenditures and taxes. Such a summit meeting would be impossible and such an approach ludicrous. What policy coordination requires is that the Western leaders reach agreement on the general nature and direction of economic policy and that they allow the individual countries sufficient latitude in selecting specific policies to achieve the overall direction. For example, if the leaders agree upon a general course of monetary constraint in order to contain inflationary pressures, they would have to accept the fact that the German policymakers are likely to interpret this goal narrowly, imposing rather stringent monetary targets, while the French are prone to adopt more stimulative monetary targets. Alternatively, the Americans and the French probably would interpret an agreement to reduce budget deficits more liberally than will the Japanese and the Germans.

It might be argued that such international policy coordination would lead to global recessions or worldwide inflation, for all of the major countries would be moving in the same direction at the same time. Would it not be far better for each country to adopt independent policies, since this might reduce the risk of simultaneous adverse economic behavior? Thus, if the United States were in a recession, a strong economy in Western Europe or Japan would act to dampen the impact of the U.S. downturn on the global economy, and vice versa. In the extreme case, one could view all countries as totally independent of one another, and recessions and inflationary periods would be randomly distributed across the global economy. In this world, strong economies would offset weak ones, some countries would be stimulating their economies to stronger growth while others were implementing policies to reduce inflation arising from growth that was too strong, and the global economy would move along a nice, stable growth path with few ups and downs.

Such a world does not exist. Nor is there enough independence left in the global economy to allow even a partially random solution to our economic problems. The world economy is too intertwined, too interdependent — particularly as far as the major industrialized countries are concerned. We face common problems that have the unfortunate characteristic of spilling across national borders. And, indeed, to continue our current independent course of action will force us toward protectionism as the solution to the world's economic problems. But such a solution has the direst of consequences, including war.

We have no choice but to acknowledge the risk of global economic cycles (especially since they are already occurring) and to take steps to reduce this risk. Such a step is the second requirement for policy coordination: that the general economic policies adopted by the major countries be somewhat moderate. In selecting their broad fiscal and monetary policies, the political leaders of these countries must strive for the middle of the road, much as the Germans have attempted in their economic experiment. Such a requirement would rule out the extremes of Reaganomics and British monetarism. There would be no room for the massive budget deficits of the Americans in a world of policy coordination and moderation.

Moderation will naturally evolve from the first requirement for policy coordination. For there to be agreement on the overall direction of economic policy among strong-willed and independent political leaders, the policies must be moderate, as extreme positions would make it impossible to reach a consensus.

Moderation dictates the third requirement involved in policy coordination: that we avoid the practice of setting unrealistic short-run and politically motivated economic goals — goals that are rarely achieved and that only serve to disillusion the public. The current economic experiments are full of such goals, but are nowhere so prevalent as in Reaganomics. This is particularly true in regard to the budget-deficit goal. The highly publicized goal of Reaganomics of balancing the budget by 1984 was never attained; quite the opposite — we incurred the largest budget deficit in our entire history.

Nor can we set a goal of reducing the unemployment rate until it is 3 percent (or some other specific target), as many Democratic politicians are suggesting. Economic targets are notoriously elusive, and for good reason. An economy is not a test tube in a scientifically controlled laboratory environment that can be regulated and manipulated. It is a highly dynamic interaction of many different economic institutions, millions of consumers, and hundreds of politicians. Economic goals are continuously changing as a result of demographics, market conditions, and external threats such as war and OPEC.

Nowhere is the futility of setting specific targets for economic performance more clear than in regard to unemployment. Because it is probably the most highly politicized and sensitive economic issue, we are prone to set a specific target for a "tolerable" level of unemployment. Twenty years ago that target was generally accepted to be 3.0 percent in the United States. Gradually, it was increased, to 3.5 percent, to 4.0 percent, then upward toward 5.0 percent. Republicans would emphasize the higher target, while Democrats would opt for a lower one. Republicans would argue that a lower unemployment target would lead to greater inflation, and the Democrats would counter that they were more concerned about the welfare of the unemployed. And so the issue seesawed.

Finally, economists agreed on the principle of a "natural unemployment rate" — the rate at which inflation would not accelerate. Currently, in our country that rate is thought to be between 6.5 and 7.5 percent. But even this is not a fixed target offering policymakers a stable economic goal. Recent evidence indicates that the natural rate of unemployment is declining as a result of the changing demographics of our labor force. No longer are young workers and women entering the labor force in the numbers they did during the 1970s; consequently, the labor force is becoming older and more stable. The rapid turnover in jobs that characterizes a growing and younger labor force has begun to slow down. And therefore the natural unemployment rate is lower than in the past.

Avoiding unrealistic short-term goals does not mean that we abandon all economic goals and simply operate our economy without any sense of where we are going and how long it will take us to get there. Our goals must be longer-term and based upon what is achievable in our economy, rather than varying according to which party occupies the White House. Such longer-term goals, for instance, would be to achieve a stable economy that grows each year in real terms between 3.0 and 3.5 percent, to keep inflation between 4.0

and 6.0 percent, and to balance the budget in the long run. When faced with a structural, long-term budget deficit, as at the present time, our goal should be to eliminate that deficit within ten years (assuming stable economic growth and high employment).

This change in attitude toward economic goals is very important to achieving the Power Economy. First of all, it removes economic policy from the arena of "goal one-upmanship" whereby politicians of one party attempt to outdo those of another in promising the American public economic results. Since such results are almost never achieved as promised, the game accomplishes little more than disillusioning us with politicians and economic policymaking. Second, it recognizes the inherent dynamics of our economy — dynamics that require a continuous process of adjustment and compromise around, ideally, a moderate course of action. Third, it places more emphasis on achieving long-term stability and results, giving us a better sense of where the economy is headed and why. And fourth, it would tend to remove much of our economic policy from the personality quirks of individual leaders — a problem that is particularly prevalent today.

Depersonalizing Economic Policies

One of the unique features of the current economic experiments of the major industrialized countries is how political and personalized they are in comparison to the economic policies of the past. All of the experiments have been imposed by strong political leaders who are stamping them with their own identity. It is difficult to separate Reaganomics in the United States from the personality of President Reagan, British monetarism from the private beliefs of Prime Minister Thatcher, or French socialism from the image of President Mitterrand. It is almost as if these leaders view the economic experiments as their own private domain, an extension not only of their political beliefs but also of their personal ideals.

Such personalization of economic policy makes it very difficult to achieve the adjustments and compromises in economic policy that are necessary in any country. Conditions change. Specific policies rarely work as intended. New information becomes available as the policies evolve. Consequently, the economic program of a country is in constant need of correction. Yet when the program is highly personalized, the political leader finds it nearly impossible to accept these corrections. Any proposal for change is viewed as a frontal attack upon the personal integrity and values of the leader.

The strong identity of economic policy with the personal values of a political leader can readily lead to the tragic results described by political scientist James David Barber in his classic study *The Presidential Character.* In predicting performance in the White House, Professor Barber wrote of a group of American leaders who so strongly adhered to a policy course that change became impossible, even "long after it began to produce terrible trouble for the country and for the man."[5]

Why? "The issue is highly moralized, a matter of principle, not prudence," stated Barber.

Therefore to compromise, to move toward any easy panacea, is seen not only as mistaken but evil. In moral terms the cost of compromise is simply too high for the President as a person: he would have to sacrifice his own integrity, his stance as a being responsible to his conscience. Furthermore, he sees the conflict as one between strength and weakness. He himself, he feels, must be tough — and others should also show their mettle, their fiber, their manhood. The soft way out is closed to him, for his fight against giving in is a double fight, against both sinfulness and weakness.[6]

For a political leader to view compromise on his or her economic policies as sinful and weak is not an ideal situation for achieving coordination of economic policies. Rather than seeking common grounds for agreement, showing flexibility and a willingness to place the requirements of global economic security and growth above personal beliefs, the leaders are far more likely to lecture each other. It is not surprising that President Reagan generally expounds the virtues of free-enterprise economics and individual initiatives when he speaks in international arenas, or that at summit conferences Prime Minister Thatcher and President Mitterrand pontificate on the merits of their respective economic programs rather than engaging in serious discussions of policy change.

Why Will Policy Coordination Work?

The requirements for policy coordination are rather demanding. To agree upon general policies that are mutually consistent, to adhere to policies that are moderate in order to achieve a consensus, and to be willing to place economic welfare above political and personal beliefs is a tall order to fill. So the question remains: Is the payoff worth the effort?

The answer is a resounding yes, for greater coordination of economic policies by the major industrialized countries will lead to a more stable global economy, and one that will grow faster. In the first place, greater coordination will result in fewer economic recessions. The extremes of current policies are creating unstable pressures both in individual economies and in the global economy as a whole. The large budget deficits of the United States are threatening to precipitate another recession in this country, the French economy has swung from one extreme to another under the Socialist experiment, and the economies of Great Britain and West Germany continue to stagnate, highly vulnerable to any recession that may occur in the United States.

It has been well documented that a significant reason for the slower growth of the United States economy during the past decade has been the serious recessions of the 1970s. These recessions greatly reduced investment by business in new plant and equipment. They were responsible for uncertainty about the future, which depressed confidence. They created a feeling of rising risk that was reflected in higher interest rates. It has been estimated that these developments accounted for one-fifth of the slower growth rate of productivity in the American economy during the 1970s as compared to the 1960s.[7]

Second, greater coordination of economic policies will go a long way in renewing confidence in the future of the world economy. Now there is great uneasiness, a feeling that the economy is in a long period of stagnation. The inability of the economic experiments of the five major Western powers to generate the growth and jobs that had been promised is only intensifying these feelings. No single experiment is going to emerge as a winner, providing a model for the other countries to follow.

Even the present strength of the United States economy is short-term, for we have not made the policy changes necessary to ensure our continued growth, such as lowering interest rates, reducing the deficit, and increasing investments. Nor can the United States operate independently from the global economy, for our dependence upon export markets is too critical to our major industries, and we rely upon imports. Also, a strong Asia and Europe are very important not only to our economic well-being, but also to our military security. Even the American economy is not large and strong enough to carry the rest of the world. An overt recognition of these facts — such as an economic summit meeting called to develop a concerted and coordinated effort to stimulate the global economy — is long overdue.

Third, policy coordination will prevent a return to protectionism. If the world's political leaders are willing to deal with mutual economic problems and adopt policies that are a help, rather than a threat, to the global economy, then we have the basis for dealing with protectionism. At present, each country imposes constraints on trade and other countries retaliate. Other than the generalized and pontifical statements on the importance of free trade that are issued at annual economic summit meetings, there is little discussion dealing with the threat of protectionism. And protectionism is a fast way to create a stagnant global economy.

Finally, policy coordination would ease one of the most serious threats to the future of the global economy: the debt of the less developed countries. This debt, already a massive $730 billion, cannot be repaid in a global economy that grows at less than 2 percent a year. Such low growth completely stagnates trade, as we learned during the years from 1981 through 1983. And without trade, the debtor countries do not earn the money to repay their debt.

A default on the debt would do far more damage to our economy than simply depressing bank profits. Nor are American depositors protected from the impact of large defaults by FDIC insurance, which guarantees payment on deposits up to $100,000. For the real damage would not be loss of these deposits in banks that might go bankrupt — government insurance has taken away this threat for most depositors — but rather the resulting damage to the economy itself: There would be a tremendous loss of confidence in the American banking system. Interest rates would rise. The central bank would be forced to inject reserves into the banking system to stabilize the situation, and this would eventually lead to higher inflation. A long and serious recession would occur.

All of these unfortunate events can be avoided if the global economy grows at a rate of 3 to 4 percent each year. At this growth rate, trade will expand about three times as fast, providing the relief that is needed to pay off the debt of the less developed countries. The higher global growth rate provides the necessary economic environment for these countries to expand. Their trade markets in North America, Europe, and Asia will be open and increasing. International banks will be able to restructure and smooth out the payments on the debt. A faster-growing economy is the only solution to the international debt problem.

Conclusion

When we place recent economic events in their historical context, it is obvious that the global economy underwent wrenching shocks between 1970 and 1980. The postwar growth era — when economic growth came remarkably easy, when the United States dominated the global economy and provided the technological model for other industrialized countries, when coordination of economic policies among the major powers flowed naturally — came to an abrupt end in the early 1970s.

In response to this change, a group of leaders emerged who launched their political fortunes on the premise that nearly everything from the past was obsolete. They blamed Keynesian economics for the problems. They pointed out the excesses of previous governments and accused them of being spendthrift. They chastised the people for losing the incentive to work and to invest. And they did not propose moderate solutions: they put into place economic policies that were untested and extreme.

On February 18, 1981, President Ronald Reagan announced a dramatic new course for the American economy. It was a "comprehensive four-point program," aimed at restoring strength and vitality to the economy. The growth of government spending was to be reduced. Unnecessary government regulations were either to be eliminated altogether or substantially altered so as to unshackle business and industry. Inflation was to be brought under control through firm monetary policy. Most important, taxes on personal income were to be slashed, providing the core of what was called the supply-side revolution. On August 13, 1981, the president signed into law a historic package of tax reductions: $750 billion to be spread over a five-year period. Never before in our history had taxes been reduced by so much for such an extended period.

Meanwhile, the Japanese were attempting to defend their economic experiment and gradually alter it to provide greater economic security and a high quality of life. It was an economic experiment that many in the West thought to be either a rebirth of old-fashioned mercantilism — invading foreign markets and accumulating massive trade surpluses — or else the overwhelming success of "Japan, Inc.," led by MITI, a government agency that practices the fine art of industrial policy and development. In actuality, the Japanese experiment was neither. Rather, it was the practice of good, solid economic management directed toward achieving economic security. Such security was based on preserving trade markets in order to pay for the critical imports without which Japan could not long survive. Furthermore, Japan's experiment was attempting to develop an indigenous technological capability and build a new welfare society for the Japanese people.

The Germans wanted no part of the excesses of the Americans, the British, or the French, the three most extreme of the five economic experiments of the major industrialized powers. Chancellor Helmut Schmidt set the tone for the German experiment on January 19, 1978, when he stated that West Germany would follow "the golden middle road" in economic policies. The size of the government was to be gradually reduced, but there were to be no significant changes in budget priorities. The money supply was to be adequate, but conservative, reflecting the long-standing German fear of inflation. And the Germans would continue to depend upon their industrial strength, which had catapulted them into the forefront in chemicals, automobiles, electronics, and heavy manufacturing, but which was beginning to show signs of age and ponderousness. West Germany set out to see if its policies of the past could be modified to meet the challenges of the future.

The British, led by the newly elected prime minister, Margaret Thatcher, approached the problem with the same irreverence for the past as did President Reagan. Nothing from the past was appropriate for the future. It was a new day. It was a time to cast aside all of the outdated policies that had guided the development of the British economy for nearly a half-century, and "start to restore incentives, encourage efficiency and create a climate in which commerce and industry can flourish."[8] But rather than relying upon tax reductions to achieve these results, as were the Americans, the prime minister put into place the first major test of monetary policy. It was a test of the famous tenet of Professor Milton Friedman that the monetary authority should adopt publicly the policy of achieving a steady rate of growth in a specified monetary total: The precise rate of growth, like the precise monetary total, is less important than the adoption of some stated and known rate. Friedman preferred a low rate, however, so that inflation could be wrung out of the economy, and the British set out to test this advice.

The French adopted an economic experiment that was totally different from that of the other four countries. It was a grand experiment in economic socialism — not a French version of the European social democracy that had been around for years, but a full-fledged attempt to "achieve a new alliance between Socialism and liberty."[9] Led by President François Mitterrand, who had joined the Socialist party just ten years before he wrested leadership of the country from the conservatives in 1981, the French set in place economic policies that had five major elements: (1) attempting to stimulate the economy to faster growth at a time when other major countries were retrenching, (2) nationalizing a substantial part of French industry and banking, (3) greatly increasing funding in order to develop high-technology industries, (4) achieving greater equality in the distribution of income, and (5) introducing greater worker democracy into the workplace. It was an audacious experiment that offered the world a dramatic alternative to the experiments being tried in the other four major powers.

The hope and promise was that one of these experiments would prove to be successful, offering the world a model for the future. But rather than leading to a more stable and secure economic future, the experiments have plunged the world into economic chaos. Even the United States, with its apparent success, is experiencing nothing more than a short-term surge from a deep and serious recession. Confrontation over trade issues, continued massive unemployment, and an undermining of confidence have been the results.

The global economy now is floundering between the extremes of economic policies put into place by such leaders as President Reagan, Prime Minister Thatcher, and President Mitterrand. The leaders of West Germany and Japan, following more traditional policies, are struggling to survive. And those challenging the current leadership are offering their own radical changes in economic direction, which suggests that we will continue to swing from one extreme to another in our search for an economy that works.

One of these extremes is protectionism. No one is openly advocating that the existing economic experiments be replaced by outright protectionism, but we are gradually being driven in that direction. Frustration over loss of jobs in basic smokestack industries such as automobiles, steel, and coal mining are leading to efforts to control imports. These controls do not take the traditional form of tariffs or duties, but come in new garb: orderly marketing agreements, voluntary trade constraints, and nontariff regulations. Many of the conditions of trade and job protection are being advanced under the banner of industrial policy. The amount of trade among the industrialized countries that is controlled is estimated to be about 44 percent, and much of this has been the result of efforts by the United States.[10] Our nation was instrumental in negotiating orderly marketing agreements for textiles in 1973, as well as similar pacts limiting imports of footwear (1977), steel (1978), automobiles (1981), and sugar (1982). Yet the European countries have far more protectionist measures than does either the United States or Japan.

The danger of protectionism is that history will repeat itself. Extreme protectionism rose during the 1920s and was a major contributor to the global depression of the 1930s and the Second World War. Trade warfare erupted, and eventually the entire global economy broke down. The United States became insular. The Europeans fought among themselves. And the Japanese moved into Manchuria and began to acquire territories throughout southeast Asia to secure stable sources of raw materials. The words of British statesman David Lloyd George are as relevant today as when stated during those treacherous days in 1933: the world "is getting nearer the brink year by year, revolution by revolution, conference by conference."[11]

If not protectionism, what? Certainly the answer is not another round of economic experiments — a highly targeted and centrally planned industrial policy put into place by the Democrats in the United States, a swing to conservatism under a neo-Gaullist leader in France, or a dramatic shift to increased nationalizations and large government spending in England. Rather, the answer is a return to certain fundamental economic axioms that form the basis of the Power Economy. These axioms are, first, that an economy operates best when it is stable and, second, that such stability can be achieved only when there is reasonable balance in economic policies.

We have learned from recent experience that recessions are not obsolete. They seem to have returned with rather troubling regularity during the past decade. There was a time, particularly during the mid-1960s, when economists and politicians announced that economic recessions were a thing of the past — that we had learned how to manipulate economic policies so effectively that we could smooth over the cyclical ups and downs of economic activity. But the economic experiments have put an end to such propitious statements.

The uncertainty that these economic experiments have unleashed on the global economy threaten its very survival. Not only is the economic impact of frequent and serious recessions costly in terms of lost investment that can never be recovered, unemployment, and deterioration in confidence, but continued recessions are highly threatening to social and political stability.

We seem to have lost much of the ability to absorb recessions that we had in the past, to roll from one economic downturn to another without undue risk. Because the global economy is inter-dependent, a recession in one major country is quickly transmitted to others and sets off political confrontations over economic policies. Continuous bickering among the leaders of the world is not con-ducive to strengthening our Atlantic ties and improving our Japanese relationships.

Furthermore, the industrialized countries are confronted with the problem of structural unemployment, so that the increased cyclical unemployment of a recession places tremendous pressures on the political system. When the number of unemployed workers averages 30 million in the industrialized economies as it does today, rather than the 15 million of a decade earlier, there is far less latitude for absorbing the impact of a recession without setting off extreme social and political responses.

And a recession, with its depressing impact on international trade, sets off pressures for increased protectionism and threatens the world with autarky and disintegration.

The question of how to return to economic stability brings us to the second basic axiom: the need to achieve a reasonable balance in economic policies. We must begin with a balance between fiscal and monetary policies, and end with a balance between short-term stabilization and long-term growth policies.

Fiscal policies are those that alter the level of taxes and govern-ment spending, and the degree to which they stimulate economic expansion is measured by the size of the budget deficit. Thus, the inordinately large federal budget deficits of the United States in-dicate that the American economy is being given a large dose of fiscal stimulation in the form of massive increases in defense spend-ing and large tax reductions.

Monetary policies are those that alter the amount of money that is maintained in the economy by the central bank. A greater supply of money is needed in an economy that is growing rapidly, in order to finance normal consumer and business transactions as well as to meet the demand for credit. If sufficient money is not provided, then interest rates rise and economic activity is dampened. And if too much money is pumped into the economy, inflation will even-tually erupt.

In a stable economy, there should be a reasonable balance between fiscal and monetary policies. When the economy is in a recession, the emphasis should be placed on stimulative fiscal policy, in order to encourage greater spending. But once full employment has been attained and inflationary pressures begin to surface, policy emphasis should shift to tighter fiscal policy. This was the problem that John Maynard Keynes addressed, and even though current politicians and many economists are prone to discount Keynesian thinking, his views in this regard are as relevant today as they were fifty years ago.

The problem is not in the theory, but in the unwillingness of politicians to implement it fully. Stimulating an economy is politically easy and fun, for it calls for tax reductions and increased government expenditures, both of which hold great appeal to the voter. But to constrain an overheated economy requires tax increases, spending reductions, or both — actions that are popular with neither the voter nor the politician.

The great weakness of Keynesian theory lies in its passive approach for dealing with the long-term growth problems of an economy. This is not surprising, for Keynes developed his theory in the depths of the Great Depression, when existing plants and millions of workers stood idle. The problem was not one of stimulating additional investments in new plant capacity, but simply putting the idle capacity back to work.

Keynesian policy as implemented during the postwar growth era assumed that the capacity of the economy to grow — what it is now fashionable to call the supply-side of the economy — would automatically take care of itself. Business managers would automatically undertake the necessary investment in research and development, and would build sufficient new plant and equipment to keep pace with the competition. Individuals would automatically save adequate funds to provide the capital the economy needed to invest in the future. Incentives to work would remain high, even though tax rates were rising.

Unfortunately, we eventually learned that the supply-side of the economy does not automatically grow. This was particularly true in the United States and Great Britain, and it is why President Reagan and Prime Minister Thatcher placed a great deal of emphasis in their economic experiments on policies to stimulate greater work effort, increased savings, and more investment. In this regard, these leaders were simply trying to redress an imbalance between short-term

Keynesian policies and long-term growth policies. But they went to the extreme in implementing their growth policies, and as a result destabilized their economies.

The current situation in the United States is a classic example of what happens when policy balance is not maintained. Our long-term policy combination is one of very large federal budget deficits and tight monetary policy, exactly the opposite of the ideal for stimulating growth in a full-employment economy. This policy imbalance has depressed productive investment — which was the original goal of Reaganomics — and as a result is jeopardizing the potential strength of the American economy. It is an example of an economic policy that has gone so far to the extreme, and is so unbalanced, that it is perpetuating the very conditions that it set out to eliminate.

The bulk of this book has been concerned with the issue of how to improve the supply-side of the economy, or the effort to enhance the performance of the economy in the long run. All of the five economic experiments had this objective. And their great failure has been their ineffectiveness in achieving a balance between their long-term growth policies and short-term stabilization problems in a globally interdependent economy. Frequently, as in the United States and France, short-term problems became so great as to overwhelm any chance for success of the long-term policies.

This book has also recommended a number of economic policies that would achieve the necessary balance for the Power Economy. These proposals are as follows:

• The United States and its allies must immediately contain the threat of protectionism through a pledge to freeze the current proliferation of such trade-restriction policies as orderly marketing agreements, domestic-content legislation, and export subsidies. Such a pledge would be formulated and administered through the General Agreement on Tariffs and Trade (GATT), the official international program for dealing with trade problems.

• The Western powers must substantially strengthen the GATT — primarily by curtailing the current practice of negotiating bilateral trade agreements between member nations and presenting the results as fait accomplis — and must extend GATT purview into the rapidly expanding area of service trade.

• The major industrialized nations must convene an economic summit meeting at which they would agree to take the lead in stimulating the global economy to achieve faster growth. A higher growth rate is needed to curtail the threat of protectionism, to keep trade markets open, and to alleviate the pressures of unemployment.

• At the economic summit meeting, the major countries must agree to coordinate economic policies more closely, to adopt policies that are generally consistent and moderate, and to avoid promising unrealistic and politically motivated economic goals.

• Rather than adopting protectionism as a means of preserving jobs and securing growth in the future, the industrialized nations must increase their efforts to develop new technology, to expand their funding of research and development, and to invest in the education of their labor force. Technology and education have been the major sources of growth for these countries in the past and will continue to be in the future.

• The United States must achieve a better balance between fiscal policies and monetary policies. Such a balance will require tax increases of approximately $100 billion and expenditure reductions of a like amount, with the long-term goal of achieving a budget balance by 1990. This change in course will enable monetary policy to be eased and interest rates to decline. Lower interest rates will have many economic benefits: they will increase productive investments in research and development, and in new plant and equipment; provide more capital for financing housing; decrease the interest costs of the federal budget; remove a major threat to the success of the economic policies in other countries; reduce the cost of debt payments for less developed countries; and bring about a decline in the value of the dollar, which will greatly improve our trade balance and ease many of the trade pressures in the United States.

• The United States must develop a more coordinated and aggressive industrial policy. Such an industrial policy would continue to place primary emphasis on broad macroeconomic policies and tax incentives; however, these macro-policies would be adjusted to protect the balance between fiscal and monetary policies recommended in the proposal just described.

An economic program of moderation as summarized above may not appeal to a politician campaigning among the unemployed steelworkers of Ohio or the out-of-work coal miners in Ruhr, West Germany. He or she might feel compelled to promise massive government industrial assistance to protect constituents' jobs, or, alternatively, might place the entire blame for their predicament on too much government. But a return to moderation and a more stable and expanding economy would be the best proposal that such politicians could offer.

In fact, such candor may find a more receptive audience than most politicians are willing to admit. The average voter, regardless of nationality, has a good sense of what can work and what cannot. People are well aware that there are no miracle solutions to our current economic problems, and they fully understand that our present economic experiments are not working. Yet they still have faith in the underlying strength of their economy to perform better than it has.

Such faith is not ill-founded, for improvement is exactly what will occur if the major industrialized countries coordinate their economic policies, return to moderation, recognize and confront the threat of protectionism, and adopt appropriate industrial policies to assist in the transition from the turbulence of the past to the Power Economy of the future.

Notes

Many works listed in the bibliography ("Major References") are listed by short title in the chapter notes and table source notes. In addition, the following abbreviations have been used:

BW	*Business Week*
CBO	Congressional Budget Office (Washington, D.C.).
ERP	*Economic Report of the President.* Washington, D.C.: GPO.
FRB	*Federal Reserve Bulletin* (Board of Governors of the Federal Reserve System, Washington, D.C.)
FT	*Financial Times* (London)
GEP 80–81	United Kingdom. Parliament. *The Government's Expenditure Plans, 1980–81.* Cmnd. 7746. Nov. 1979.
GPO	Government Printing Office (Washington, D.C.)
HMSO	Her (His) Majesty's Stationery Office (London)
IMF	International Monetary Fund (Washington, D.C.)
MITI	Ministry of International Trade and Industry (Tokyo)
NYT	*New York Times*
OECD	Organization for Economic Cooperation and Development (Paris)
OMB	Office of Management and Budget (Washington, D.C.)
SFC	*San Francisco Chronicle*
"SUMER"	Ronald W. Reagan. "State of the Union Message on Economic Recovery." 18 Feb. 1981. As transcribed in *NYT,* 19 Feb. 1981, sec. 2, 8.
WSJ	*Wall Street Journal*

Introduction

1. Benjamin J. Cohen, "Putting the Squeeze on World Trade," *SFC,* 16 Feb. 1983.

2. *NYT,* 10 Dec. 1981, 26.
3. Rumberger and Levin, "New Technologies."
4. *Europe,* Sept.–Oct. 1981, 30.
5. *NYT,* 22 May 1981, 10.
6. *NYT,* 20 Jan. 1978, sec. 4, 1.

Chapter One
The Tumultuous Seventies

1. *NYT,* 16 Aug. 1971, 14.
2. *NYT,* 21 Oct. 1973, 28.
3. *OECD Economic Outlook,* Dec. 1973, 5.
4. IMF, *International Monetary Fund: Annual Report, 1974* (Washington, D.C., 1974), 1.
5. *NYT,* 13 Oct. 1974, sec. 3, 1.
6. Helmut Schmidt, "The 1977 Alastair Buchan Memorial Lecture," 28 Oct. 1977, as reported in *Survival* (International Institute for Strategic Studies, London) 20 (Jan.–Feb. 1978): 2–10.
7. Helmut Schmidt, "Germany in the Era of Negotiations," *Foreign Affairs* 49 (Oct. 1970): 40
8. *OECD Economic Outlook,* 1978, v.
9. *Economist,* 6–12 June 1981; 25 Sept.–1 Oct. 1982; 3–9 June 1981.
10. Reported by Walter W. Heller, chairman of Kennedy's Council of Economic Advisors, in Heller, *Political Economy,* 35.
11. Friedman, "Monetary Policy," 8–9.
12. *BW,* 3 Sept. 1979, 23.

Chapter Two
The United States Flirts with Reaganomics

1. "SUMER."
2. *NYT,* 19 Feb. 1981, sec. 2, 9.
3. 'SUMER."
4. Senator Lloyd Bentsen, quoted in *NYT,* 19 Feb. 1981, sec. 2, 5.
5. *NYT,* 30 July 1981, 7.
6. Ibid., 1.
7. Norman B. Ture, "The Economic Effects of Tax Changes: A Neoclassical Analysis," in Fink, *Supply-Side Economics,* 36.
8. Ibid., 37.
9. Arthur B. Laffer, "Government Exactions and Revenue Deficiencies," in Fink, *Supply-Side Economics,* 191.
10. The proposition that a trickle-down effect results when economic growth is stimulated had been advanced many years earlier by Professor W. H. Locke Anderson. A more recent examination of the proposition has been made by James R. Thornton et al. See W. H. Locke Anderson, "Trickling Down: The Relationship between Economic Growth and the Extent of Poverty among American Families," *Quarterly Journal of Economics* 78 (Nov. 1964): 511–524; and James R. Thornton, Richard J. Agnello, and Charles R. Link, "Poverty and Economic Growth: Trickle Down Peters Out," *Economic Inquiry* 16 (July 1978): 385–394.

11. Laffer, "Government Exactions and Revenue Deficiencies," 201.

12. David Hume, "Of Taxes," in *Writings on Economics,* ed. Eugene Rotwein (Freeport, N.Y.: Books for Libraries Press, 1955), 85.

13. Smith, *Wealth of Nations* (Cannan ed.), bk. 1, 91.

14. Ibid., bk. 2, 414.

15. Say and Mill quoted in Robert E. Keleher and William P. Orzechowski, "Supply-Side Fiscal Policy: An Historical Analysis," in Fink, *Supply-Side Economics,* 138.

16. *ERP,* Feb. 1982, 116.

17. Ibid., 121.

18. Smith, *Wealth of Nations* (Cannan ed.), bk. 1, 358.

19. David Ricardo, *Principles of Political Economy and Taxation* (London: John Murray, 1821), 166.

20. Ronald W. Reagan, "Inaugural Address of President Ronald W. Reagan," 20 Jan. 1981, as transcribed in *NYT,* 21 Jan. 1981.

21. These major themes were stressed in OMB, *Major Themes and Additional Budget Detail, Fiscal Year 1983* (Washington, D.C.: GPO, 1983).

22. *ERP,* Feb. 1982, 84.

23. *NYT,* 3 Jan. 1983, 1; ibid., 26 Jan. 1982, B9; ibid., 7 Feb. 1982, 28.

24. *NYT,* 15 Jan. 1982, 1; ibid., 28 Jan. 1982, D13.

25. "SUMER."

26. *ERP,* Feb. 1981, 22–23.

27. "SUMER."

28. Testimony by Paul A. Volcker, Chairman, Board of Governors of the Federal Reserve System, as reported in *FRB,* Feb. 1981, 135; ibid., Apr. 1981, 237.

29. *FRB,* Apr. 1981, 237–241.

30. Smith, *Wealth of Nations* (Modern Library), 653, 669, 681. Subsequent Smith quotations are ibid., 667, 668, 681, 682, 716, 689, 693, 147.

31. See note 20 above.

32. "SUMER."

33. Ibid.

34. *ERP,* Feb. 1982, 6.

35. Ibid., 3–5.

36. OMB, *Major Themes* (see n. 21 above), 21. Quotations in the following three paragraphs are ibid., 22, 22, 18, 13.

37. *ERP,* Feb. 1982, 27.

38. "SUMER."

Chapter Three
Japan Seeks Economic Security

1. *NYT,* 14 July 1978, sec. 4, 7.

2. *NYT,* 5 Feb. 1978, sec. 11, 56.

3. *NYT,* 4 May 1979, sec. 4, 14.

4. *NYT,* 30 Apr. 1978, sec. 3, 1.

5. *NYT,* 27 Mar. 1982, 29.

6. Yukio Matsuyama, "Advice to Japan," *NYT,* 15 Feb. 1978, 25.

7. *NYT,* 28 Dec. 1980, sec. 4, 2.

8. *NYT,* 27 Mar. 1982, 29.

9. Hall, *Japan,* 349.

10. Allen, *How Japan Competes,* 12.

11. *NYT,* 17 Nov. 1973, 1.

12. Fukuda quoted in *NYT,* 2 Dec. 1973, 23; MITI officials quoted in *NYT,* 15 Dec. 1973, 43.

13. Japan, Economic Planning Agency, *Seven-Year Plan,* 77.

14. Lawrence B. Krause and Sueo Sekiguchi, "Japan and the World Economy," in Patrick and Rosovsky, *Asia's New Giant,* 387.

15. OECD, Ojimi, 15.

16. Ibid., 37.

17. Ibid., 58.

18. Ibid., 58–59.

19. Ibid., 61.

20. William V. Rapp, "Japan's Industrial Policy," in Frank, *Japanese Economy,* 44.

21. The Japanese will undoubtedly be as assertive in pursuing export markets for these new industries as they were in the past with their older industries. Even in the area of housing construction, an industry that is typically indigenous and one in which the Japanese do not have an international reputation, they have behaved aggressively, having moved into the California residential market in the early 1980s.

22. OECD, Ojimi, 46.

23. Japan Trade Center, *Industrial Policy in Japan: A Question and Answer Overview* (New York: JTC, under the auspices of MITI, n.d.), 5.

24. Magaziner and Hout, *Japanese Industrial Policy,* 41.

25. Ibid.

26. Vogel, "Guided Free Enterprise," 164.

27. Magaziner and Hout, *Japanese Industrial Policy,* 43.

28. OECD, Ojimi, 30.

29. Ibid.

30. MITI officials' characterization of the Japanese economy, as quoted in Magaziner and Hout, *Japanese Industrial Policy,* 47.

31. OECD, Ojimi, 17.

32. Haitani, *Japanese Economic System,* 39.

33. OECD, Ojimi, 19.

34. Japan, Economic Planning Agency, *Seven-Year Plan,* 103.

35. One of the "Seven Spirits of Matsushita" that is recited every morning by the employees of the seven hundred Matsushita plants in Japan. Reciting in unison beliefs or statements of loyalty and dedication is common practice throughout most plants and offices in Japan.

36. OECD, Ojimi, 30.

37. Magaziner and Hout, *Japanese Industrial Policy,* 37.

38. Feigenbaum and McCorduck, *Fifth Generation,* 105.

39. Johnson, *MITI,* 233.

40. Feigenbaum and McCorduck, *Fifth Generation,* 2.

41. Quoted ibid., 124.

42. Ibid., 103.

43. Edwin Reischauer, *The Japanese* (Cambridge: Harvard University Press, 1977), 226.

44. Quoted in Feigenbaum and McCorduck, *Fifth Generation,* 133–134.

45. Ibid., 132.

46. Japan, Economic Planning Agency, *Seven-Year Plan,* 7.

47. Ibid., 32–34.

48. Ibid., 34, 43, 46.

49. Ibid., 32, 5.

50. OECD, Ojimi, 14.

Chapter Four
West Germany and the Golden Middle Road

1. Helmut Schmidt, "Policy Statement to the Bundestag," 19 Jan. 1978, as reported in *NYT,* 20 Jan. 1978, sec. 4, 2.

2. *NYT,* 1 Feb. 1978, sec. 4, 1.

3. Otto Lambsdorff, "West Germany's Economic-Growth Program," *NYT,* 2 Mar. 1978, 19.

4. "After two German monetary upheavals and reformations in this century, the psychological limit [to stronger economic stimulation and the resulting threat of inflation] will be reached before the economic limit," Armin Gruenewald, deputy spokesman for the West German government, told the American press (*NYT,* 16 May 1978, 47).

5. Helmut Kohl, "Policy Statement to the Bundestag," 13 Oct. 1982, as reported in *Foreign Broadcast Information Service Daily Report: Western Europe,* 14 Oct. 1982.

6. OECD, *OECD Economic Surveys: Germany* (1979), 31.

7. Hanrieder, *Helmut Schmidt,* 120.

8. The money supply can grow faster than the MCB owing to a jump in the "velocity of circulation" — the ratio of money to GNP. This measure tends to rise when interest rates go up as the holders of currency attempt to increase "turnover," or efficiency in the use of money. Such behavior is standard, for holding "idle cash" that earns no interest is expensive.

9. Hanrieder, *Helmut Schmidt,* 116.

10. *Monthly Report of the Deutsche Bundesbank,* Jan. 1978, 8.

11. Ibid., July 1978, 6.

12. Ibid., Nov. 1978, 5.

13. Ibid., Jan. 1979, 5.

14. *Report of the Deutsche Bundesbank,* 1981, 3.

15. Ibid., 1982, 30.

16. Ibid., 35.

17. OECD, *14 Member Countries,* 16.

18. Hanrieder, *Helmut Schmidt,* 120.

19. OECD, *14 Member Countries,* 11.

20. Erhard, *Economics of Success,* 171.

21. Hanrieder, *Helmut Schmidt,* 121.

22. Heinz Riesenhuber, "German Technology Policy: A New Orientation," in

United States–German Economic Survey, 1983 (New York: German American Chamber of Commerce, 1984), 95.

23. OECD, *14 Member Countries,* 17.

24. Hanrieder, *Helmut Schmidt,* 107.

25. *NYT,* 25 Jan. 1976, sec. 3, 62.

26. Sloman, *Socialising Public Ownership,* 20.

27. OECD, *14 Member Countries,* 14.

28. Ibid., 33.

29. Riesenhuber, "German Technology Policy," 98.

30. Ibid., 97.

31. Pinder, Hosomi, and Diebold, *Industrial Policy,* 31.

32. Markovits, *Political Economy,* 20.

33. Ibid.

34. OECD, *14 Member Countries,* 25.

35. This does not mean that the Germans do not accept any governmental intervention in their economy. As discussed under "Industrial Targeting," West Germany has been decidedly interventionist in providing assistance to certain industries; however, this is microeconomic rather than macroeconomic intervention.

36. Knott, *Managing the German Economy,* 15.

37. Helmut Schmidt, "A Policy of Reliable Partnership," *Foreign Affairs* 59 (Spring 1981): 743. The first Schmidt quotation in the following paragraph is ibid., 743.

38. Hanrieder, *Helmut Schmidt,* 83–87.

39. Schmidt, "Policy of Reliable Partnership," 755. Schmidt on several occasions emphasized these objectives as essential ones for political leaders trying to manage in a time of crisis, after first stating them publicly in a speech before the Tenth Special General Assembly of the United Nations, 26 May 1978.

40. Schmidt, "Policy of Reliable Partnership," 744.

Chapter Five
Great Britain: The Iron Lady Imposes Monetary Discipline

1. "Tories and Labor vs. Spring," *NYT,* 22 Apr. 1979.

2. *NYT,* 11 Feb. 1979, sec. 4, 2.

3. Anthony Lewis, "A Choice, Not an Echo," *NYT,* 26 Apr. 1971.

4. Attributed to conservative analyst Peregrine Worsthorne and quoted in "Tories and Labor" (see n. 1 above).

5. *NYT,* 5 May 1979, 6.

6. See n. 1 above.

7. Attributed to a director of the merchant bank Kleinwort-Benson and quoted in *NYT,* 5 May 1979, 6.

8. Queen Elizabeth II, speech to Parliament, 15 May 1979, as transcribed in *Daily Telegraph* (London), 16 May 1979, 11.

9. Geoffrey Howe, budget message to the House of Commons, 12 June 1979, as transcribed in *FT,* 13 June 1979, 18. (Subsequent quotations in this section are from the same source.)

10. *GEP 80–81,* 1.

11. J. R. Sargent [Group Economic Advisor, Midland Bank], "Mrs. Thatcher's Monetarism: The Theory and the Practice" (paper presented at the International Conference of Commercial Bank Economists, Budapest, June 1982).

12. *Monetary Control,* Cmnd. 7858 (Mar. 1980), iii.

13. Ministry of the Treasury, *Economic Progress Report,* no. 123 (London: HMSO, 1980), 1.

14. Ministry of the Treasury, *Financial Statement and Budget Report, 1981–82* (London: HMSO, 1981), 15.

15. Ministry of the Treasury, *Economic Progress Report,* no. 144 (London: HMSO, 1982), 1.

16. Friedman, "Monetary Policy," 12. Unless otherwise indicated, the statements of Friedman quoted subsequently are from the same source.

17. Friedman's allusion is to John Stuart Mill's famous statement that money "is a machine for doing quickly and commodiously, what would be done, though less quickly and commodiously, without it; and like many other kinds of machinery, it only exerts a distinct and independent influence of its own when it gets out of order."

18. See note 9 above.

19. See note 12 above.

20. *Monetary Control* (see n. 12 above), 2.

21. Milton Friedman, "Hooray for Margaret Thatcher," *Newsweek,* 9 July 1979, 56.

22. Geoffrey Howe, as quoted in *NYT,* 19 Aug. 1979, sec. 4, 3.

23. *NYT,* 27 July 1979, 3.

24. *NYT,* 19 Aug. 1979, sec. 4, 3.

25. Sloman, *Socialising Public Ownership,* 20.

26. Ibid., 90.

27. Kelf-Cohen, *British Nationalisation,* 93.

28. Ibid., 260.

29. Sloman, *Socialising Public Ownership,* 101.

30. Ibid., 99.

31. U.K., National Economic Development Office, *Nationalised Industries,* 8, raises these points.

32. Sloman, *Socialising Public Ownership,* 24–25.

33. U.K., Trades Union Congress, *Public Ownership.*

34. U.K., National Consumer Council, *Nationalised Industries,* 53.

35. *Coal Industry Commission: Minutes of Evidence,* Cmd. 359 (1919), 324.

36. U.K., Trades Union Congress, *Public Ownership.*

37. Sloman, *Socialising Public Ownership,* 57.

38. Ibid.

39. *The Government's Expenditure Plans, 1983–84 to 1985–86,* Cmnd. 8789, vol. 2 (Feb. 1983), 106.

40. Quoted in *FT,* 29 Mar. 1979, 10.

41. *NYT,* 26 Apr. 1971, 42.

42. Margaret Thatcher, speech delivered at the Guildhall, London, 12 Nov. 1979, as quoted in R. W. Apple, Jr., "Is Maggie Thatcher Just Making Things Worse?" *NYT,* 16 Dec. 1979.

43. *NYT,* 13 June 1979, 1.

44. Ibid.

45. *GEP 80–81,* 1.

46. *NYT,* 16 Dec. 1979, sec. 4, 42.

47. Data are from *GEP 80–81* and Ministry of the Treasury, *Financial Statement and Budget Report, 1980–81* (London: HMSO, 1980), 19.

48. *GEP 80–81,* 1.

49. Ibid., 2.

50. Ibid., 3.

51. *NYT,* 5 May 1979, 22.

52. See note 21 above.

53. *NYT,* 16 Dec. 1979, sec. 4, 49.

54. *ERP,* Feb. 1982, 3.

55. See note 9 above.

56. Geoffrey Howe, budget statement, 26 Mar. 1980, as transcribed in *FT,* 27 Mar. 1980.

57. See chapter 2, note 20.

Chapter Six
France Does Things Differently

1. *Europe,* Sept.–Oct. 1981, 30.

2. Ibid.

3. Ibid.

4. "Election Shock Grips Bourse," *NYT,* 13 May 1981.

5. Friedrich Seythal, "François Mitterrand: The New Strong Man of Europe," *U.N. Plaza,* Sept. 1981, 33.

6. "Text of Address by Mitterrand," *NYT,* 22 May 1981.

7. "Mitterrand Opts for the Middle Way," *FT,* 25 Nov. 1981.

8. "Mitterrand Team Moves Quickly on Social Programme," *FT,* 28 May 1981.

9. *WSJ,* 21 Apr. 1982, 1.

10. *NYT,* 16 Sept. 1981, sec. 4, 15.

11. Ibid.

12. André Fourcans, "France — The Strategy Remains Unchanged," *Banker,* July 1982, 51.

13. "Can Mitterrand Remake France's Economy?" *BW,* 10 Jan. 1983.

14. *NYT,* 22 May 1981, sec. 4, 1.

15. *BW,* 10 Jan. 1983, 67.

16. All quotations in this paragraph are from "Can Mitterrand Remake France's Economy?" *BW,* 10 Jan. 1983.

17. *BW,* 24 May 1982, 66.

18. David Housego, "Mitterrand's First Year: Socialism, More or Less," *FT,* 10 May 1982.

19. *BW,* 10 Jan. 1983, 47.

20. Malcolm Rutherford, "The Consequences of Mitterrand," *FT,* 15 May 1981.

21. *NYT,* 23 June 1981, sec. 4, 1.

22. Ardagh, *France in the 1980s,* 72.

23. *Time,* 28 Sept. 1981, 74.

24. *NYT,* 23 June 1981, sec. 4, 1.

25. Ibid.

26. The decision was made on 9 Sept. 1981, and the statement is quoted in *NYT,* 10 Sept. 1981, sec. 4, 1.

27. *BW,* 10 Jan. 1983, 52.

28. Ibid., 55.

29. *FT,* 25 Nov. 1981, 5.

30. Ardagh, *France in the 1980s,* 34.

31. OECD, *Industrial Policy of France,* 35.

32. Cohen, *Modern Capitalist Planning,* 75.

33. OECD, Suleiman, 28.

34. Ibid., 30.

35. Ardagh, *France in the 1980s,* 37.

36. *BW,* 10 Jan. 1983, 47.

37. Ardagh, *France in the 1980s,* 90.

38. Jacques-A. Kosciusko-Morizet, *La Mafia Polytechniciéne* (Paris: Le Seuil, 1973).

39. Ardagh, *France in the 1980s,* 85.

40. Ibid., 86.

41. Granick, *European Executive,* 147.

42. Karl Marx, "Address to the Communist League," in Howe, *Socialism,* 56.

43. Howe, *Socialism,* 24.

44. Oskar Lange, "The Economist's Case for Socialism," ibid., 708.

45. Ibid., 710.

46. Irving Howe and Lewis Coser, "Images of Socialism," in Howe, *Socialism,* 847.

47. Oscar Wilde, "The Soul of Man under Socialism," in Howe, *Socialism,* 413.

48. Lange, "Economist's Case for Socialism," 700.

49. Henry M. Pachter, "Three Economic Models: Capitalism, the Welfare State, and Socialism," in Howe, *Socialism,* 788.

50. George Orwell, "A Footnote to Wilde," in Howe, *Socialism,* 429.

51. Lange, "Economist's Case for Socialism," 706.

52. Marx, "Address to the Communist League," 51, 56.

53. Daniel Bell, "Work, Alienation, and Social Control," in Howe, *Socialism,* 608.

54. Ibid., 610.

55. Jean-Pierre Cot, minister delegate to the Minister of External Relations for Cooperation, as quoted in *Le Monde,* 29 Dec. 1981.

56. *BW,* 10 Jan. 1983, 51.

57. These income distribution data are for the period 1969–1973, a time of relative full-employment and economic stability, and therefore probably give a clearer picture of the situation than data from a later period, when the industrialized economies were experiencing high unemployment and economic recessions.

58. Ardagh, *France in the 1980s,* 384.

59. OECD, Sawyer, 14.

60. Ardagh, *France in the 1980s,* 384.

61. Ibid., 386

62. Ibid., 95.

Chapter Seven
The Economic Experiments Fail to Deliver

1. "EEC Attacks U.S. over Interest Rates," *FT,* 12 Feb. 1982. All quotations in this paragraph are ibid.

2. Jean-Pierre Cot, as quoted in *Le Monde,* 29 Dec. 1981.

3. "SUMER."

4. U.S. Secretary of Treasury, "A Program for Economic Recovery," Feb. 1981.

5. Greider, "Education of David Stockman," 38. Subsequent Stockman quotations are ibid., 32, 32, 54.

6. "Special Report: The Built-in Deficit," *BW,* 16 Aug. 1982.

7. *NYT,* 20 Aug. 1982, 1.

8. Henry S. Reuss and James K. Galbraith, "Supply-Side's Sunk," *NYT,* 30 Aug. 1982.

9. *NYT,* 22 Aug. 1982, 38.

10. Peter Field, "The Death of Reaganomics," *Euromoney,* Sept. 1982.

11. Norman B. Ture, "An Erosion of 1981's Gains," *NYT,* 12 Sept. 1982.

12. See note 10 above.

13. Brookings Institution, *The Future Course of U.S.-Japan Economic Relations* (Washington, D.C., 1983), 55 (hereafter cited as *Future Course*).

14. Ibid., 49.

15. U.S. Department of Commerce, International Trade Administration, *Domestic Employment Generated by U.S. Exports* (Washington, D.C.: GPO, 1983).

16. *Future Course,* 45.

17. Response to Senator Danforth by Henry Owen, in *Future Course,* 107.

18. *Future Course,* 94.

19. *Quarterly Economic Review of Germany* (The Economist Intelligence Unit, London), no. 1 (1983): 14.

20. Gregor Mettinger, "Venture Capital in the U.S. and Germany: A Comparison," in *United States–German Economic Survey, 1982* (New York: German American Chamber of Commerce, 1983), 147.

21. *NYT,* 6 June 1983, D7.

22. "Special Report: What Hath Thatcher Wrought?" *BW,* 6 June 1983.

23. "The 364 Economists' Attack on Government Policy," *Barclays Review* 56 (May 1981): 27.

24. Sir Keith Joseph, *Monetarism Is Not Enough* (London: Center for Policy Studies, 1976).

25. See Laurence H. Meyer and Robert H. Rasche, "On the Costs and Benefits of Anti-Inflation Policies," *Monthly Review of Federal Reserve Bank of St. Louis,* Feb. 1980. These costs are the discounted value of the cumulative output loss in 1972 dollars. They therefore indicate relative magnitudes of estimated loss, suggesting that the monetarists obtain a loss about one-third that obtained by the neo-Keynesians.

26. Stephen J. Lewis, chief monetary economist at London stockbrokers Phillips and Drew, in *BW,* 4 Apr. 1983, 67.

27. *BW,* 11 Apr. 1983, 44.

28. Ibid.

29. Attributed to Jean François Demieau, sales director for a hospital-supply concern in Bagnolet, France, in *NYT*, 27 Mar. 1983, 1.

30. *NYT*, 22 Mar. 1983, 3.

31. Ibid.

32. *NYT*, 16 Mar. 1983, 3.

33. *Economist*, 15 Oct. 1983, 14.

34. Ibid., 26 Mar. 1983, 30.

35. Ibid.

36. *BW*, 11 Apr. 1983, 44.

37. *WSJ*, 17 Oct. 1983, 35.

38. *Economist*, 26 Mar. 1983, 11.

39. Ibid., 30.

40. *Future Course* (see n. 13 above), 47.

41. "U.S. Rhetoric over Trade Wearing Thin in Japan," *Houston Post*, 9 Nov. 1983.

Chapter Eight
The Threat of Protectionism

1. King George V, opening speech to the World Economic Conference, as published in *NYT*, 13 June 1933, 1.

2. *NYT*, 12 June 1933, 1.

3. Ibid., 2.

4. Many economists and groups of experts believed in 1933 that the depression was over. The *World Economic Survey* of the League of Nations, released on 4 Oct. 1933, stated that the world recovery "in progress in the Summer of 1933 is more substantial than that a year ago" (*NYT*, 5 Oct. 1933, 31). The National Industrial Conference Board in the United States also issued a positive verdict, noting that "since the Summer of 1932, when the low point of the world depression was reached, a marked improvement in business activity in the principal industrial countries has taken place, accompanied by a recovery in world prices of staple commodities" (*NYT*, 7 Oct. 1933, 26).

5. *NYT*, 26 June 1933, 3.

6. *NYT*, 4 June 1933, sec. 4, 1.

7. *NYT*, 4 July 1933, 1.

8. *NYT*, 28 July 1933, 1.

9. Ibid.

10. Hall, *Japan*, 335.

11. *NYT*, 16 Nov. 1933, 47.

12. Yoshihiko Seki, "Why Japan Should Heed the Lessons of the Past," *SFC*, 16 Feb. 1983, sec. 3, 1 (excerpted from *Sankei Shimbun*).

13. "The Latest Battle of Poitiers," *NYT*, 14 Jan. 1983, sec. 4, 13.

14. American Chamber of Commerce in Japan, *Report on 1981/82 Trade-Investment-Barrier Membership Survey* (Tokyo: ACCJ, 1982).

15. "Text of Williamsburg Declaration on Economic Recovery," *NYT*, 31 May 1983.

16. "Text of Versailles Joint Communique," *NYT*, 7 June 1982.

17. "Text of the Ottawa Summit," *NYT*, 22 July 1981.

18. *WSJ*, 2 Dec. 1982, 1.

19. Ibid.

20. Bergsten and Cline, *Trade Policy*, 32.

21. Ibid., 11. (Cost estimates in the 1982 Bergsten-Cline study have been updated to 1984 by JOW.)

22. Benjamin J. Cohen, "Putting the Squeeze on World Trade," *SFC*, 16 Feb. 1983.

23. "Electronics Execs Bitter at Japanese," *SFC*, 27 Apr. 1982.

24. "Japan's Farmers Protest Imports," United Press International, 13 Jan. 1983.

25. *NYT*, 29 Apr. 1983, 1.

26. *NYT*, 28 Apr. 1983, sec. 4, 2.

27. *NYT*, 1 Aug. 1982, sec. 3, 1.

28. *NYT*, 22 Jan. 1983, 28.

29. For a complete discussion of this proposal, which is only briefly summarized in the text, see Bergsten and Cline, *Trade Policy*, 66–70. The action was endorsed in 1982 by a group of international finance and trade experts convened by the Institute for International Economics (IIE) in Washington, D.C. The experts, who clearly recognized the growing threat of protectionism, recommended that a "Standstill Agreement" be signed that "would obligate all participating countries to avoid imposing new trade barriers (or other distortions) for its duration." The conference was held just prior to a high-level meeting of the GATT ministers in Nov. 1982. See IIE, *Promoting World Recovery*.

30. John Hein, "A New Protectionism Rises," *Across the Board* (Conference Board, New York), Apr. 1983, 23.

Chapter Nine
The Issue of Industrial Policy

1. Jimmy Carter (statement setting forth his "Economic Program for the 1980s"), 28 Aug. 1980, as quoted in Wachter and Wachter, *U.S. Industrial Policy?*, 497.

2. Reginald H. Jones, "Toward a New U.S. Industrial Policy," ibid., 14.

3. Schultze, "Industrial Policy," 10.

4. Quoted in "Industrial Policy: What Is It? Do We Need It?" *U.S. News and World Report*, 3 Oct. 1983, 46.

5. CBO, *Federal Support of Business* (Washington, D.C.: GPO, 1984). As noted in the CBO study, the true total may be less than the sum of the individual tax provisions because of interactions between different tax provisions for business.

6. Hiroya Ueno, "Industrial Policy: Its Role and Limits," *Journal of Japanese Trade and Industry*, July–Aug. 1983, 34.

7. Robert S. Ozaki, "How the Japanese Industrial Policy Works," in Johnson, *Industrial Policy Debate*, 48.

8. Chalmers Johnson, "The Idea of Industrial Policy," in Johnson, *Industrial Policy Debate*, 8.

9. Denison and Chung, *Japan's Economy*, 40.

10. Jeremy Bernstein, "Profiles: Allocating Sacrifice," *New Yorker*, 23 Jan. 1983, 45, 78.

11. Aaron Wildavsky, "Squaring the Political Circle: Industrial Policies and the American Dream," in Johnson, *Industrial Policy Debate*, 32.

12. Kelf-Cohen, *British Nationalisation,* 260.

13. Schultze, "Industrial Policy," 9.

14. Denison, *Sources of Economic Growth,* 73.

15. Denison, *Accounting for Economic Growth,* 79.

16. Eugene Bardach, "Implementing Industrial Policy," in Johnson, *Industrial Policy Debate,* 101.

Chapter Ten
The Power Economy

1. Johnson, *Industrial Policy Debate,* 14.

2. Ibid., 154.

3. *WSJ,* 17 June 1983, 1.

4. Ibid.

5. Barber, *Presidential Character,* 43.

6. Ibid., 56.

7. John W. Kendrick, "Productivity Trends and the Recent Slowdown," in *Contemporary Economic Problems* (Washington, D.C.: American Enterprise Institute, 1979).

8. See chapter 5, note 8.

9. See chapter 6, note 6.

10. See chapter 8, table 18.

11. *NYT,* 26 June 1933, 3.

Major References

Allen, G. C. *How Japan Competes: A Verdict on Dumping*. London: Institute of Economic Affairs, 1978.

Ardagh, John. *France in the 1980s*. London: Secker and Warburg, 1982.

Barber, James David. *The Presidential Character: Predicting Performance in the White House*. Englewood Cliffs, N.J.: Prentice-Hall, 1972.

Barro, Robert J. "Second Thoughts on Keynesian Economics." *American Economic Review* 69 (May 1979): 54–59.

Benedict, Ruth. *The Chrysanthemum and the Sword*. Tokyo: Charles E. Tuttle Co., 1979.

Bergsten, C. Fred, and William Cline. *Trade Policy in the 1980s*. Washington, D.C.: Institute for International Economics, 1982.

Bluestone, Barry, and Bennett Harrison. *The Deindustrialization of America*. New York: Basic Books, 1982.

Bowe, Collette, ed. *Industrial Efficiency and the Role of Government*. London: HMSO, 1977.

Broadway, Frank. *State Intervention in British Industry, 1964–68*. Rutherford, N.J.: Fairleigh Dickinson University Press, 1969.

Business International Research Report. *France in Transition*. Geneva, 1979.

———. *Socialist France: The New Business Environment*. Geneva, 1983.

Chigusa, T., ed. *A Reorganization of Industrial Structure*. Tokyo: Shunju Publishing Co., 1963.

Cline, William. *International Debt: Systemic Risk and Policy Response*. Washington, D.C.: Institute for International Economics, 1984.

Cohen, Stephen. *Modern Capitalist Planning: The French Model*. Cambridge: Harvard University Press, 1969.

Dean, James W. "The Dissolution of the Keynesian Consensus." In *The Public Interest, Special Issue, 1980: The Crisis in Economic Theory*, 19–34.

Denison, Edward F. *Accounting for United States Economic Growth, 1929–1969*. Washington, D.C.: Brookings Institution, 1974.

Denison, Edward F. *Sources of Economic Growth in the United States.* New York: Committee for Economic Development, 1962.

Denison, Edward F., and William K. Chung. *How Japan's Economy Grew So Fast: The Sources of Postwar Expansion.* Washington, D.C.: Brookings Institution, 1976.

Erhard, Ludwig. *The Economics of Success.* Princeton, N.J.: D. Van Nostrand Co., 1963.

Eckstein, Otto, Christopher Catch, Roger Brinner, and Peter Duprey. *The DRI Report on U.S. Manufacturing Industries.* New York: McGraw-Hill Book Co., 1984.

Feigenbaum, Edward A., and Pamela McCorduck. *The Fifth Generation: Artificial Intelligence and Japan's Computer Challenge to the World.* Reading, Mass.: Addison-Wesley Publishing Co., 1983.

Feldstein, Martin, ed. *The American Economy in Transition.* Chicago: University of Chicago Press, 1980.

Fink, Richard H., ed. *Supply-Side Economics: A Critical Appraisal.* Frederick, Md.: University Publications of America, 1982.

Frank, Isaiah, ed. *The Japanese Economy in International Perspective.* Baltimore: Johns Hopkins University Press, 1975.

Friedman, Milton. "The Role of Monetary Policy." *American Economic Review* 58 (Mar. 1968): 1–17.

Granick, David. *The European Executive.* New York: Doubleday, 1964.

Greider, William. "The Education of David Stockman." *Atlantic Monthly,* Dec. 1981.

Hadley, Eleanor M. *Antitrust in Japan.* Princeton, N.J.: Princeton University Press, 1970.

Haitani, Kanji. *The Japanese Economic System.* Lexington, Mass.: Lexington Books, 1976.

Hall, John Whitney. *Japan: From Prehistory to Modern Times.* Tokyo: Charles E. Tuttle Co., 1971.

Hanrieder, Wolfram F. *Helmut Schmidt: Perspectives on Politics.* Boulder, Colo.: Westview Press, 1982.

Heller, Walter W. *New Dimensions of Political Economy.* New York: W. W. Norton and Co., 1967.

Howe, Irving, ed. *Essential Works of Socialism.* New Haven, Conn.: Yale University Press, 1976.

Institute for International Economics. *Promoting World Recovery: A Statement on Global Economic Strategy.* Washington, D.C., 1982.

Japan. Economic Planning Agency. *New Economic and Social Seven-Year Plan.* Tokyo, 1979.

———. Export-Import Bank. *The Export-Import Bank of Japan: Its Object and Functions.* Tokyo, 1963.

———. External Trade Organization. *White Paper on International Trade.* Tokyo, 1980.

———. Ministry of International Trade and Industry (MITI). *Discussion Paper on the Vision of MITI's Policies in the 1980s.* Tokyo, 1979.

Johnson, Chalmers. *MITI and the Japanese Miracle: The Growth of Industrial Policy, 1925–1975.* Stanford, Calif.: Stanford University Press, 1982.

————, ed. *Industrial Policy Debate*. San Francisco: Institute for Contemporary Studies, 1984.

Kelf-Cohen, Reuben. *British Nationalisation, 1945–1973*. London: Macmillan and Co., 1973.

Knott, Jack H. *Managing the German Economy*. Lexington, Mass.: Lexington Books, 1981.

Kohl, Wilfrid L., and Giorgio Basevi. *West Germany: A European and Global Power*. Lexington, Mass.: Lexington Books, 1980.

Kojimi, Kiyoshi. *Nontariff Barriers to Japan's Trade*. Tokyo: Japan Economic Research Center, 1971.

Lawrence, Robert Z. *Can America Compete?* Washington, D.C.: Brookings Institution, 1984.

Lewis, Ben W. *British Planning and Nationalization*. New York: Twentieth Century Fund, 1952.

Magaziner, Ira C., and Thomas M. Hout. *Japanese Industrial Policy*. Berkeley, Calif.: Institute of International Studies, 1980.

Magaziner, Ira C., and Robert B. Reich. *Minding America's Business: The Decline and Rise of the American Economy*. New York: Vintage Books, 1983.

Markovits, Andrei S., ed. *The Political Economy of West Germany*. New York: Praeger Publishers, 1982.

Morrison, Herbert. *Socialisation and Transport*. London: Constable, 1933.

Nakazawa, Kazuo. *Japan's Foreign Economic Policy: Options for the Seventies*. Washington, D.C.: U.S.-Japan Trade Council, 1970.

Okita, Saburo. *Causes and Problems of Rapid Growth in Postwar Japan and Their Implications for Newly Developing Economies*. Tokyo: Japan Economic Research Center, 1967.

————. "Natural Resource Dependency and Japanese Foreign Policy." *Foreign Affairs* 52 (July 1974): 714–724.

Organization for Economic Cooperation and Development (OECD). "Adjustment Process Since the Oil Crisis." *OECD Economic Outlook* (Paris), July 1977.

————. *Economic Outlook*. Paris, published biannually.

————. *Economic Surveys*. Paris, published annually for individual countries.

————. *Industrial Policy of France*. Paris, 1970.

————. *Industrial Policies of 14 Member Countries*. Paris, 1971.

————. Ojimi, Y. *Industrial Policy of Japan*. Paris, 1972.

————. Sawyer, Malcolm. *Income Distribution in OECD Countries*. Paris, 1976.

————. Suleiman, Ezra N. "Industrial Policy Formulation in France." In *Industrial Policies in Western Europe*. Paris, 1975.

————. *United States Industrial Policies*. Paris, 1970.

Palmer, John L., and Isabel V. Sawhill, eds. *The Reagan Experiment: An Examination of Economic and Social Policies under the Reagan Administration*. Baltimore: Urban Institute Press, 1982.

Patrick, Hugh, and Henry Rosovsky, eds. *Asia's New Giant: How the Japanese Economy Works*. Washington, D.C.: Brookings Institution, 1976.

Pinder, John, Takashi Hosomi, and William Diebold. *Industrial Policy and the International Economy*. New York: Trilateral Commission, 1979.

Roberts, Paul Craig. "The Breakdown of the Keynesian Model," *Public Interest* 52 (Summer 1978): 20–33.

Rumberger, Russell W., and Henry M. Levin. *Forecasting the Impact of New Technologies on the Future Job Market.* Stanford, Calif.: Stanford University School of Education, 1984.

Schultze, Charles L. "Industrial Policy: A Dissent." *Brookings Review* (Brookings Institution, Washington, D.C.), Fall 1983.

Shehan, John. *Promotion and Control of Industry in Postwar France.* Cambridge: Harvard University Press, 1963.

Sloman, Martyn. *Socialising Public Ownership.* London: Macmillan and Co., 1978.

Smith, Adam. *An Inquiry into the Nature and Causes of the Wealth of Nations.* Edited by Edwin Cannan. Chicago: University of Chicago Press, 1976.

———. *The Wealth of Nations.* Modern Library. New York: Random House, 1937.

Stein, Herbert. "The Never-Never Land of Pain-Free Solutions." *Fortune,* 31 Dec. 1979.

Tobin, James. "How Dead Is Keynes?" *Economic Inquiry* 15 (Oct. 1977): 459–468.

United Kingdom. National Consumer Council. *Consumers and the Nationalised Industries.* London: HMSO, 1976.

———. National Economic Development Office. *A Study of UK Nationalised Industries.* London: HMSO, 1976.

———. Trades Union Congress. *Public Ownership: An Interim Report.* London, 1953.

United States. Department of Commerce. International Trade Administration. *Domestic Employment Generated by U.S. Exports.* Washington, D.C.: GPO, 1983.

Vogel, Ezra F. "Guided Free Enterprise in Japan." *Harvard Business Review* 56 (May–June 1978): 161– 170.

Wachter, Michael L., and Susan M. Wachter, eds. *Toward a New U.S. Industrial Policy?* Philadelphia: University of Pennsylvania Press, 1983.

Index

Abu Dhabi, 4
Accelerated Cost Recovery System, 238
AEG Telefunken, 188
AFDC (Aid to Families with Dependent Children), 46
AFL-CIO, 229
Africa, 102
agriculture, 218–220, 226, 230–232
Aircraft and Shipbuilding Industries Bill of 1974, 117
Air France, 150
air-quality control, 39
Allegheny Ludlum, 214
Allen, G. C., 52
American Chamber of Commerce in Japan, 213
antitrust laws, 98
Argentina, 222
artificial intelligence, 69–73
ASEAN (Association of Southeast Asian Nations), 102
Associated European Capital Corporation, 190
Atlantic Monthly, 171
Ayres, Bud, 214

baby boom, 12–14, 139
balanced budget, 27–28, 127–128. *See also* budget deficits
Baldrige, Malcolm, 214
Bank of England, 196–197
Bank of Japan, 183
banking: in France, 151; in Great Britain, 109; in West Germany, 96–98
Banque Rothschild, 144

Barber, James David, 266
BASF, 187
basic industries, 92–93, 239–240
Bayer, 187
Bell, Daniel, 160
Bergeron, André, 199
birthrate, 138–139. *See also* baby boom
BNOC. *See* British National Oil Corporation
Brazil, xii, 11, 222–224, 227
British Aerospace, 111
British Airways, 111, 192
British Economic Advisory Council, 208
British Leyland, 192
British National Oil Corporation (BNOC), 111, 118
British Shipbuilders, 111, 192
British Steel, 192
British Telecom, 118
British Transport Docks Board, 118
Britoil, 118
Brock, William, 214
Brookings Institution, 230, 244
Budget-Accompanying Laws, 80
budget deficits: in France, 135, 137, 138; no-recession, 80; Reaganomics and, 168, 169, 171–176; in United States, 79, 166, 263, 267; in West Germany, 79–80. *See also* balanced budget
Bundesbank, 83–86, 166

Callaghan, James, 103, 104
Canada, 162
capitalism vs. socialism, 156, 159
Carter, Jimmy, 77, 229

Environmental Protection Agency (EPA), 39

Erhard, Ludwig, 88, 230

Euromoney, 172–173

Europe, Western. *See* Western Europe

European Economic Community (Common Market), 152–153, 201, 213, 218–219; coal imports and, 93; criticism of United States by, 222; Japanese trade and, 49; West Germany and, 102

European Monetary System (EMS), 136, 200–201

export credits, 217

export promotion, 240–241

exports: current-account balances and, 7–8; dependence of U.S. economy on, xii; of Japan, 48–50, 54, 177–180, 209–210; limits on, 216; of United States, 181, 255; of West Germany, 188. *See also* export credits; export promotion

Fabius, Laurent, 137, 204

farm subsidies, 218–220, 231–232

Federal Housing Administration (FHA), 242

Federal Republic of Germany. *See* West Germany

Federal Reserve Bank, 40–41, 108, 169, 196–197, 224

Federation of German Labor Union, 97

Feigenbaum, Edward A., 70

Feldstein, Martin, 18

FHA (Federal Housing Administration), 242

Fifth Generation Computer System, 51, 69–73

fiscal policy, 195; defined, 233; industrial policy and, 233, 237–238; monetary policy and, 84–85, 110, 273–274, 276; in West Germany, 84–85

Food Stamp Program, 46

Force Ouvrière, 199

franc (French), 130, 136, 198, 199, 200, 202, 203, 205, 270–271

France, xiv–xv, 130–165, 198–204; birthrate in, 138–139; budget deficit in, 135, 137, 138; criticism of, 167; criticism of United States by, 222; consensus forming in, 248; disposable income in, 134–135; economic-policy coordination and, 260; employment in, 133, 134, 138–142, 155; entrepreneurship in, 146–147; export credits and, 217; foreign competition and, 152–153; government spending in, 137; high technology in, 147, 151; income distribution in, 162–164, 165; incomes policy in, 135; industrial base in, 186; industrial concentration in, 152; industrial policy in, 203–204, 253; inflation in,

France *(continued)* 135, 136–137, 200, 202; job training in, 141; Keynesian economics in, 15, 134; labor issues in, 138–142; lack of global view by, 101; large-scale industry in, 151–153; management in, 147–148; management education in, 153–154; monetary policy in, 137; nationalization of industry in, xv, 132–133, 142–154, 165, 202; Nazi occupation of, 149, 150; nontariff barriers to trade in, 212–213; oil embargo and, 5; productivity in, 141–142; projected economic growth rate in, 203; public investment by, 239; real growth in, 198; socialism in, 137, 142, 146–148, 155–165; social programs in, 134; social security in, 140–142; tax evasion in, 163; tax policy in, 135, 163; telecommunications in, 147, 148; trade deficit in, 136, 199, 200, 202; unemployment in, 138–142

free market economy, 15–16, 87–89, 213–214

Friedman, Milton, 18, 105, 107–111, 125, 193, 270

Fukuda, Takeo, 52

full employment, 15–16

GATT (General Agreement on Tariffs and Trade), 217, 221, 224–225, 275

GDP (gross domestic product). *See* gross national product

General Theory of Employment, Interest, and Money, The, 14

George V (king of Great Britain), 207

George, David Lloyd, 208, 272

Germany. *See* West Germany

Giscard d'Estaing, Valéry, 130, 134, 148, 164, 203

global economy, 101–102; cycles in, 263; debt and, 268; Great Depression and, 208; growth rate of, 180–181, 268; interdependence of, 185, 200, 252, 254–259, 263; problems confronting, 208–210; protectionism and, 217; recessions and, 273; stimulation of, 225–226, 275–276; United States and, 249. *See also* Power Economy

GNP. *See* gross national product

"golden middle road" policy, 77–102

gold standard, 3–4, 208

government: investment in industry by, 36–38, 68, 80–81, 91–102, 230–231, 238–239; Japanese economy and, 56–76; Reaganomics and, 42–47; role of, in economic policy, 16–18. *See also "government" entries below*

government investment bank, 241–242, 249

government procurement, 217, 243

government regulation, 39, 114–115; reduction of, 21, 33, 38–40